THE PUBLIC MANAGER

Contemporary Challenges and Responsibilities

Donald P. Crane, Ph.D.
Department of Management
Georgia State University

William A. Jones, Jr., Ph.D.
Department of Management
Georgia State University

1991

Georgia State University Business Press
College of Business Administration
Atlanta, Georgia

Library of Congress Cataloging-in-Publication Data

Crane, Donald P.
The public manager : contemporary challenges and responsibilities / Donald P. Crane, William A. Jones, Jr.
p. cm.
Includes bibliographical references (p.).
ISBN 0-88406-223-6
1. Public administration. I. Jones, William A., 1934-
II. Title
JF 1351.C68 1991 91-6981
CIP

Published by:
Georgia State University Business Press
College of Business Administration
University Plaza
Atlanta, Georgia 30303-3093
Telephone: 404-651-4253

Revised Edition

First edition published in 1982 by The Bureau of National Affairs, Inc. as The Public Manager's Guide.

95 94 93 92 91 5 4 3 2 1

Printed in the United States of America.

Cover design by Patton H. McGinley, Jr.

Contents

Preface

Instructors are always searching for the "right" textbook. We are no exception. Having taught for many years, both in graduate-degree programs and in organizational training environments, we developed a clear vision of what we feel is a needed public management text.

The result, *The Public Manager,* has a pragmatic orientation. It is written to reach practicing public managers as well as students. It would be appropriate for academic courses at the graduate and undergraduate levels and, especially, for use in governmental training programs.

While it is well-grounded in public management research, it is intentionally written in a straight-forward, easy-to-read style. For the interested reader, we have included a complete bibliography of the many works that were consulted in developing the book. Recognizing, however, that footnotes are of minimal interest to most readers, we have resisted detailed citations. Instead, we have tried to synthesize much of the mainstream of this literature in an easily accessible fashion. For the most part, this mainstream is not time-bound information.

To provide perspective on contemporary issues, we have included a variety of carefully-selected readings. Also included are a number of application-oriented case situations. These should be useful for illustration and analysis, either for the individual reader, or for the classroom.

We would like to thank the many public managers that we have learned from over the years. Gerri and Winola should be included among this number, though their management skills are exercised in subtle ways. Special thanks to our publishing team: Cary Bynum, director; Peggy Stanley, managing editor; and Edith Kilgo, assistant editor, Georgia State University Business Press; and Lucy Hayes.

CHAPTER 1

Achieving Public Purpose: Public Management

"Management is management is management is . . . " say some observers. According to this view, planning, staffing, leading, controlling and other management functions must be performed—whatever the specific situation.

Yes. We agree. Managerial functions do, indeed, have a universal character. However, we must look beyond such activities to understand the true essence of management. As an applied field with a professional orientation, its real meaning must be understood in terms of its purpose. Why did such a thing as public management arise? Why does it exist?

Public management must be seen as the link between government goals and government accomplishments. Goals translate into actions only through the coordinated application of human effort and economic resources. This process of translation is the central purpose of the public manager's job. For government's work to be accomplished:

- Policies, plans, and organizations must be created.
- Money must be obtained, budgeted, and expended.
- People must be hired, trained, assigned, and supervised.
- Programs must be monitored, evaluated, and guided.

Whether the goal is traveling to the moon, protecting the environment, or paving a street, public management is a crucial component. When we look to government to do anything, we are looking toward public managers.

Contrary to the popular view, government organizations generally are managed quite well. This does not negate the continuing need to seek improvement. Just as we want business to be well run in order to provide a good product for a reasonable price, we want efficient and effective returns for our tax dollars.

This book is about American public managers in the last decade of the twentieth century. The purpose of the book is not to provide a detailed and definitive exposition. Rather, the authors seek to capture the nature and flavor of the public manager's job and to stimulate the reader's appetite for further investigation into the subject.

Public management in the United States is an extremely diverse enterprise. It is a part of all three branches of government—executive, legislative, and judicial. It is a part of all levels of government—national, state, and local. Beyond these traditional categories, public management is a part of newer governmental categories that have emerged in recent years— special districts, councils of governments, regional planning commissions, and others. All of these categories of public agencies, both traditional and contemporary, provide the means through which society pursues its goals.

Societal Goals and the Public Manager's Role

To exist in proximity to others, we form governments. In an effort to make our governments work, we constantly attempt to define our public goals—a process commonly referred to as politics. Political scientist Harold Lasswell termed this process of politics a matter of "who gets what, when, how" as a result of governmental practices, policies, and goals.[32]

While details and dollar amounts vary, we ask government to do many different things, including the following:

- Provide for the national defense.
- Inspect elevators and chickens.
- Build public housing.
- Fight fire and crime.
- Regulate the stock market.
- Educate us.
- Require a health warning on cigarettes.
- Conduct foreign relations.
- Maintain public roads and sell automobile tags.
- License us for driving, hunting, and fishing.
- Research health problems.
- Tax us.

The list could be extended for several more pages. The jurisdictions and complexities of modern government are such that an enumeration of things where government is *not involved* would probably yield a much shorter list. Governmental complexity is one reflection of the nature of modern society.

Each of the activities just listed is a pursuit of a specific goal already established by society. Much of the literature of political science deals with the various ways in which goals come into existence. Without detouring to explore this literature, it should be noted that public goals evolve in many ways; they may have varying degrees of clarity, they may even be contradictory, and they may remain in effect when we no longer need them.

Alternative Ways to Pursue Goals

While the central concern of this book is public managers and their efforts to achieve public goals, action in relation to goals can be achieved in other ways. One alternative would be for government to choose "no action" on a particular matter. The president, mayor, governor, Congress, city council, or other pertinent person or group could decide that a problem is temporary, unimportant, or for some reason does not require action. Inaction might also be government's response because the involved persons are unable to decide, or to agree, on what to do.

Assuming agreement to take action can be reached, a range of choices is possible. This range can be depicted on the following scale, with each point representing an increase in the amount of government involvement:

Level 1—Government acts to inform private persons who then may or may not take appropriate action (example, a government pamphlet urges mothers to keep dangerous items out of baby's reach).

Level 2—Government provides financial assistance to influence private action (example, a small business loan).

Level 3—Government regulates the behavior of private organizations (example, inspections of restaurants).

Level 4—Government at one level financially supports a government agency at another level (example, the Federal government provides support to state and local government housing agencies).

Level 5—Government creates an agency to pursue a particular goal or goals (example, the U.S. Department of Energy).

One central point is evident from this scale. No matter how little or how much government chooses to become involved, public managers are required at every level. Whether the action involves a small staff to work on public information announcements or an entire new agency, public managers are required if government is to act. The more action desired, the more public managers will be required.

The Variety of Public Managers

As noted in the preceding discussion, public managers are found in every branch, level, and function of government. To add an additional element to our frame of reference, the reader should keep in mind the range of activities in which public managers are engaged. Examples of the diverse job categories of public management include the following:

- Personnel administration specialists
- Budget analysts
- Casework supervisors
- City managers
- Program or project monitors
- Research administrators
- Investigators
- Grant makers
- Hospital administrators
- Police chiefs
- Park and forest managers
- Inspectors
- Public information officers
- Tax collectors

These and other public management categories will be used as examples throughout this text. Despite the obvious diversity of public managers' jobs, there are also many commonalities. These commonalities are the primary concern of this book.

Nature of the Public Manager's Job

It would be convenient for both the reader and the authors were it possible to begin with a clear and simple definition of the term *public manager.* Unfortunately, repeated efforts by many writers have failed to produce such a definition. Attempts to develop definitions have usually centered on efforts to define *public administration.* After years of such efforts, it almost appears that we are now less able to define this term than we were at the close of the nineteenth century. The earliest writers seemed to be the most confident about their definitions.

The first recognized article on public administration was written by a young scholar, and "good government" activist, Woodrow Wilson. Although Wilson is generally remembered as president of the United States (and, by many, as the president of Princeton University), he played a major role in making this book possible.

Wilson's article, published in the *Political Science Quarterly* in 1887, argued that administration is "a field of business."[58] He saw it related to "political life only as the methods of the counting house are part of the manufactured product." Wilson viewed public administration as the "latest fruit of the study of politics," and he called for administration to become a science. The conventional interpretation of Wilson's position is that he was asserting that politics is politics, and administration is administration—that the two are essentially separate activities. Politics tended to be equated with the making of policy, while administration referred only to its implementation. Some scholars, however, have drawn different conclusions from Wilson's essay. Political scientist Herbert A. Simon, for example, argues that Wilson was making a normative claim rather than reporting an empirical observation about the way things are in government.[52] According to Simon, Wilson meant that governmental administration "ought to be" an activity removed from the strife of politics. According to this interpretation, Wilson's essay should not be understood as a naive claim that administration and politics are separate; rather, it should be interpreted as one of the early reform statements on behalf of neutrality in administration, aimed at improving the capacity of the executive branch to provide responsive and responsible government. Regardless of how one interprets Wilson's view of politics and administration, one thing is clear: his essay called attention to the importance of administration as a central activity of government. That is its most important legacy.

While academicians may debate Wilson's position, Frank Goodnow asserted throughout his book, *Politics and Administration,* that administration could and should be separated from policy-making and partisan political activity.[23] More recent writers have demonstrated the importance of politics in the administrative process. Through interaction with clientele groups, the exercise of discretion, and the development of expertise, public managers are involved in politics and policy-making that is difficult, if not impossible, to distinguish from administration.

In *Papers on the Science of Administration,* (12–13), classic management writer Luther Gulick took quite a different approach to developing a definition of administration.[25] He began by asking what is the work of the chief executive? What does he or she do? Gulick identified the answer with an acronymn: POSDCORB. The initials stand for the following activities:

> *Planning,* that is working out in broad outline the things that need to be done and the methods for doing them to accomplish the purpose set for the enterprise;
> *Organizing,* that is the establishment of the formal structure of author-

> ity through which work subdivisions are arranged, defined and co-ordinated for the defined objective;
> *Staffing,* that is the whole personnel function of bringing in and training the staff and maintaining favorable conditions of work;
> *Directing,* that is the continuous task of making decisions and embodying them in specific and general orders and instructions and serving as the leader of the enterprise;
> *Co-ordinating,* that is the all important duty of interrelating the various parts of the work;
> *Reporting,* that is keeping those to whom the executive is responsible informed as to what is going on, which thus includes keeping himself and his subordinates informed through records, research and inspection;
> *Budgeting,* with all that goes with budgeting in the form of fiscal planning, accounting, and control."

In his approach, Gulick emphasized the generic nature of the administrator's role. He was less interested in searching for unique aspects of the public administrator's job.

Paul Appleby, a distinguished practitioner and scholar in public administration, saw government work as emphatically unique. In his book, *Big Democracy* (p. 1), he considered government to be completely different from every other activity in society.[2] He saw "so big a difference that the dissimilarity between government and all other forms of social action is greater than any dissimilarity among those other forms themselves." He pointed to three related features of government. These were its breadth and impact on all citizens, its political character, and its public accountability.

A Working Definition

The debate over definition continues today. Rather than continue to trace its development, suffice it to say that there is no one best definition of public administration or public management. The ground covered so far does suggest that public management involves such things as:

- Working with and through other people
- Striving to achieve public goals
- Applying management skills and knowledge

With this review as background information, it is necessary to enumerate the dimensions of a definition that we can use—and build on.

The focus of this book is on the *public manager* rather than on public administration or public management. Its purpose is to emphasize the role and responsibilities of *individuals* working in the field of public administration. Much current literature focuses on defining public administration and on listing and dissecting its various dimensions and elements. While such a focus has merit, the perspective of this book is different. Many who study public administration hope to be (or already have become) public managers. Others hope to gain an understanding of public managers and their behavior. Regardless of which goal motivates the reader, this book should enable him or her to better understand the world of the practicing public manager.

Public managers are the persons who must, in the final analysis, do the work of government. Legislators enact laws, judges judge, and presidents proclaim, but until public managers swing into action, little will actually be accomplished.

It is useful for us to draw on the work of the United States' largest public employer—the federal government. Its personnel agency, the Office of Personnel Management (formerly the Civil Service Commission), defined the term "managerial position" in its *Federal Personnel Manual Letter Number 412-2* (29 January 1974). While this definition may not meet every sophisticated test that could be designed, it is both helpful and workable, and needs to be paraphrased only slightly to become equally applicable to positions at all levels of government.

Three dimensions are stressed in this definition. Each incumbent of a managerial position must be

- involved in directing the work of a governmental organization.
- accountable for specific programs, functions, activities, or projects.
- involved in monitoring and evaluating progress toward organizational goals and in making appropriate adjustments based on this evaluation.

As part of these three basic dimensions, the public manager must perform most of the following duties:

- Develop goals and plans, either jointly with higher management or independently.
- Contribute significantly to determining resource needs and their allocation, and account for their effective use.
- Recommend or make important changes in the organization, such as basic structure, key positions, or operating costs.
- Consider such broad factors as legislative relations, public policy, economic impact, public relations, and labor-management relations, when making (or recommending) decisions.
- Coordinate agency programs and efforts with the activities of other agencies.
- Assess the impact of organizational development on the agency and its programs, on other government units, and on the private sector.

- Establish organization policies in determining program emphases and guidelines.
- Understand and communicate agency policies and priorities throughout the organization.
- Deal with personnel policies and decisions affecting the organization and key employees, or deal with matters having possible serious repercussions.
- Delegate authority to subordinate supervisors and hold them responsible for the performance of their units.

Careful reading of these duties gives considerable added depth to the three dimensions mentioned earlier, all of which will be discussed in following chapters.

Some Unique Aspects of Public Management

As noted in our introduction, many people would argue that "management is management is management." To a degree, our working definition accepts that there is much validity to such a statement. Management is a "people" process and all organizations are, by definition, conglomerations of people. The organization may be public or private, large or small, centralized or decentralized. Its goal may be profit, service, control, religion, or other. Whatever the distinction, the manager's concern in every instance is to foster cooperative interactions and contributions toward matters of organizational concern. In each case the manager must develop people skills, such as communication, analysis, motivation, persuasion, and strategy.

Why Public Sector Management Is Different

The working definition we have adopted also recognizes that, despite the generic aspects of the role performed by all managers, management in government also has its unique dimensions. The writings of political scientist Frederick Mosher are especially helpful in emphasizing these. Mosher agrees that many jobs are similar, or even identical, in both government and business organizations.[40] He then notes that transfers from one to the other are frequent, and that training and experience requirements may be similar. Beyond these similarities, however, Mosher emphasizes the special aspects of the public sector. Some of these he sees as differences in degree while others are more basic differences of kind.

As the first point of departure from the private sector, the sovereignty of government must be emphasized. Government represents the highest power in a particular society or jurisdiction; it derives its authority from "the law of the land." Government managers are expected to swear or affirm a special kind of loyalty to their employer and to the authority that the employer represents.

A second distinct feature of employment as a public manager is the concept of political neutrality. Some top management positions in government jurisdictions are political appointments. Appointees are usually active participants in the politics of the mayor's office, of the governor's office, or of the president's office. However, a much larger number of managers hold nonpolitical, or career, appointments. These managers, who are the major concern of this book, are generally expected to refrain from active political involvement. The public manager is expected to serve the people and the cause of public programs but to avoid seeking political influence. While the complexity of modern society makes it increasingly difficult, the public manager is expected to be politically neutral and occupationally competent.

A third feature of the public manager's job is political responsiveness. This requires the manager to strive for goals established by the appropriate political bodies. Carried to an extreme, this concept would suggest a distinction between policy-making and policy implementation that simply does not exist. We expect to find policies and goals set by legislative bodies, chief executives, and the judiciary, while managers strictly implement them. There obviously is no such distinction. Managers recommend to, and otherwise interact with, legislative, executive, and judicial bodies as they reach their decisions. Managers also set policy and establish goals as an integral part of the implementation process. Despite the haziness of jurisdictional distinctions, the public manager must respond to the basic political goals and directions set by elected superiors. Consequently, political responsiveness is a prerequisite for the successful public manager.

A fourth feature of public service suggests that it should be representative of the total population. Representativeness requires an equitable distribution of employment throughout society and equal representation with regard to policy-oriented phases of the management process. Ideally, all levels of an agency would contain a mixture of race, color, creed, and national origin proportionate to the population of the geographic area it serves. Bureaucracies may be said to be representative in yet another way—to the extent that their policy decisions conform to what is believed to be prevailing public opinion. As important as demographic representativeness in selection and promotion of personnel may be from a human rights perspective, agencies that are representative in this sense of the larger society may not necessarily be more representative of public opinion in their policy decisions—nor should it be inferred that they will be less representative.

Government has been dubbed by some as a goldfish bowl. While this is not exactly true, the nature and degree of public scrutiny, or the possibility of it, is endemic in public management. Mosher suggests that public employment may be as much related to social purposes, and in some cases more so, as it is to getting the job done in the most efficient way. Government programs to reduce unemployment, rehabilitate the handicapped or disabled, and even to allow veterans' preference in employment are examples. In addition, government has some degree of responsibility to lead the way as a model employer, setting an example for other employers. The use of merit systems, emphasis on equal employment and treatment, minimum wages, and retirement systems are relevant examples.

Some would argue that the features which distinguish public management are becoming more important with the passage of time. Others would oppose such a view and perceive all large organizations as becoming more and more alike. Regardless of the position one takes, the precise meaning and importance of these features change over time. Despite this, however, each feature exists and demands our awareness.

Why Study Public Management?

There are both personal and professional reasons why almost everyone should have a basic understanding of public management. As government increasingly pervades our society, it touches every individual. The activities of public managers influence, coerce, reward, or control all of us in various ways. Public organizations, and the management of them, are a significant part of our life.

It is easy to criticize "big government," "red tape," or "bureaucracy" without considering the need for public organizations. Our modern way of life simply could not exist without them. The task before us, either as citizens or as managers, is to find ways to make our public organizations more proficient—to make them responsive and responsible to our needs, and effective in their performance.

Persons who are concerned about the state of the world today, or about the human condition, must take special interest in public organizations. If we are to make major improvements (progress, if you will), we must understand, and work through, organizations. Even when we dislike organizations, we find that we must organize to fight successfully for change.

Much of our knowledge about public management also applies to business, religious, educational, not-for-profit, and other kinds of organizations. The study of public management is especially concerned with organizations that are large. Government organizations are definitely not alone in this category. Large-scale business organizations—such as IBM, GM, AT&T, and others—are in many ways like public organizations. In such structures, it is impossible, for example, to use profit as the focus for measuring the performance of individual managers. Many of the problems of managing such organizations differ little from those of public agencies.

Finally, it is necessary to encourage capable people to study public management and managers in the hope that they will aspire to be public managers. The needs and challenges of government are continuing to grow, as is the need for competent public managers. To make public organizations work— indeed, to make government and society work—nothing is more important than the quality of these managers.

A Brief Case Study—to Illustrate—to Ponder

The "Success" of I.M. McDougal

I.M. was proud of his past accomplishments and eager for the challenges that he saw ahead. Fifteen years ago, fresh out of college with a business degree, he had opened a small fast-food restaurant. His specialty, and trademark, was, "the good old American hamburger."

From the beginning he was a very successful businessman and within ten years his restaurants were located in 31 different states. A total of 75 restaurants had been opened and not one had failed. I.M. was also happy that none of these were franchised locations. He had complete ownership and control over the restaurants, and each one proudly displayed both the American flag and I.M.'s personally designed hamburger pennant.

About five years ago, having become quite comfortable financially, I.M. began to develop an interest in politics. His initial interest grew out of an annoyance with government licensing, inspection, taxes, and red tape. As he became more informed about government, his involvement grew both deeper and broader. He began to attend political party meetings and to contribute to election campaigns.

This involvement continued, and over the last year I.M. played a prominent role in the gubernatorial campaign. His candidate won an overwhelming victory and is now the governor-elect. He will take office in two weeks and has just appointed I.M. to be secretary of the state's Department of Health and Human Services. I.M. is anxious to experience a period of public service. He visualizes such an opportunity from a dual perspective. It would give him a chance to repay society for all the success he had enjoyed, and he knows he could improve the efficiency of this state agency.

Because of your reputation as a public management consultant, I.M. has now approached you for advice about the post he will soon assume. What suggestions and recommendations can you offer? Consider such things as:

1. Self-concept and personal goals—are they changing, or should they?
2. Goals of private and public organizations—how are they similar, and how are they different?
3. Day-to-day concerns and pressures relevant to public and private organizations—how are they similar, and how are they different?
4. Evaluations of "success" in public and private organizations—how are they similar, and how are they different?

CHAPTER 2

The Context of Public Management: Nature of the Environment

To understand public management, one must first understand the context within which it takes place. This context is, in a word, politics. It is the arena in which decisions are made that affect the entire society—decisions that carry the force of law, decisions that can be legitimately carried out by force if necessary. Depending on the perspective, government can be viewed as synonymous with politics or as the primary *result* of politics. Both politics and government are often discussed as though they were contemporary forms of American sin. In reality, of course, both have always been pervasive parts of all group life. By definition, the basis for every nation is its government, and the most descriptive term, rather than sin, would be necessity. The governing process provides every society with the mechanisms to

- decide on common goals.
- provide for the common defense.
- promote the common welfare.

In the United States, we pride ourselves on our democratic form of politics. The Founding Fathers are seen to have developed a government based on equality and representation. While the study of American history actually reveals this to be somewhat of a myth, it is one we like to perpetuate. The point, however, is that every nation has its own particular political form and process. To understand public management in a given nation, we must begin by looking at the nature of the political, governmental, or public environment.

The Nature of American Government and Politics

Government and politics are favorite subjects of discussion for Americans, and few avoid them entirely. Like sports and sex, they are mainstays of conversation. In all instances, it is correct to say that people will talk about things that are important to them and to their self-interest.

As mentioned earlier, government has a monopoly in its ability to make and enforce rules that apply to everyone in the society. Force can be used if necessary, and its use is legitimate. The real key to government's survival is, of course, acceptance by its citizens. The application of force could rapidly lose its legitimacy if it were to be applied too often.

Government is important to every citizen because it can, and does, provide for and take away from everyone. It offers services such as streets, mail service, national defense, parks, social security, and disease control. In return, it makes demands on citizens such as taxes, restrictions, and licenses. Sales and income taxes, driving and fishing licenses, and the penalties prescribed by government for crimes are examples of these. Government acts to protect, regulate, license, tax, and inspect in a variety of ways. Its objective is to provide important services for society at large. To achieve this objective requires that some rights be taken away. Citizens find it much easier to get accustomed to the services than they do to the costs.

Pluralism and Elitism

In times of war or other national (or local) emergency, the primary challenge of government becomes quite clear. The citizenry can quickly rally to the common defense when there is general agreement on how it is defined. This is not to say that there are no difficulties and complexities in such cases, but rather that in normal everyday government, consensus may be more difficult and complex to attain.

Governing is a process of competing, trading, bargaining, and compromising. Some hold that this process is widespread and functions through the many groups and organizations in American society. Individuals and groups are seen to be well-represented in the political process through their membership in various organizations and larger groups. This view is popular in modern political science and is called *pluralism.*

Pluralism perceives the American political system as overlapping economic, religious, ethnic, and geographical groupings, competing for and sharing power. The political process serves as the mechanism for dynamic interaction among these groups. Pluralism is seen to benefit minorities as well as majorities, and decision-making activities are seen to be divided among many competing groups.

Congress, state legislatures, and other legislative bodies are composed of people who represent a variety of interests. Legislators depend on votes to get elected, and they are especially sensitive to the concerns of the groups within their constituencies.

Supporters of pluralism argue that it opens up the decision-making process to the vast majority of the electorate. Citizens can support interest groups that are consistent with individual beliefs; the interest groups then evolve consensus views and air them in political forums comprised of other interest groups. Final decisions thus represent a compromise of diverse interests.

The *elitism* perspective divides society into two groups: the elites and the masses. Persons with power, prestige, and money are elites, and everyone else is considered to be the masses. Decisions flow from the actions and interactions of society's elites. In this system, the larger population segment, or the masses, has little meaningful participation in government decision making.

A significant part of political science literature deals with arguments for and against pluralistic or elitist interpretations of American democracy. While interesting reading, the two explanations can best be labeled as opposing ideologies. Both views are no doubt right in part, but they also represent some degree of distortion of reality.

A Systems View

A useful way to visualize how American government functions is the "Open System" approach or model. This perspective, originally developed by David Easton in his book *A Framework for Political Analysis,* provides a guide for both understanding and analysis.[18] This framework, depicted in exhibit 2–1, illustrates a number of important ideas, including the following:

- A system is composed of various units, or parts, and each unit plays a unique role.
- The different units of the system interact to produce outcomes.
- Actions and interactions of units are affected by information, resources, and demands that flow into the system from the surrounding environment.
- System outputs filter through the environment and feed back into the system as new inputs.

EXHIBIT 2-1. **Key Elements of the Political System**

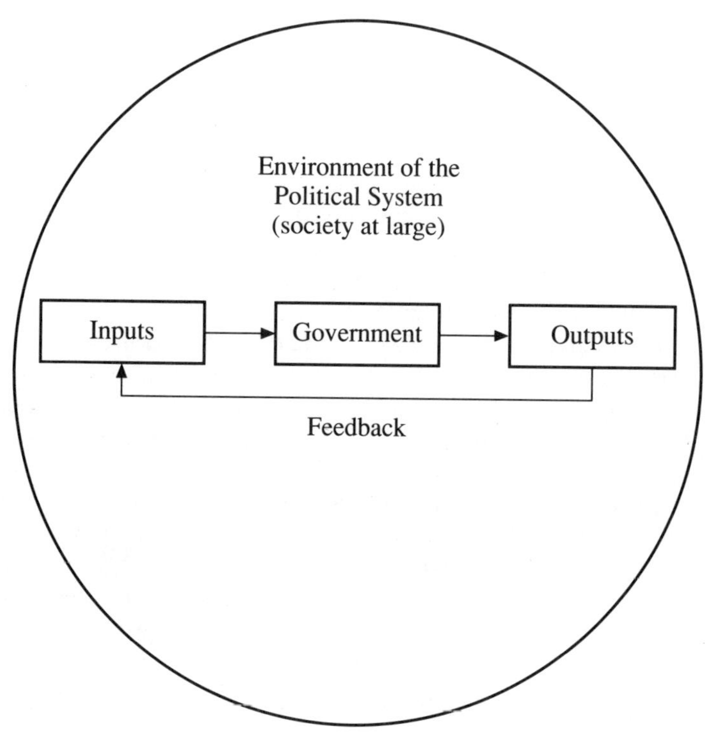

By using this model as a simplification of reality, one is better able to grasp the concept of American government.

Public managers are central elements in this systems model. They deal with inputs and produce outputs, which flow back into society. Other figures, or actors, in this role are the following, with examples:

- The elected chief executive (president, governor, mayor)
- Political appointees (commissioner, secretary, director)
- Elected legislators (senators, representatives, council members)
- Judges

These five sets of actors make up what we call "the government."

A variety of inputs constantly flow into government. Some support the system and others demand from it. Support inputs include:

- Elections and voting
- Payment of taxes
- Jury duty
- Military service

Demands on the system also take a variety of forms, such as:

- Filing a Social Security claim
- Writing a letter of complaint to an elected official
- Applying for a federal grant
- Forming organizations to get government action on environmental problems

It should be remembered that demands and supports come from both individuals and organizations. Organizations can range from a "save-the-oak-tree-in-front-of-city-hall" group to a multimillion-dollar interest group that is highly organized and well financed. Also of special significance on both the demand and the support sides are political parties and the mass media.

A continuous flow of supports and demands shapes the thoughts and actions of government actors. Most of these actors are also aware of latent demands and supports in the society. These represent the unspoken boundaries of government action. For example, a taxpayer revolt begins to take hold at a certain point; aggression by a foreign nation results in citizen support for the military; or corrupt actions by a politician force his resignation.

Outputs are government's response to assorted problems in the society, which are the items we read about in the daily newspaper: inflation, housing, health and welfare, education, energy, pollution, and urban problems. These matters are constantly on the government agenda because of their common or public nature. They are acted on by government repeatedly (government rarely deals with a problem only once).

The output side of the system yields such things as:

- Laws, rules, and regulations
- Expenditure of government dollars
- Policy objectives and preferences

Now that some key dimensions of the systems model have been surveyed, our illustration can be revised (see exhibit 2–2). The reader should note that this represents only small steps toward a full analysis of the model. For example, legislatures are usually divided into two houses and various committees; interest groups are of many types and function in varied ways; political parties have similarities and differences. The important role of the various communications media has not been developed. The model is still very much a simplification of reality.

EXHIBIT 2-2. **The Political System**

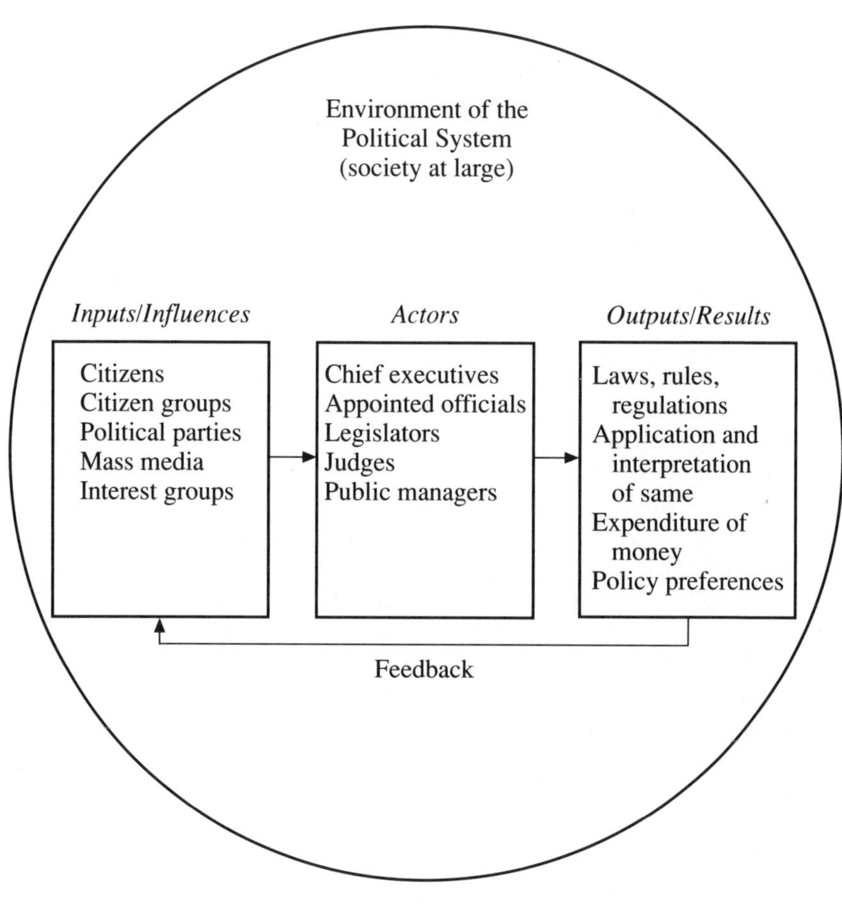

Although simplified, the model is a useful tool for locating the public manager within the governmental system. Some of the important units and forces that surround the typical public manager can be seen more clearly. The interaction of all components of the system is the political process. The public manager is at the center of this process and has a complex role. A multiplicity of interest groups, with various expectations, are anxious to influence public managers.

It is helpful to think of society as a collection of systems constantly interacting. One can, for example, speak of the American

EXHIBIT 2-3. **Society as a Group of Systems**

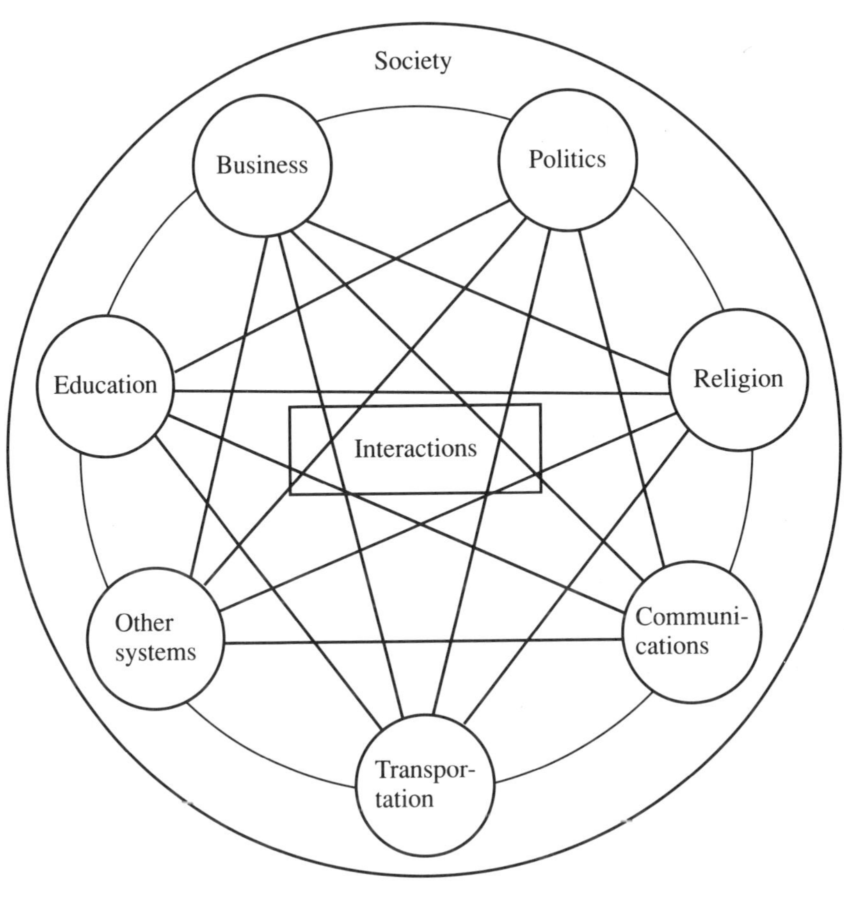

public education system, business system, communications system, transportation system, religious system, and others. Each of these can be described in terms of their multiple subsystems or parts. Teachers (as members of the education system), for instance, actively seek pay raises by lobbying in the legislature (the political system). At a higher level, society can be viewed as an interactive organism composed of multiple systems, as shown in simplified form in exhibit 2–3.

Various people, depending on their backgrounds and biases, assign different degrees of importance to these systems, although for the present purpose, they are considered equal in the total scheme of society. Interactions are given center stage to indicate their pervasive nature—moving in all directions at once.

Functions of Government

One primary difficulty with the systems view is that it is too neat and organized. While useful as a device to help develop a perspective or orientation, it fails to capture the complex and fragmented nature of a system. It is a good snapshot, but does not convey the dynamic operation of the political process over time. Political activities and outcomes are as diverse as the content of our daily newspapers. Despite this, there are some specific functions being continuously performed.

Decisions, for example, are constantly made through the workings of the political system or process. Conflict is continually resolved through the activities of politics. As issues and opportunities become public, decisions are made about them. Often these decisions are made slowly, perhaps painfully, and in some instances not made at all. This too is a decision. Political and/or other forces may be unable to agree for any number of reasons. For example, knowledge limitations can severely restrict decision making on such key matters as the energy crisis, inflation, unemployment, criminal justice, health, environmental concerns, or urban problems. Individuals and groups will often disagree as to what ultimate goal is sought. How much should government do, for example, and how much should be left to private interests.

In addition to providing the mechanism for society's collective decision making, government makes it possible for private persons and organizations to function. A monetary system makes commerce possible; courts and legal provisions make it possible to negotiate and enforce private contracts; public roads encourage the private production of automobiles; a social security system helps relieve older persons of financial burdens; military protection reduces the threat of outside aggression. Many things become possible by virtue of the fundamental services that government provides for the society.

Lloyd Musolf has explored the notion that government acts in a variety of ways in making public decisions and facilitating private ones.[41] For example, government *promotes and encourages* scientific progress, home ownership, rural electrification, minority business, international trade, and airport construction. Government also *regulates and controls* interstate commerce, nuclear energy, television, and automobile emissions. The direct market activities of government *buying and selling* are also significant—it makes huge purchases of land, vehicles, buildings, aircraft, ships, rockets and missiles, pencils, and paper clips. In addition, sales are made continually, including postage stamps, TVA electricity, water and sewage, and military equipment sold to foreign governments.

Another constantly debated function of government is that of guardian of the morals of society. Some argue that cigarettes and liquor should be heavily taxed because they can be harmful. Sunday blue laws, pornography, dangerous drugs, and prostitution are other areas where the role of government is debated.

It should also be noted that building support for itself becomes an important function of every government. This reflects the self-interest of each person within the system. Politicians want to be reelected, high officials desire to be reappointed, administrators and staff hope to be promoted, and so forth. While we talk about a government of laws, first and foremost we have a government of people, and people aspire to be successful and to get ahead.

The Structure of American Government

The reader should keep in mind the fragmented nature of power in the U.S. system of government. The Founding Fathers were careful to avoid establishing a strong, central source of power. While the events of history have moved us rapidly in that direction, fragmentation is still the most distinguishing feature of the American government.

Framers of the Constitution (which the reader might wish to review) sought to establish and maintain a separation of power in government organization through a system of checks and balances. By separating the government into branches, they ensured that each holds the power of the others in check. The chief executive can veto bills enacted by the legislature; the legislature can override the veto, and it has the authority to review major appointments of the president; the judiciary has the right to review the constitutionality of the actions of the other branches. Any member of these branches can be removed from office by impeachment should he or she act improperly, and political pressures can be brought to bear within a branch or by another branch to force the recall or resignation of an elected official. The House and Senate Watergate hearings forced the resignation of President Nixon in 1974, and the Speaker of the House of Representatives, Jim Wright, was influenced to step down in 1989 as the result of investigations and adverse publicity.

Further control over power in government has been maintained through a bicameral legislature (the federal House and Senate) where measures passed by one body must be reviewed and approved by the other. In addition, elected officials are the ultimate authority in administrative agencies, program implementation is defined by law, and Congress and the chief executive must approve proposals for new or revised programs. Similarly, the budgeting process follows legislated procedures that must be approved by officials in legislative and executive branches.

State governments have an even more complicated separation of power. Governors, in making their own appointments of department heads, must work with officials who are elected or appointed by boards or commissions. State legislatures are also constrained in their activities. Short sessions limit the depth and scope of the bills they can enact; and constitutions, federal legislation, and commissions restrict their borrowing and spending.

The greatest diversity of organizational and power arrangements appears at the local level. Of the estimated 80,000 local governments, the mayor-council form is the most common. The executive and legislative branches share power, department heads are appointed by the mayor, and budget requests of the various departments are acted on by the council. The commission form departs from the typical local organization because elected officials who comprise the council perform both the executive and legislative functions, and the council administers the affairs of the municipality. About 40 percent of cities of 5,000 or greater population use the council-manager form. With the increasing complexity of social and economic problems faced by cities and counties, the use of professional managers may become more prevalent.

Persons interested in a particular activity of government, such as health, transportation, or criminal justice, usually find that it is dispersed throughout the national, state, and local levels of government. Intergovernmental relations, or federalism, has become a major topic, and a considerable body of literature has developed. Political scientist Deil S. Wright has provided a useful representation under the label "picket fence federalism."[59] An illustration of this approach is provided in exhibit 2-4.

The picket fence is designed to show the flow of money, program authorities, and guidelines from the national to local governments. Like the systems view, the picket fence is a device to help grasp the notion of federalism or intergovernmental relations. Again, it is a "still" view and should be thought of as a place to begin developing an understanding—not as the definitive picture. Many of the prob-

EXHIBIT 2-4. **Example of "Picket Fence Federalism"—Highways and Education**

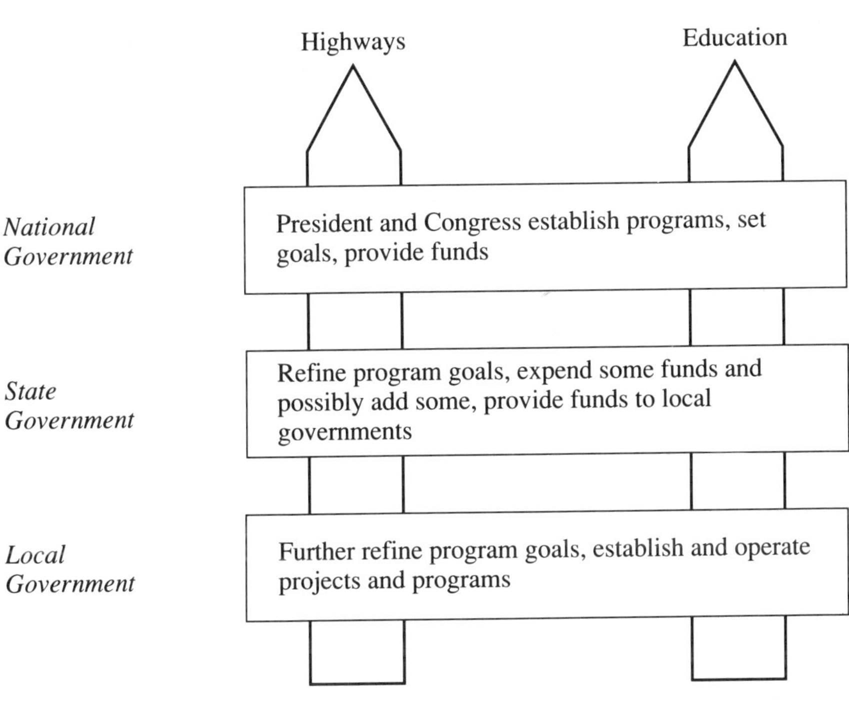

lems of our society, for example, are found in urban areas. When we examine a metropolitan area, we will find, for example, that

- the "local" Social Security office is operated by the federal government, the employment service office by the state, and the welfare office by the county.
- the sewer and water systems may be parts of local government or they may be "special districts" established apart from city and county government.
- the school system and the local hospital may also be "special districts," or part of either city or county government.
- the financial support for each of these comes from a mixture of federal, state, and local government sources.

The Impact of Ideas and Values on Public Management

Politics and public management are culture-bound activities. The ideas and values that pervade society set definite boundaries for the governmental process in a representative, democratic society. Such a society strives to fulfill human needs that cannot be met individually, and to do so in a collective manner that reflects the society at large. A number of contemporary phenomena have had major impacts upon the prevailing ideas and values of American society. These include:

- Movement toward larger size (bigness) in many sectors—government, business, labor, religion, and others
- Population changes in both size and composition
- Increases in white-collar and service-related jobs and decreases in agriculture and manufacturing
- Consumerism
- Environmental and energy concerns
- Decline in authoritarianism and greater interest in consensus/group decision making
- Organized efforts to achieve greater equality
- Increased interest in "professionalism" in almost all occupations
- Belief that analysis and planning can yield solutions to most problems, and that people can control their own destinies

Phenomena such as these are constantly forcing individuals and groups to reassess their value systems and beliefs. As change occurs, evolution in ideas and values is reflected in the nature of governmental systems.

In this century, a leading notion has been that public managers should not be involved in politics or policy-making. This idea calls for public management to be purely an instrument or tool for routine policy execution. Like any other instrument, it is expected to be competent and efficient in its use but neutral regarding important decisions. As pointed out earlier, this concept is not realistic in modern government. Legislative bodies, chief executives, judges, political candidates, and others commonly invite or require nonpartisan public managers to become involved in the policy process. This takes such forms as drafting new laws and regulations and serving as knowledgeable witnesses in various areas. When a public issue develops in a particular field, it is quite natural to ask the persons working in that field to become involved. Unfortunately, experts in government service, like their private counterparts, do not always agree. Even when they do, political evaluations often dictate amending their advice. Regardless of the outcome in particular cases, public managers will often find themselves involved in policy issues. This might occur at any stage in the governmental process—from problem identification to evaluation of a completed program.

Public managers also find that laws, policies, and rules developed through the political process are usually far from complete. In administering a public park or forest, for example, the public manager may well have to balance conservation and recreation interests. At a more elementary level, the traffic policeman must decide how specific he must be in enforcing the speed limit on a suburban street. Should the motorist who travels at 36 miles per hour in the 35-mile-per-hour zone be ticketed?

Closely related to the notion that public managers should not be policy-makers is the admonition that public managers always act in the public interest. While this phrase has a nice ring, it is impossible to define it for purposes of day-to-day application. In the example just mentioned, for instance, how does one balance the conflicting goals of conservationists and recreationists in terms of the public interest?

A Brief Case Study—to Illustrate—to Ponder

On the Firing Line

Jack Sanderson is fully aware that his task is going to be difficult. After many successful years of dealing with complex problems as a public manager, he is about to face an audience that, in some ways, will be one of his toughest. This audience, the Young Entrepreneurs Club, is almost totally antigovernment. The members are outspoken and quite aggressive in their view that "the only good government is no government." Their position is essentially that citizens should be left alone and allowed to function without government interference.

Jack has never taken time to think about this basic issue. He began his public-sector career at an early age and has always accepted government as a given part of society. His college work was in psychology, and he is now wishing that he had studied government.

As his new staff assistant, and one who has studied public management, your task is to provide Jack with eight or ten central ideas for his presentation. Jack doesn't expect to convert the Young Entrepreneur membership, but he does hope that they will better understand the role and importance of government at the national, state, and local levels. Perhaps some of them can even become convinced of the need to participate in the political process. In preparing your material for Jack, be sure to spend some time anticipating the questions and criticisms he will likely receive.

CHAPTER 3

The Organizational Context: Nature of the Public Management Process

The nature of our society and the political influences that interact with government bodies create a complex and sophisticated environment. The organizational context operates within a political system and continuously interacts with it. The various components comprising the organizational context are discussed in this chapter.

To understand the operation of public organizations, we need to appreciate the uniqueness of government administration. As discussed in Chapter 1, public managers are different from those in the private sector. They are continuously subject to public scrutiny, and their actions must consider a myriad of special and general interests as well as the possibility of investigation. Persons inside or outside the organization may become disgruntled with their performance. In his classic writing, *Big Democracy,* Paul Appleby—a longtime public servant—concluded that governmental organizations are unique because they are so publicly accountable.[2] Everything they do is subject to public scrutiny, debate, or investigation. He claimed that government has concern for everyone, is dependent on everyone, and deals with those psychological intangibles that reflect popular economic needs and social aspirations. While other types of organizations may not be free from politics, "government *is* politics," Appleby claims.

Organization and the Manager's Role

Organizational theorists generally agree that organizations provide the vehicle for accomplishing goals or objectives, operate through human relationships that are divided into roles which contribute to the attainment of goals, and contain *hierarchies of authority* that direct, limit, and control the activities of lower-level members toward goals. The definition of the organization contains each of these elements: *Organization consists of a group of individuals with specific roles and defined authority who interact to coordinate their efforts toward the accomplishment of articulated objectives.* The need for a hierarchy of authority makes management the key to the functioning of organizations. But why are they formed in the first place?

Since the beginning of recorded history, people have formed organizations to satisfy needs that could not be satisfied independently. People engage in cooperative group efforts when the benefits promise to outweigh the costs. Today, organizations range from informal, ad hoc gatherings to formal, highly structured bureaucracies. Formal military groups have been organized to protect the populace; governmental agencies have been developed to accomplish specific tasks; and voluntary associations have attracted members for social, religious, recreational, philanthropic, or other reasons.

Organizations cannot act by themselves; they require management by people in positions of authority. Managers are needed to coordinate and integrate human, financial, and physical resources for the accomplishment of objectives.

When Roy Ash served with the Office of Management and Budget, he observed that in any organization, management is a rare and prized commodity.[3] He lamented that a lack of managerial talent coupled with the complicated nature of governmental organizations had led critics to argue that our government may have become ungovernable. John B. Miner's research on the "motivation to manage" concluded that there has been a general decline in this motive among younger managers and students that will eventually lead to a critical shortage.[37] But even more alarming is his finding that government managers typically have less overall motivation to manage than business managers.

As this condition becomes acute, the opportunity for the aspiring (and managerially motivated) manager to rise in government service will greatly increase. This phenomenon admonishes any upwardly mobile public manager to develop to the limit of his or her potential. Enlightened agencies are expanding development opportunities through such programs as Certified Public Manager, educational leave, management development seminars, and numerous other activities.

Let us examine the nature of organizations in general, and more specifically, the elements that comprise public organizations. Perhaps this discussion will enlighten managers on the organizational aspects of their jobs and will inspire others to seek public management responsibility.

Nature of Organizations

Organizations can be viewed in terms of the results they achieve and can be deemed effective if they achieve their intended results. But effectiveness is diminished unless it is attained efficiently at a low, or at least a reasonable, cost. If the United States wants to land a scientific exploration team on Mars, an organization will be needed to accomplish the task. Any number of organizations could carry out the mission at different costs in money, time, manpower, and materials, but only a limited number could carry it out efficiently. We can conclude from this that different types of organizations are appropriate for different tasks.

The nature of organizations can be viewed as a continuum. At one extreme there are organizations that perform routine or programmed tasks such as statistical recording or monitoring where efficiency is a primary concern. These types focus on the task and, hence, are inclined to be "mechanistic" or "closed." At the opposite extreme are "open" or "sociotechnical" organizations in which creativity and flexibility are emphasized because of the varied and nonroutine nature of the work. Organizations that deliver services such as health care to the public exemplify this type of organization. In the middle are organizations that have attributes of both the predictable/routine and the creative/flexible, or that fluctuate between these two extremes. They lean toward closed or open organizations, depending on various factors, such as the work being performed at the time, the philosophy of the ranking managers, and the nature of the people in the organization. Personnel staff organizations that maintain employment records as well as deliver services—training, testing, collective bargaining—might be an example of this middle category.

The nature of organizations also can be classified depending on their fundamental orientation. Gulick and Urwick in their classic *Papers on the Science of Administration* identified four categories of organization [25]:

1. Organizations oriented toward accomplishing a specific purpose, such as a sanitation department that maintains a city's or county's cleanliness.
2. Process organizations that perform certain tasks. A city law department, for instance, has a group of lawyers who serve other departments (one might represent the city's urban renewal—another defend the city's public works department).

3. Organizations classified as *place* because they service a specific geographic area. The regional bureaus in the U.S. Department of State are good examples of this type. Five Assistant Secretaries are responsible for foreign affairs activities in major regions of the world.
4. Clientele-oriented organizations designed to serve a particular group of people. The Bureau of Indian Affairs that handles needs of American Indians throughout the nation is typical of this type of organization.

Public organizations can be classified by a variety of schemes as indicated in this discussion. However, the one characteristic they all have in common is their bureaucratic nature. Federal, state, and municipal agencies, by and large, follow the bureaucratic model originally espoused by Max Weber. Because of its widespread adoption in public management, it is perhaps the core of the public organization's conceptual framework. The Weber model is summarized in the following section.

Bureaucratic Organizations: The Weber Model

Max Weber was raised in an affluent and politically influential German family. As professor, editor, author, and consultant to government, he exemplified the leading scholar at the turn of the century. Through his writings he sought to influence the adoption of a rational basis for the management of large-scale enterprises, and he conceived his bureaucratic model as the ideal approach. Weber attacked the traditional use of political control and favoritism in emerging capitalistic economies, particularly in Germany. He felt that bureaucracy would emphasize rules and competence and would lead to a high degree of efficiency and reliability in management. Although Weber's writings on bureaucracy did not emerge in America until the late 1940s, they are credited with having a profound impact on organization theory [22].

The Weberian model of the ideal bureaucracy contains the following elements:

- Fixed, clearly defined, and divided jurisdictional duties that are given sanction by laws or administrative regulations.
- A system of graded authority organized in a hierarchy in which the lower offices are supervised by the higher.
- Authority clearly defined and limited to the functions necessary to carry out the organization's task. (Weber claimed that this form of rational-legal authority was the basis for a bureaucracy.)
- Members of the organization—except elected officials—selected

and appointed on the basis of their technical qualifications verified by formal examination, and/or by certification of expert training and education.

- Materials and written documents comprise the files for the operation of the bureau or office.
- Managers (administrative officials) work for fixed salaries on a career basis. They are subject to strict rules of conduct and controls that are consistently and uniformly applied [22].

To Weber, management meant the exercise of control on the basis of knowledge. Qualified by their technical competence, managers lead their organizations by rationality rather than by whim, by ability rather than by favoritism. Rationalism in modern management expresses itself in constant self-appraisal. How often have you heard managers ask "How does this promote our mission?" The growing influence of scientific and technical professionals in organizational decisions also contributes to this spirit of rationalism.

The hierarchical nature of bureaucracies creates a factoring of goals into subgoals and specialization (even routinization) of organizational activity. Operationally, the bureaucratic model gives the appearance of plodding inefficiency because an activity has to go through many procedural steps before it is complete. It may also appear impersonal because of the formal specialization of functions. Perhaps the latter points up an inherent deficiency in the "ideal" blueprint, and even Weber recognizes that it is impractical to expect any organization to reach that ideal. Dysfunctional consequences, the behaviorists point out, become evident when the idiosyncracies of people come into play. It follows logically that organizations do not operate like well-oiled machines. Consequently, public managers would be well-advised to assign a high priority to the human factor in the organization.

The bureaucratic model applies to both private and public organizations. One unique feature of the public organization, as previously pointed out, is that it operates within a political environment. A few comments about this relationship might be appropriate.

Management—Political Context Relationships

In Chapter 2 it was noted that public managers play a political role and affect public policy through their participation in formulating as well as implementing programs. In public organizations there is a dependence upon other organizations (agencies, legislative and executive bodies, citizen groups, and so on) for goal definition, resource allocation, jurisdiction, and exertion of influence.

Political disagreements often center in these areas. For example, public dismay over the alleged mismanagement of one state's health and welfare agency led to the agency's reorganization and the dissolution of several of its units. Thus, the degree to which politics are a positive or negative influence depends on how well managers establish linkages with other organizations. By acting as "boundary agent," the public manager attempts to reconcile the political and management environments to reduce the threats of uncertainty posed by dependence on other organizations.

Politics also exist within organizations as evidenced by struggles for personal survival, power, and prestige. Hence, the public manager's success often depends on his or her skill at real politics—the ability to determine who gets what, when, and how. The internal political system consists of groups and individuals who compete for the power to decide policy and gain favors. As shown in the Weber Model, bureaucracy is designed to deal with politics through a clear division of labor, a hierarchy of authority, clearly defined rules, and impersonal and rational modes of behavior. Bureaucracy, by promoting opportunities for its people to advance and by minimizing unfairness and favoritism, decreases what Stephen Robbins, a writer on administration, characterizes as "dysfunctional politics."[50] The values and beliefs of top managers determine what behavior will be rewarded by the organization. The Iran Contra affair is one example of what can occur when upper-level managers abuse the system and influence others to conspire with them in dysfunctional political activities. Bureaucracies are not immune from such behavior, but the organizational context makes it more visible and consequently more difficult.

There are no hard-and-fast rules for gaining power and influence within one's organization; but successful public managers recognize early in their careers that sensitivity to the internal and external political environments is crucial to their effectiveness. This is especially true in local government. At this level public managers are closest to their constituencies and more responsive to the pressures within the political environment. In addition to politics, a variety of other elements comprise the organizational context. Each of these elements is discussed in detail in the following section.

Components of the Organizational Context

Exhibit 3–1 depicts the organizational context and its various components. We see the organizational context functioning in a political setting. The management context itself consists of the organizational structure, functions performed by managers, people, management systems, physical factors, and policy. At the focal point is the public manager who is responsible for goal achievement.

Organizational Structure

Classical management theory contends that organizational objectives can be accomplished through the efficient structuring of tasks. Organizations are viewed as products of rational thought that perform coordinated tasks and that are governed by a hierarchy of authority.

In his classic text, *The Functions of the Executive,* Chester Barnard presented a model of the formal organization.[4] The model stressed that people were key to the functioning of organizations.

EXHIBIT 3-1. **The Organizational Context**

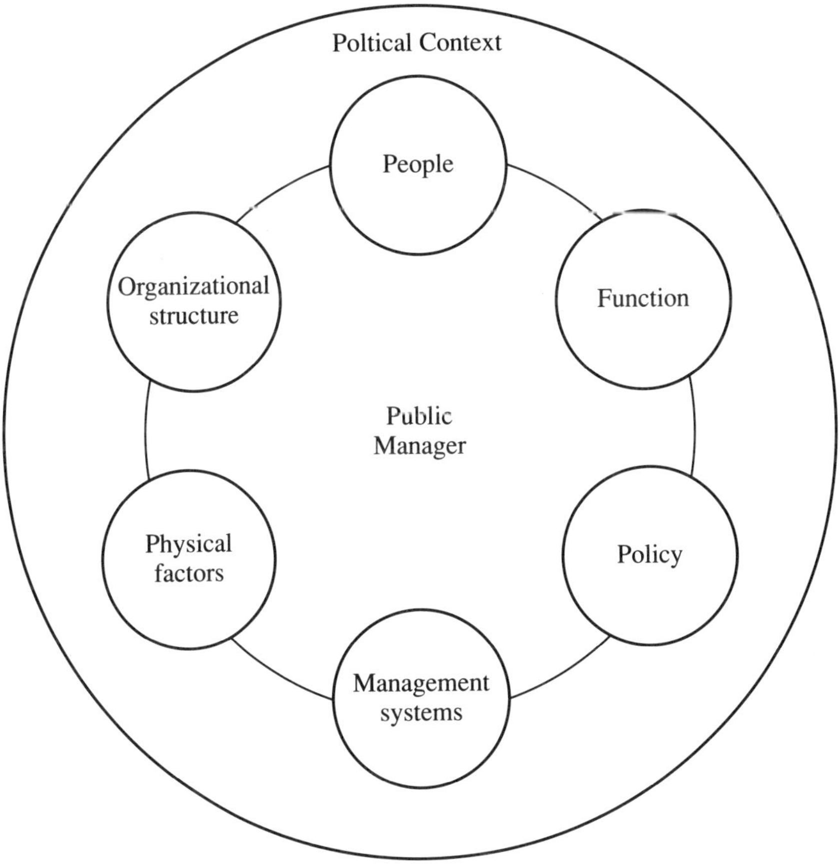

Their cooperation in achieving the organization's objectives was gained through communicating the performance expected and the satisfactions to be gained. Barnard's model emphasized that executives, or managers, were key to its successful implementation.

The classical school also defined other principles related to organizational structure. In a hierarchy of graded authority, individuals normally report to one superior for any given assignment (unity of command); the work is clearly defined and divided jurisdictionally; managers must have authority commensurate with responsibility to accomplish their assigned duties (parity); and they must be accountable for the results. With the enactment of the Civil Service Reform Act in 1978, all levels of government rededicated themselves to making managers accountable for *results.* From this stemmed the need for reliable performance data to judge managers' efficiency and effectiveness in utilizing people and other resources to accomplish designated goals. Consequently, agencies have developed quantitative data from work measurement, productivity, and cost systems in order to gauge performance against established goals and provide a basis for evaluating the effectiveness of public managers, including:

- *Cost/benefit analysis* to measure efficiency—the emphasis being on more and better output per dollar invested.
- *Unit cost information* to appraise resource utilization, compare operations, and analyze personnel requirements. Agencies' accounting systems often record obligations and disbursements for appropriations, programs, functional activities, and organizational segments by object class (for example, salaries, travel, equipment).
- The *budget process* to facilitate accountability by enabling a comparison of expected performance with actual performance.
- *Performance standards* to serve as expectations for managers' performance. For instance, managers can be required to state that their units will produce a certain number of units of output for a given dollar level.
- *Appraisal and review* to incorporate all the foregoing methods. By consulting descriptions of the manager's duties, the manager and his or her supervisor can identify key result areas and set goals for definite accomplishments within each area. Suffice it to say that the performance appraisal is an essential tool for managerial accountability.

In practice, public agencies exhibit many of the structural attributes of classic management paradigms. However, certain unique conditions, such as political involvement, size, and constitutionality present a real challenge to public managers. The following discussion of the structure of public organizations demonstrates some of the problems in translating theory into practice. It should give public managers a greater appreciation for the management context and make them more keenly aware of the principles associated with structuring organizations.

Political Involvement

In public agencies at all levels of government, elected officials and career managers must function together in the same organization. The elected officials' actions often conflict with the managers' operational effectiveness because these officials have political obligations. They must satisfy or appease their constituents if they desire to be reelected. Similarly, legislative committees and the chief executive might send conflicting directives to a manager that could easily create a conflict of loyalty. Such loyalty conflicts can upset a manager's control over an agency and inhibit control by either the chief executive or by the legislature.

Size

As government agencies expand, their management becomes increasingly difficult. Critics of government's size cite program proliferation, overregulation, and burdensome reporting requirements. The federally funded social programs have demanded astronomical growth of state and local payrolls and employees. Today there are more than 16 million people working in government compared to only 3 million in 1930. Payroll dollars soared from less than $1 billion in 1940 to over $30 billion today. Government spending is the center of debate in public and private forums and the federal deficit is a political football. Our government expenditures ballooned from 12 percent of the gross national product in 1929 to 20 percent today.

Former New York State Governor William Carey points out that there are over 80,000 units of state and local government.[10] He warns: "This tangle must be thinned out and rationalized. The welter of states, counties, cities, municipalities, townships, special districts, and miscellaneous clutter serves only to produce a web of redundancy."

Perhaps some of the hodgepodge and confusion stems from the very nature of government organization. Within the labyrinth of bureaus and agencies, some exist by design, some by mistake, and still others by evolution.

Functions

According to classic management theory, all managers perform common managerial functions in carrying out their roles (the universality of management concept). Managers universally perform the functions of planning, organizing, staffing, directing, and controlling; each of these functions will be covered in detail in Chapters 5 through 9. For the purpose of our discussion, each function is briefly defined here:

- *Planning—defining the agenda:* Public managers plan by working out in general terms the things that need to be accomplished and the strategy for achieving goals to reach the agency's mission. In carrying out the planning function, public managers establish objectives and policies for the organization and detail plans that will achieve those objectives.
- *Organizing—preparing the resources:* This function involves the determination of activities necessary to achieve the organization's objectives, defining the work to be done and assigning it to subdivisions (departments or units), delegating the necessary authority, and coordinating the activities.
- *Staffing—managing human resources:* This is the personnel function that determines of the kinds and numbers of people needed to carry out the organization's mission, placing them where they can make the greatest contribution to objectives, training the employees to be effective and efficient, and creating a work environment conducive to maintaining employee commitment.
- *Directing—moving toward results:* In this function public managers direct employee efforts and coordinate their activities to contribute optimally to the organization's objectives. In directing the work force, public managers communicate information up, down, and across the organization, resolve conflicts between and among employees, and maintain order through constructive or corrective discipline.
- *Controlling—assuring results:* Here the public manager verifies that the entire management process functions as planned. In controlling, the manager measures performance against the organization's objectives, determines causes of deviations, and takes the necessary corrective action.

Schools of management and special management development programs teach managers how to perform these functions more effectively. Since the basic principles, concepts, and techniques of managing have some general applicability to management situations and can be learned in a classroom, public managers can take the initiative to become educated in management. Schooling alone, however, does not make a manager; there is no substitute for broad-based, in-depth experience. Only by performing these functions does the practitioner develop managerial capabilities.

People

It takes people to run organizations. One key to public managers' effectiveness is their ability to get people in the organization to support its mission willingly and enthusiastically.

Considerable insight into the ways people behave in organizations has resulted from the studies of behavioral scientists. Research in human behavior in organizations was stimulated by the Hawthorne experiments of 1927–32, undertaken by a team of Harvard social scientists. They found that social and psychological influences in the work environment had a significant influence on performance.[49] Since that time sociologists have studied group dynamics, cooperation, and conflict in organization. Psychologists have developed theories of motivation, leadership, and human behavior patterns. The body of literature that emerged from these studies formed the behavioral school of management thought.

According to behavioral theory, behavior is influenced by an individual's needs, wants, and desires, and people form associations (informal organizations) with others who have mutually supportive or common needs and interests. In directing the work force, then, the public manager can influence the behavior of employees by exercising leadership and by providing an environment that stimulates desired performance.

Systems

The systems concept or approach views the organization as a network of components that work in a coordinated manner toward goal achievement. The essence of this approach is operations research that utilizes mathematical models to quantify organizational problems and facilitate planning and control functions. Computers enable managers to use systems models to simulate real-world conditions and to manipulate extraordinary amounts of data in order to arrive at more objective decisions. The systems approach also is viable for addressing behavioral, social, and political problems in the management context.

As an illustration of the systems approach, we might envision the management context system. Essentially, it is a microcosm of the political system discussed in Chapter 2. The management context works as a system in the following manner:

Inputs to the management system include the resources—human (people), financial, and physical—and the information and regulations that influence the public manager in working toward the achievement of the organization's goals. The manager then interacts with other actors within the environment. For example, an elected or appointed official may serve as liaison with the political environment and often influences the manner in which the public manager functions. In addition, the public manager's functions involve the direction of people over whom he or she has authority, as well as communication and coordination with peer managers and higher-level officials within the organization.

The public manager also interacts with the management context at-large to achieve system results. One example of the public manager interacting with the environment (context) is the process of co-optation. In co-optation new elements are absorbed into the leadership or policy-determining structure of an organization as a means of averting threats to its stability or existence. At the Tennessee Valley Authority, through its grass roots policy, local agricultural interests were able to influence major changes in overall policies on public land management and conservation as well as participate in specific activities, such as fertilizer distribution. TVA shared with agricultural interests the exercise of authority over a segment of its operation.

Outputs are the programs produced by the system in response to demands. Citizens continue to demand more and more from the government in protection, housing, health care, education, economic growth, public works, stability, technology, and an ever-widening array of services. And the system responds, with the result that costs soar and government continues to grow. The options seem to be, consequently, to cut services or to increase taxes, but in a national policy statement (*Improving Productivity in State and Local Government*) issued by the Committee for Economic Development, a third option was suggested: "that more intelligent use be made of existing resources to achieve desired goals; that is, increase government productivity."[11]

However, many services provided by the government defy objective measurement, and the outcome of many programs is not completely predictable. The Medicare program is a classic example. According to recent figures published by the Social Security Administration, Medicare covers about 33 million people at a cost exceeding $86 billion. The duration of incapacitation of elderly Americans covered by Medicare has been reduced from an average of eight days a year to five days a year. But the program resulted in the federal government becoming the leading purchaser of health care. Doctors responded by raising their fees, causing a significant jump in the cost of medical care. The unanticipated consequence has been the imposition of controls on the ways doctors practice medicine. The federal requirement for peer review of physicians in federally assisted hospitals, for example, threatened to close down almost one-third of the hospitals in the state of Oklahoma because there were not enough doctors to make up the review boards.

Feedback provides the system with a dynamic environment for the public manager. Programs and services produced by the organization have an impact on individuals and groups inside and outside of the organization. Through various means, public opinion or scientific measures, for example, the outputs are recorded, measured, and evaluated. The results elicit citizen response in the form of praise, protest, and so forth, which place further demands on the system. This response becomes the influence and information that cause change in priorities and goals and eventually affects the operation of the organization. Feedback introduces dynamism to the system—constant and changing demands maintain a state of flux. Thus, the system components of public demands, of management, and of programs interact to affect an original purpose. Similarly, the outputs (programs) of the system are a reflection of the inputs (resources). Evaluation of the results (outputs) forms a basis for appraising the performance of the inputs—this is especially true for appraising people's performance.

Applications of the systems approach: Concern for better government has resulted in a number of systems applications pertinent to public organizations. Productivity programs are making major inroads at all levels of government. Basically these programs serve to identify and analyze problems and to monitor progress toward performance improvement. Systems applications are used to measure efficiency, such as calculating ratio of work accomplished to inputs; introducing engineered work standards; and utilizing effectiveness—measurement procedures through citizen or client ratings of various service characteristics, or through use of predeveloped rating scales.

There are a variety of productivity programs in effect. For example, the city of Detroit has a productivity center that implements a continuing productivity effort through an expert staff; Phoenix performs program analyses and reviews through a planning-programming-budgeting system; and a Tacoma, Washington, program for productivity improvement involves extensive use of organizational development. In state government, Washington involves citizen task groups in planning future programs, all of which involve productivity programs; and Wisconsin has decentralized its productivity efforts in order to actively involve and stimulate each manager throughout the state. In the federal government, through the National Center for Productivity and Quality of Working Life, there is a systematic review of all federal activities that affect the performance of the economy as well as a national productivity policy.

Policy

The impact of public policy on organizations and the ways that public managers influence public policy was discussed earlier in this chapter and in Chapter 2. Similarly, organizational policies guide the operation of the organization. They emanate from organizational objectives and implement the intent of the formulators, for example, the managers. Policy-making is an integral part of the planning function of management, and policy—both public and organizational—has a significant bearing on the management context.

Physical Factors

This component of the management context refers to every physical condition within the organization. Technology plays a significant role in public management. Computers help managers retrieve information and manipulate data useful to decision making. Sophisticated equipment improves managerial and organizational performance. For example, video programs permit communications and training on a decentralized basis, and artificial organs help sustain patient life in health-care agencies. In recent years, environmental aspects of work locations have gained attention. Safe, healthy surroundings enhance performance; and comfortable temperatures, pleasing visual effects, and absence of distracting noises contribute to employee efficiency. Behavioral scientists have studied the effect of the physical grouping of people on productivity, and operations researchers have developed work-flow systems to enhance efficiency. Physical factors also include the materials and supplies available within the organization. Papers, pencils, forms, manuals, and files are essential to the operations of the bureaucracy. Information is recorded, communiques generated, and information filed to maintain a smoothly running organization. Even though government may be criticized for creating a paperwork jungle, agencies would cease to operate without some measure of it.

Integration of the Components: Contingency Theory

Public managers must consider myriad implications within a constantly changing environment. Each component of the environment interacts with others, and the entire environment in turn interacts with the political context. Not only is each component variable, but there is a multitude of possible interactions among them. How then should public managers view the management context?

Contingency management means that the style of management or the design of the organization depends on variables and their interactions in the situation. The approach to leadership, motivation, or decision-making would vary in different situations. Essentially, contingency theory stipulates that there is no single best way to manage—the environment or situation must be analyzed to determine an appropriate course of action.

Perhaps contingency management will be the integrating theory for the classical, behavioral, and systems approaches. It is a rational systemwide way of thinking; yet it includes behavioral, economic, and technological variables. The contingency approach makes sense for public managers who must operate in a dynamic environment.

A Brief Case Study—to Illustrate—to Ponder

The New Office Manager

When George Teasel retired as manager of the Social Security Administration's (SSA) district office in Metropolis, Loretta Compton was appointed as his replacement. Loretta had been the assistant manager, in the Chicago office, so her appointment from outside the local office created quite a stir.

Mr. Teasel had been the Metropolis District Manager for the past ten years, and he had worked his way up from field representative. He was a popular manager and most of his staff had been with him the entire time he was manager. The policy at SSA had traditionally been to promote from within, but a year ago it changed to one of selecting managers on a nationwide basis. As might be expected, Metropolis staff was reluctant to accept the new policy; they were a tightly knit group with long service in SSA and most of them were middle-aged. John Stoner, the assistant manager, was particularly upset because he felt that he had been developed for the manager's position by George Teasel and that he was more deserving of the appointment.

SSA commissioned Loretta Compton to improve the productivity of the office. There was a substantial backlog of disability and health insurance claims which took 60 to 70 days to process (the national standard was 30 days), the error rate on claims forms processed by this office and detected by the payment center was the highest in the region, and complaints from clients were well above the norm.

Soon after she assumed her position as manager, Loretta Compton met with her staff (clerical people, field and claims representatives, unit supervisors, and department managers) to brief them on the need to improve production and to solicit their cooperation. Everyone seemed to be in agreement with Ms. Compton's plans, which included performance improvement, a training program, rearrangement of the work flow on claims processing, and the institution of management by objectives.

Despite these efforts performance did not improve. Supervisors seemed to irritate employees in the way they initiated changes, absenteeism began to increase, and the claims backlog got worse, not better. Loretta found herself working longer hours in an effort to correct the situation. After six months as manager she was wondering if she could ever get the full support of her staff and get the situation to turn around.

1. What management functions is Loretta Compton performing here?
2. How can Loretta set performance standards for the SSA office?
3. In this case what might Loretta apply from the various management schools of thought (functional, behavioral, systems, contingency) to help turn the situation around?
4. Why do you suppose employees were irritated with the way changes were initiated? What can SSA do to influence the employees to accept changes?

CHAPTER 4

Determining Problems and Opportunities: Policy-making

Contemporary America is confronted with a broad assortment of major problems and opportunities. Daily newspapers devote much of their space to such items as budget and trade deficits, environmental and pollution concerns, inflation, unemployment, health and welfare, urban problems, and a multitude of other public concerns. The public nature of such issues inevitably forces them onto the agenda of government.

As our daily lives have become increasingly complex in the twentieth century, so have the agenda and activities of our many governments. We see more demanded of the public sector, whether it be local, state, or national government. In addition, many demands turn into paradoxical situations. Even when sufficient consensus develops and government takes action, the result may not solve the problem. In fact, the ultimate result will probably be a change in the nature of the problem. We want a cleaner environment, for example, but we also want to increase production and consumption. We want lower taxes, but we also want defense, police, health, parks, and better roads. Most conflicts that come to government for resolution have no easy or simple solutions. In addition, it is rare when government is able to act on a particular issue with finality.

None of the public manager's roles is more unique, nor more important, than that of policymaker. The public manager is deeply involved in policy-making at two interrelated levels. First, and most obvious, is the making of policy about the internal operation of his or her agency. Decisions must constantly be made about practices and procedures within the agency. Second, but perhaps less obvious, is the manager's participation in policy that directly affects the world outside the confines of the agency itself. This second category, public policy-making, is the primary concern of this chapter.

Historically, public managers were seen as implementing, but not making, public policy. Today's understanding is considerably revised, enlarged, and more realistic than this earlier view.

A Broad View of Public Policy

While the central interest of this chapter is the implementation of societal goals and policies through public management, this interest must be viewed in a broader context. Two important aspects to keep in mind are

- the overall nature of politics and policy-making within our total political system, and
- the fact that public agencies represent only one of the many ways society can choose to deal with a public problem.

A complete review of the ways in which policies develop would require a thorough exposition of the American political system. The existence of our particular democratic system is itself the result of an evolving public policy process. All political systems stem from ethical assumptions; democracy is no exception. A primary assumption is that the individual is the basic unit of value, thus government should facilitate the pursuit of individual needs and interests. In their excellent book on American government, Thomas Dye and Harmon Ziegler discuss democracy in terms of five values or policy preferences.[17] Paraphrased somewhat, these include:

1. Popular participation in decisions that shape the lives of persons in society
2. Majority rule
3. Recognition of minorities' rights to try to become majorities—including such specific rights as freedom of the press, freedom of speech, freedom to form opposition parties, freedom to assemble, and freedom to run for office
4. Commitment to individual dignity and to preserving the values of life, liberty, and property
5. Commitment to equal opportunity for all persons to develop their capabilities

Our Constitution sets forth fundamental elements of how these policy preferences are attained. From time to time the Constitution has been amended to clarify or change policies or the ways they can be achieved. Thus, the public manager needs a clear understanding of the assumptions about democracy. While there is much distance between the Constitutional framework and the operation of specific agencies, it must be remembered that public agency goals and policies arise within the context of the political system under which we live.

Alternative Ways to Pursue Public Policies

A governmental system can choose to address problems or needs in various ways. Establishing a public agency and setting in action a public management process is only one possible outcome. In response to a particular problem, there is a range of choices available to government; it can

1. Decide to do nothing
2. Encourage voluntary action by citizens
3. Give individuals tax credits or other specific incentives to take individual action
4. Contract with private organizations to accomplish the desired action
5. Provide grant-in-aid dollars to lower governmental levels (for example, from federal to state and/or local)
6. Create a new program within an existing agency
7. Create a new agency

Each of these options represents a basic policy direction taken with respect to a particular need or problem. All seven can easily be found in our society. Government actions in such areas as tobacco, automobile safety, environmental issues, health, and international relations provide a wide range of examples. In general, as a problem becomes more visible and more severe, and as politicians and others (including voters) begin to agree on what should be done, there is a movement from item 1 toward item 7.

The Public Agency Choice

Public agencies are obviously established for the purpose of pursuing public policies. For such agencies to function effectively, however, more than broad policy is required. The Congress or state legislatures may legislate, and the president or governors may approve, a new program. It becomes a reality only as organization charts are developed, goals for component units are established, office space is secured, and staff is hired. As these steps are taken, more precise policies (or goals) are created, aimed at putting the original broader policy into operation. This process of policymaking is depicted, in a simplified form, in exhibit 4-1.

In viewing this process, the reader should try to identify additional

EXHIBIT 4-1. **A Simplified View of Government in Action**

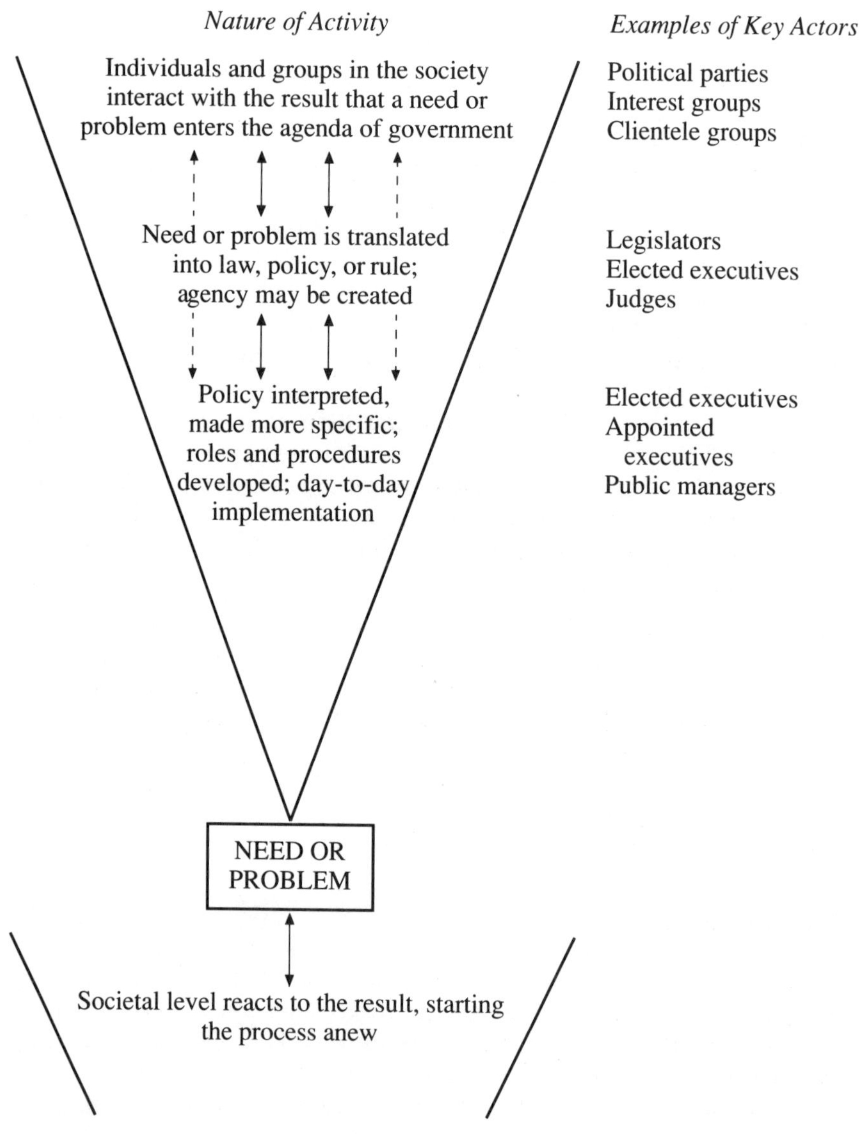

Note: While the large arrow indicates the direction of movement, smaller arrows point out the continuing interactions between the various levels.

"primary actors" at the various levels. A few moments of reflection on the nature and significance of interaction between levels would also be very useful. This simplified view is equally applicable in considering local, state, or federal government. It is also applicable to whatever function of government one considers — from aviation to zoos.

Policy-making and the Public Manager

Policy can be defined in various ways. It is, for example, "a big decision governing how little decisions will be made." Another view might simply be "whatever governments choose to do." Policy is essentially government's steering process. It has to do with moves made or not made and with the resultant course and direction that is charted.

The charted course is a central output of the political system described in Chapter 2. All of the societal systems identified there participate in the policy-making process. Key actors in the policy arena include:

- Elected and appointed government executives
- Legislators
- Judges
- Career public managers
- Political party leaders
- Media persons in the press, radio, and television
- Lobbyists and special interest groups
- Religious leaders
- Clientele served by government agencies (for example, veterans, farmers)
- Community leaders and citizens
- Leaders in professions and occupational groups (for example, business, education, law, science)

While the first four on this list are the official actors, who are directly and legally responsible for government actions, the other seven also play important parts. The influence of individuals and groups in the policy process depends upon many factors, including:

- The general nature of the subject matter (changing the Social Security program as compared to building a highway or a park)
- The intensity of feeling about an issue or problem
- The resources available to the interested parties (for example, money, voters, expertise, time)
- Success in attracting other persons and groups as allies
- Luck and circumstance

The degree of success of persons and groups in influencing policy is illustrated in almost every daily newspaper or news broadcast.

Why Public Managers Are Policymakers

In addressing the public manager's role as policymaker, it is useful to begin, in a sense, at the end. How does the policy activity of the public manager ultimately affect the average citizen? While the impact has been diversely illustrated by authors, none have caught the essence better than political scientist William Boyer in his book *Bureaucracy on Trial:*

> A typical day in the life of an average person illustrates the importance of administrative policies. If he drives his car to work, it is probably equipped and maintained to satisfy minimum requirements and specifications as determined by an administrative agency. His car is insured by a company regulated by an administrative agency. He must abide by administratively created traffic regulations involving such matters as speed zones and stop signs. If he should travel by bus, trolley, or railway, he must pay a fare fixed by a regulatory agency.
>
> If he works in an office building, he probably ascends to his office in an elevator constructed and maintained in accordance with an administrative code. The building itself was probably planned by a licensed architect and constructed under the supervision of registered engineers pursuant to the administrative regulations of a building code; it was wired as prescribed by an electrical code, heated and ventilated according to another code, and equipped and fitted with plumbing fixtures as required by plumbing code. He lunches at a restaurant where the equipment complies with health rules. The food he eats was produced and marketed under agricultural regulations, transported by means of regulated carriers, and processed according to administrative food standards. (p. 3)[7]

Although the role of the public manager is pervasive in this example, this is only part of the story. In addition to conducting the day-to-day affairs of government, public managers are central actors in the long-range decision-making and policy-making process. Public managers bring a variety of skills to the policy process. These include skills that are necessary both for making and for implementing policy decisions. The purpose of creating large organizations is to enhance human competences by providing for a division of labor. The resulting opportunity for concentrated attention gives public managers significant advantages over political officials who deal with a variety of matters, spending relatively little time on any one. In this sense, public managers often have a near monopolistic control of information about the area in which they work. In addition to specialized knowledge, their continuity in dealing with particular matters leads to further development of their expertise. Public managers have many opportunities to use their specialized knowledge. They are often asked, or required, to advise chief executives and legislators in the deliberation of policy issues. In addition, as the foregoing example suggests, laws and policies generally leave room for discretion to those who implement them. The city council, for example, may determine the speed limit for a particular street, but the real policy is determined by the decisions of the police chief and his or her staff in enforcing the ordinance.

Most legislation passed by legislatures is drafted in the offices of various executive agencies. This is common practice whether the draft is requested by the president or the Congress. Both look for the most knowledgeable agency when a proposal is needed.

Another source of power is the political support acquired and developed by public managers. Many agencies have their particular group, or what may be called a constituency, that has great interest in the agency's activities. Agencies in areas such as labor, agriculture, and veterans affairs will rarely take a stand opposing the interest of the group they serve. The interest and support of outside groups obviously translates into political support and appropriations in the Congress.

Political support can be sought in any one, or in any combination of, three areas:

- The executive branch itself—the president, governor, mayor, or other highly visible powerful person
- The legislative body—influential individuals or groups who have special interest in any agency and its work
- The public—interested, and politically active outside groups, or the public at large

In seeking political support, one source of danger for an agency is the potential cost associated with it. Support-seeking can become deference to particular persons or groups, and the agency can find that a high price is exacted in the political arena. In return for support, political persons and groups often want to influence the agency's decision-making process.

In the final analysis, public managers are involved in the policy process because they are needed. They bring critical knowledge and expertise in their particular field to the process. Few know as much about the work of government agencies as the people who manage them. If a chief executive, or a legislative body, seeks information on transportation, housing, or conservation, what better and more accessible place to look than in the agency itself?

The public manager's knowledge and expertise are based on a combination of education, training, and experience. Tenure and continuity are important dimensions. Often the public manager has seen his or her field evolve through many policy changes. This enables the manager to develop a significant grasp of particular public problems, of the agency's capacity for dealing with such problems, of what has worked and what has failed. As the size and complexity of government have grown, so has the importance of the public manager's knowledge. To achieve governmental purposes the public manager must, by the nature of his or her task, be a significant and continuing participant in the making of public policy.

Policy Analysis

In recent years political scientists, economists, and others have become increasingly interested in policy analysis. Interest has focused on examination and improvement of the policy-making process as well as the evaluation of specific choices and outcomes. This reflects a change in emphasis from the way politics and government traditionally have been studied.

Historically, the institutions and structures of government and political behavior and processes have been the central concerns. Policy analysis strives to achieve an interdisciplinary approach and to focus on society's activities and problems. While some persons pursue policy analysis as scholarly research or out of personal curiosity, more people are interested in policy analysis for action-oriented reasons. They hope to bring a higher degree of rationality and scientific analysis to the process of making public policy. The analyst likes to think of his or her work as objective, rigorous, and important. The result of such analyses may well be all of these, however, and still not be used or usable.

While policy analysts and evaluators focus on issues and problems, political actors are more concerned with people and with creating advantages for competing groups. While the analyst may believe that he or she is the "purveyor of truth," the politician may see him or her as "just another lobbyist." This does not mean that the politician is anti-analyst, or even unappreciative of the work that has been done. It is simply a product of the politician's role under our form of government and reflects the fact that "truth," as determined through the political process, is a very subjective matter.

Policy analysis is concerned with several general areas. First, it is concerned with the assessment of policy impacts and outcomes. Second, it is concerned with the evaluation of failures and successes of policy on specific problems. Third, it must apply analysis to policy improvement and reform.

Methods of Analysis

A basic problem in the analysis of public policy is how to do it in the most systematic and effective manner. To develop broad understanding of the policy process and its products, there is a need to develop methods to sort out and categorize information and to make certain the right questions are asked. Here are four approaches to the study of policy that currently are being used:

- Case study of specific situations
- Input-output analysis
- Criteria-based evaluation
- Process approach

In the case-study approach, the analyst becomes immersed in a selected policy matter to learn as much as possible about it. This approach has the obvious advantages of detail and specificity. The biggest disadvantage is that many case studies must be completed and compared before general conclusions can be reached.

The second method, input-output analysis, attempts to apply the systems model outlined in Chapter 2. The goal is to explain outputs by analyzing inputs. As an example, one might compare policy decisions made by states with predominantly rural voters to those of states where the majority of voters live in urban centers.

The third approach, criteria-based evaluation, attempts to identify and apply "yardsticks" or measures that are deemed relevant. Yehezkel Dror, in his *Public Policymaking Reexamined,* [16] has provided a good list of the most frequently used criteria:

1. Past quality (are we doing better?)
2. Quality of other systems (how do we compare?)
3. Desired quality (is the result what we hoped for?)
4. Professional standards of quality (how do the experts in this area view our result?)
5. Survival quality (can we, or the organization, continue at this level?)
6. Planned quality (is this the result we paid for?)
7. Optimal quality (how far are we from the "ideal"?)

While standard 7 is the most desirable measure to use, unfortunately, it is also the most difficult to achieve—and often the least practical.

The fourth approach, analysis of the policy process, will probably provide policymakers with the best understanding over time. It has the advantage of breadth and the potential for integrating the other three methods discussed above. Policy analysis attempts to evaluate alternative policy options. It involves the collection and interpretation of information and attempts to predict the consequences of alternative choices.

One scholar who has provided a useful synthesis of the policy analysis approach is Charles Jones.[30] He has developed a model that includes:

- How problems develop and get on the agenda of government
- What happens within government
- Government's response to the problem
- The result and feedback that follows

In developing his ideas, Jones emphasizes the never-ending nature of the policy process. Issues and problems change and evolve, but rarely is a policy matter dealt with and dispatched once and for all.

A Brief Case Study—to Illustrate—to Ponder

A Policy Problem in Dawson City

Members of the City Council of Dawson City continue to receive citizen complaints about police actions on Memorial Drive. This controversy has been going on ever since this street was built and opened three years ago. Approximately 50 percent of the complaints are from citizens who have received speeding tickets. The other 50 percent complain that not enough tickets are being given.

Memorial Drive was developed to serve as a link between two state highways that pass through Dawson City. Both commercial and residential development has grown along the new street.

The controversy has become the number one policy problem of both the Police Chief and the City Manager. Prepare a plan of action that they can use to work toward an appropriate speed limit—a workable public policy.

CHAPTER 5

Defining the Agenda: Planning

Planning is concerned with the development of objectives and their accompanying programs. Planning is future-oriented in that a manager decides in advance what is to be done, how and when it is to be accomplished, and who is to be responsible. It is a conceptual process that involves anticipation of future events that can be predicted. Because these events are generally affected or often even imposed by factors beyond the control of the manager, they cannot be predicted with absolute certainty. In this respect, planning includes an exchange process between the organization and its environment in which the organization attempts to work the exchanges to its advantage. Planning presumes the existence of alternatives—even for circumstances beyond the control of the manager—from which objectives can be selected. Thus, the planning process provides a rational approach to the determination of the organization's objectives.

Planning also provides the basis for controlling operations. With measurable objectives, the managers can clearly determine how well programs are moving toward their intended ends. Thus, both planning and control look to the future; planning anticipates future events, and control ensures that those events occur as they were planned.

Importance of Effectiveness in Public Programs

Although plans do not guarantee the success of a program, they do greatly enhance the probability of success. When desired results are conceived in advance of the performance of activities, experience has shown that the results are far better than when a haphazard, unplanned approach is taken. Effectiveness and efficiency in public programs are far more likely to occur when objectives are carefully thought out and prioritized, and when strategies with supporting activities are delineated in advance of implementation.

When public programs fall short of their intended purpose, society suffers. Since 1969, this country has endured three recessions in quick succession. In past years, the unemployment rate has hovered near 6 percent, and according to many economists, inflation continues to be a major concern. These adverse conditions have given rise to a push for centralized, comprehensive, economic planning. On another dimension, several years ago the U.S. Army recognized a lack of effectiveness in its "people" capabilities, such as, poor leadership, lack of meaningful and challenging work, a pervasive rejection on the part of some soldiers of individual responsibilities, and other shortcomings. The Army instigated a remedial program for organizational effectiveness, and the centralized planning effort corrected many of the deficiencies.

Society expects its public agencies to be effective, and this expectation places the onus on public managers to deliver the necessary goods and services. Managers are accountable to society for the performance of their organizations. It is from society that managers derive their authority because society—taxpayers—supplies the resources for the operation of the organizations. From society's viewpoint, effectiveness is the degree to which a public agency achieves its objectives, given the resources available to it. But, as previously discussed, efficiency is a corollary to effectiveness. The manager must achieve the organization's ends, but at a reasonable cost. Effectiveness without efficiency is still untenable. For example, if the costs of protecting health and safety become excessive, citizens will demand that alternative or replacement programs be developed. Obviously, this would mean replacing the management of the inefficient program.

Achieving organizational effectiveness is especially challenging for public managers because they often must show results in a relatively short time, attain massive objectives with limited resources, and operate with people whose careers may be outside of their control. Despite these and other constraints, many public managers have helped their organizations achieve effectiveness. The first appointed head of the Environmental Protection Agency, William Ruckelshaus, managed to achieve the standards promulgated in the Clean Air Act within a relatively short time. Similarly, Gordon Chase, the widely respected former administrator of New York City's Health Service Administration, involved the medical establishment and the voluntary sector in an effective program to combat a host of social and environmental dangers that affected enormous numbers of people. The key to the effectiveness of these public managers was that they were able to influence the purpose, structure, and people of their organizations by developing clearly stated, measurable goals that were politically acceptable. In the words of Harvard professor Joseph Bower, "To be effective in the public sector, you must be a politician. But (perhaps what they have argued is wise) you must not play for political power. Rather, it is through use of analytic and operating skills, supported by staff, that a substantive program can be developed and implemented."[8]

The Planning Process

The planning process is depicted graphically in exhibit 5–1. It has its basis in a management *philosophy.* Emanating from the philosophy are the organization's *objectives,* the ends toward which activities are directed. To implement these objectives managers are guided in their decision making by *policies,* but they must develop *strategies* that direct activities toward the attainment of objectives. Lower-level managers then disseminate *procedures* that detail the intended methods of handling these activities. *Rules* are promulgated to delineate specific required actions to support the activities or programs. Each of these elements of the planning process is a type of plan itself because it is chosen from among alternatives, it is oriented toward the future, and it helps determine the results of the organization. In the same regard, a budget is also a plan; it expresses expected results in numerical terms.

Determining a Management Philosophy

Although the management literature does not yield a consistent definition of the term *management philosophy,* the one offered by administration theorist Ralph C. Davis appears to be most widely accepted. In his classic, *The Fundamentals of Top Management,* he contends that a philosophy is a "body of doctrine . . . [which] refers to any formal statement, either express or implied, of objectives, ideals, principles, points of view, and general modes of procedures."[15] For a manager, a philosophy helps bridge the gap between theory and practice. It becomes a way of thinking that influences the way an individual behaves as a manager. Thus, organizational efficiency is facilitated because managers with well-defined philosophies can focus on specific desired ends. And when top management's philosophy is articulated in writing, it guides the organization in the development of objectives and of supporting plans and programs. Since the environments in which public managers operate are dynamic, the development of a management philosophy logically becomes a continuous self-development process.

EXHIBIT 5-1. **The Planning Process**

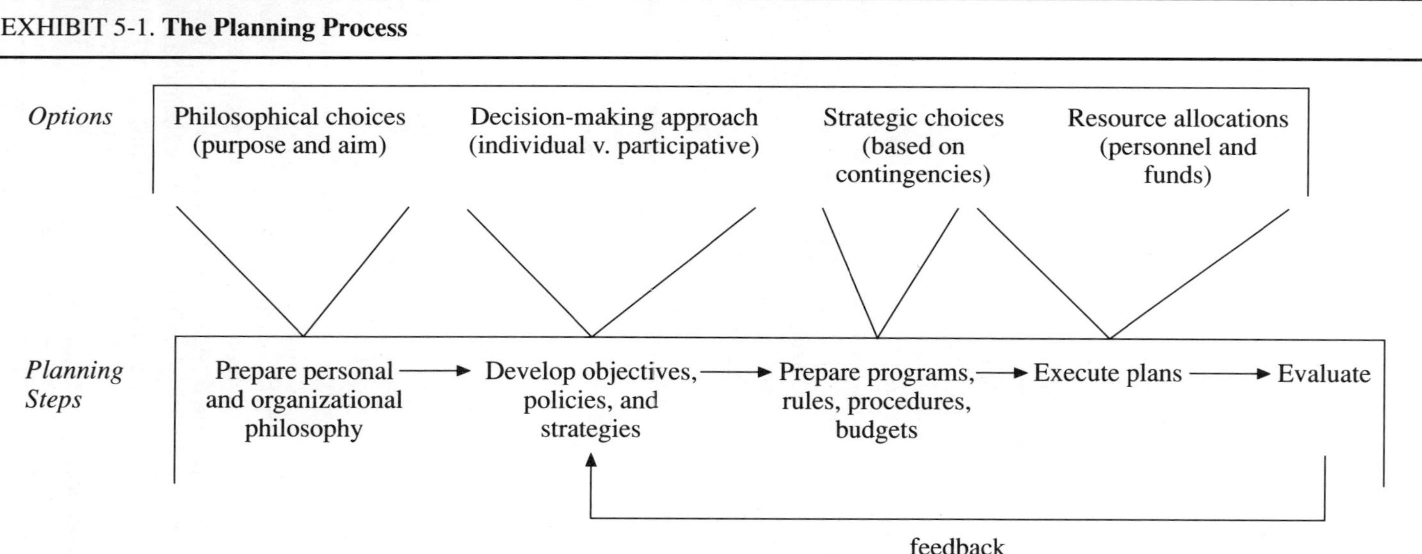

Note: The arrow at each planning step represents communication.

The process of developing one's management philosophy is portrayed in exhibit 5-2. The process involves the following:

Assimilation of thoughts from a vast reservoir of ideas derived from theory, beliefs about practices, and attitudes of the manager. Even the experienced practitioner with a pragmatic outlook would be well-advised to integrate the theoretical dimension with the practical and personal dimensions.

Conception, or the formulation of a mental image or impression that can be translated into a model to serve as a framework or design. This is the most difficult phase of the process. It requires the manager to identify the key elements that form his or her way of thinking about the job of managing the organization. These might be classified into sets of thoughts that become the primary components of the philosophy. Defining the relationships among components integrates the philosophy into a tentative model. Once the model is described, the manager can test it against existing conditions. Time devoted to developing a strong, clear concept can pay important dividends when the thoughts are reduced to writing.

Description involves the written articulation of one's philosophy. This is the step between concept and reality. There is no prescribed format for a written philosophy. It can take the form of an essay, a concept paper, or a pronouncement. But whatever form it takes, a written philosophy is an essential first step in the planning process.

One example of a public management philosophy is the following excerpt of an Annual Posture Statement of the Department of the Army: "Simply put, the Army's role, its purpose, and its reason for existence, is to serve the United States interests in this uncertain and unsettled world. Among those interests are National survival and the freedom of interaction with people of the world in peaceful pursuits." Were there an official Army philosophy, the statement would be substantially expanded to include the details necessary to relate the various parts into a unitary whole.

A search of the literature on the basic criteria for a philosophy of management, indicates that essentially a management philosophy should

- be practical and workable.
- be based on an acquired body of knowledge in conjunction with personal experience.
- incorporate the functions of management.
- be based on sound evidence from other disciplines.
- be flexible to take account of changing environmental conditions.

- consider and be congruent with existing organization objectives.
- enhance the general welfare of the organization and its personnel.
- be communicated openly.
- be based on equity, morality, and human dignity.
- have an orientation toward the future.

Setting Objectives

It has already been noted that setting objectives is an essential step in the planning function that guides the organization toward specific, intended results. Regardless of the approach one takes to establishing objectives, the essential point is that a definition of objectives is the critical first step in making rational decisions.

EXHIBIT 5-2. **A Process for Developing a Personal Management Philosophy (A Manager's Way of Thinking About the Job of Managing an Organization)**

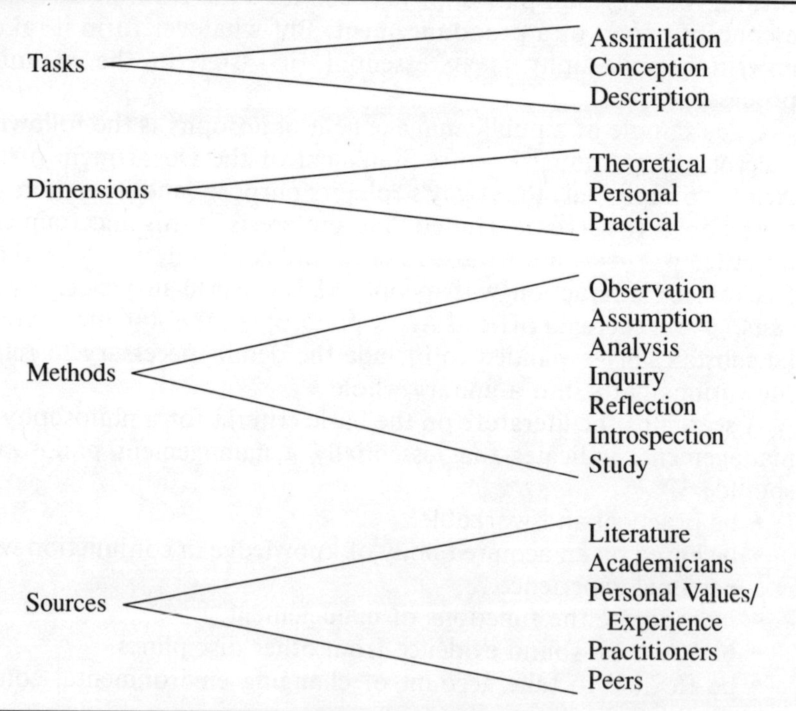

Policies: Policies are guidelines for action. They emanate from organizational objectives and implement the intent of the formulators. Properly conceived policies consist of two parts: first, a principle or a group of related principles; and second, rules of action. Together, these two parts support the objectives toward which they are directed.

Principles: A principle is a significant truth that is usually stated as a cause-and-effect relationship. Years of experience with organizational problems have led to generalizations about effective administration; these generalizations have become the principles that channel organizational activities. Principles in organizations increase efficiency and crystallize the nature of management, but most important, they explain the intent of the policy. Examples of principles related to public management might include:

- Public employees perform better when they have a voice in determining matters that affect them.
- The authority, duties, responsibilities, and relationships of everyone in the organization should be clearly and completely spelled out in writing and communicated so that everyone's efforts can be directed toward a common goal.
- A public manager's performance is determined by the quality of service his or her agency delivers to its constituents.

It should be emphasized at this point that these examples are not absolute. Managers have operated successfully in violation of some principles. For example, matrix organizations violate the principle of the unity of command yet are a viable form of organization.

Rules: When policies are implemented in the form of rules and procedures, the principle is only implied. If the reason behind a rule is not explained, the rule becomes an edict. As the public service employs increasing numbers of younger, better-educated people who often do not obey orders blindly, agencies find it necessary to explain the reasons behind policy statements. Employee understanding and acceptance of the meaning of rules are essential in eliciting cooperation.

A statement of principle can clarify the meaning of a rule. Take, for instance, this rule on attendance: "The workday begins at 7:30 a.m. All employees are expected to be at their duty station and ready to work promptly at the beginning of the workday." Such a matter-of-fact announcement is likely to elicit a negative response from employees. However, if management explains the principle behind the rule, voluntary conformity is much more likely to result. Consider this version of the rule: "The public relies on us to serve their needs. A starting time of 7:30 a.m. has been designated so that we can be prepared when our clients call. Experience has shown that a 7:30 a.m. starting time allows us to provide the best possible service. You are, therefore, asked to be at your work station promptly at 7:30 a.m."

Systems analysts Hinrich and Taylor, in their text *Systematic Analysis*, have devised a scheme of systematic analysis, a decision-making process that focuses on utilizing limited means to achieve unlimited ends.[27] They propose to convert societal values into objectives, or quantified desired outputs that are measurable or prioritized. Setting these objectives is no easy task, but it calls for answering questions such as: What are the "wants" of society? What are its primary values? The alternative choices in setting public managerial objectives include:

1. *Maximize.* Ignore special interests and attach value only to common needs of individuals.
2. Ensure that *everybody gains* in welfare, for example, satisfaction and achievement of individual preferences.
3. Ensure that at least *one individual gains and nobody loses.*
4. Ensure a *net gain,* for example, gains outweigh losses.
5. *Maximize the minimum possible gain.* For example, U.S. defense strategy could be premised on achieving a minimum effective deterrent.
6. *Minimax,* or minimize the maximum possible loss.

Achieving Objectives

Strategies: Traditionally, the military utilized the concept of strategy to develop plans in light of the adversary's anticipated movements. From a public-management standpoint, strategy is a plan of action that specifies the resources and the allocation of those resources required to achieve organizational goals.

The U.S. Army has a national objective that seeks to reduce the chance and risks of war with emphasis on prevention of nuclear war. It also desires to maintain a general freedom of action in international relations. The military strategy to support that approach is based on collective security, deterrence, forward defense, and flexible response. The Army's concept of strategy in that overall scheme is flexibility, usability, and visibility of force—these being the characteristics of land warfare.

The concept of strategy implies competition, and one might argue that public agencies are not viewed as competitive. Yet public agencies do compete for programs and for the funds to support them. As mentioned in the previous discussion of the context of public management, political considerations cause some programs to be adopted while others are dropped. Consequently, the public manager needs to think strategically in order to promote the continuation of desired programs.

Here is an example of strategic thinking that paid off. A large metropolitan area that was designated a prime sponsor under the Comprehensive Employment and Training Act (CETA) included in its strategy for implementing its manpower program (1) a detailed forecast of local industry's employment needs, and (2) a Labor Market Advisory Committee that included executives from a representative sample of local firms. The committee guided the CETA staff in developing programs that would be meaningful to local industry. The large number of CETA program graduates who subsequently were hired attested to its success.

Procedures: We are all familiar with manuals containing procedures that detail the manner in which an activity is to be carried out. While policies are broad guidelines for managerial thinking, procedures are step-by-step methods to guide action. An agency might have a policy on reimbursement for official travel expenses; the procedure would detail the method for filing for reimbursement and describe how to fill out and process the necessary forms.

Program: The ultimate step or outcome of the planning process is a program. Programs seldom stand by themselves. To carry out a plan of action, a complex array of programs is usually required. Any one program affects and depends on others. The interdependence of programs calls for coordination and timing so that each program will be supportive of the other.

Management by Objectives

Management by objectives (MBO) has been a somewhat controversial approach to management and has been discussed pro and con for several years. The discussion has also involved some variation in the definition applied to MBO by various management writers. Some have claimed that MBO is simply a new group of words which have the same basic definition as management itself. Others have focused on the process of enhancing employee commitment and participation in the organization as being a primary goal of MBO. Others have attributed planning and planning processes as being the central and most important keys in the MBO process. Still others have considered the process of evaluation and control itself as being the central focus of an effective MBO program.

One source of information on MBO and its application in government is George L. Morrisey's *Management by Objectives and Results in the Public Sector.*[39] According to Morrisey, management methodology can generally be placed on a continuum between two extremes. At one extreme is management on the basis of activity or reaction, and at the other is management on the basis of objectives and results. Morrisey feels that government is all too often managed on the basis of activity and reactions. The activity- or reaction-oriented manager simply counts the number of widgets that are processed or judges the flurry of activity when a visiting dignitary arrives as being an indication of productive effort. The manager who has an objective and results orientation, however, is more geared to results and the action plans required to achieve such results. Basically, planning is central to the difference in these two approaches. Morrisey recognizes, of course, that neither extreme will exist in its purest form. He also recognizes that in any management situation, some of both will exist. His goal, however, is to urge the manager to move in the direction of managing by objectives and results rather than by reacting to problems and emergencies. A forward-looking orientation prevents many of these situations from ever occurring. Proper planning also provides for and facilitates the handling of such situations that do occur.

Morrisey depicts the MBO process as going from the general to the specific. It begins with roles and missions and works through key result areas, indicators, objectives, action plans, and, finally, controls. Morrisey sees the management process as focusing more and more specifically on things to be done and verifying that those are in fact done. He sees the process as basically very simple, commonsensical, logical, and as a way to arrange and to practice the proven principles and techniques of management.

Jong S. Jung gives a different emphasis to the MBO processes, defining management by objectives as "a process whereby organizational goals and objectives are set through the participation of organizational members in terms of results expected."[31]

The basic idea is that of participative management. Goal-setting processes are seen as the key factor, and Jung stresses individual participation, self-management, and decentralization within the organization. Strong communication and feedback processes are considered critical to an integrated approach to management.

One of the founding fathers of MBO, George S. Odiorne, has described the basic elements of MBO in government by identifying the following five items[44]:

- *Goal setting.* Each administrator works with his or her superior in a mutual agreement as to what kinds of results are expected.

- *Budgeting.* To the extent possible, objectives are related to necessary resources and budgets related to tasks and responsibility.
- *Autonomy.* Individuals are left alone to the extent possible once goals and resources are agreed upon.
- *Feedback.* The individual manager is provided with information on his performance, and on what corrective action is needed, or what shortcomings exist.
- *Payoffs.* Rewards are provided for accomplishment, and the remuneration of managers is based upon incentives to improve their own performance, rather than on political affiliations or on some other factor, such as personality.

Perhaps the most significant thing about all of the techniques or approaches to large-scale management is not so much the specific accomplishments of each method but simply the focus on the system itself. In many respects, these and many other management techniques are like successive waves: each has its moment of triumph but will be superseded by later techniques. The important lesson for the public manager to learn and to remember is the analysis of the management process, particularly in the consideration of planning. In addition to planning with respect to goals and programs, it is necessary for the manager to be constantly aware of the need planning on the management process itself, whether it be a process of management by objectives or some other kind of system. It is desirable to set goals and objectives, but the process itself must be made increasingly effective. In this context, MBO certainly demonstrates the complexity of the management process, identifies those points at which improvement is necessary, and aids in understanding the difficulties in obtaining such improvements.

Evaluating and Controlling Plans

After plans have been put in motion, it is crucial that they be monitored to determine the organization's progress toward its objectives. In this respect, the record of the organization's performance is examined to see how current results compare to past performance. Trends are indicators of needed change in future plans. Monitoring plans make managers aware of potential problem areas and the actions that need to be taken should these problems arise. Anticipation of problems helps managers avoid crises. Unfortunately, few public managers track their plans once they have been implemented. Plan evaluation and control are areas on which many public managers need to work.

Decision Making

Regardless of their classification or level in the hierarchy, public managers are required to make decisions, either individually or as members of a decision-making group. In each managerial function (planning and organizing, controlling, and so forth), the public manager is called on to make decisions. Decision making is especially relevant to the planning process because the manager must select appropriate objectives for the organization and must determine the appropriate courses of action to achieve the objectives. Public decision making is a dynamic process because the solution of one problem often gives rise to another. For example, as managers seek to correct environmental problems, they may find that unemployment increases. Or as federal funds are expended on welfare programs, the resulting strain on the economy may increase the risk of inflation. Consequently, today's solutions do not resolve tomorrow's problems.

Conceptual (decision-making) skill is one of the basic skills of a successful administrator, or manager. Conceptual skill relates to the ability to recognize the relationships among the social, economic, and political elements in the management environment and to take action that advances the welfare of the organization. This skill is perhaps the most difficult to apply. It involves making decisions whose outcomes are extremely uncertain.

In any government agency, there is a maze of clientele groups that have a basic influence over the organization. For instance, county governments must be mindful of citizen needs when planning programs. However, they are also influenced by state legislation and administrative guidelines, and by basic requirements of federal funding sources. In addition, the internal politics of the organization impinge on the decision-making process. Each of the clientele groups has its own expectations as to the outcome of the programs being planned or replanned by the county, so that the ultimate decision must, somehow or other, consider—or at least not violate—the wishes of each of the clientele groups. This is more easily said than done.

Group Decision Making

Considerable controversy surrounds the issue of group decision making. Proponents claim the approach is conducive to employee involvement in decisions that affect them and yields a high degree of commitment. They also find an advantage in encouraging creative thinking through maximization of a variety of inputs. The group approach gains much of its support from the popular notion that it is good management style to have your people participate in the decision-making process.

But there are also disadvantages to the group approach. Conflicts are likely to occur, especially when diverse interests are present in a group. Consequently, a consensus may be the product of the most vocal, but not necessarily the most knowledgeable, members. All of this activity is time-consuming, may be frustrating to some members of the group, and may not produce desirable results. Furthermore, when groups make decisions, if the desired outcome does not materialize, there is a tendency to "pass the buck" rather than accept responsibility for the decision.

An alarming but interesting phenomenon related to group decision-making behavior was identified by social commentator Irving Janis. He studied a number of fiascos (among them, the Bay of Pigs, the Cuban Missile Crisis, the Korean War, and the escalation of the Vietnam War) that resulted from high-level political decision making. His studies, which are reported in his book, *Victims of Group Think,* led to the coining of the phrase "group think," which refers to "a mode of thinking that people engage in when they are deeply involved in a cohesive in-group, when the members striving for unanimity override their motivation to realistically appraise alternative courses of action."[29]

Many of the drawbacks of group decision making can be overcome to make the process more effective. Various research studies provide the following pointers for facilitating group decision making:

- *Clear definition of objectives.* Public managers involved in decision making should be knowledgeable of the group's goals. In a similar sense, when any group, whether it be employees or citizens outside the agency, participates in the decision-making process, the outcome is more likely to be positive when it understands the goal. For example, if the group is a coalition on urban housing, the goal would be stated in terms of a certain number of additional low-cost housing units to be disbursed throughout the area. The coalition then might decide how to accomplish building and locating the units given the resources of the group.
- *Accountability.* Public managers who have experienced success with group decision making cite accountability of the group as a key. When the group recognizes that it will be held accountable for its action, self-imposed peer pressure usually brings deliberations to an action stage within a reasonable time, and each member of the group seems to accept the decision as if he or she had made it alone.

- *Size of group.* Although research findings are not consistent on the optimum size of a decision-making group, it appears that in general such groups function best with five to seven members. One researcher claims the ideal size is five. Writing in the *Academy of Management Journal* L. L. Cummings and his colleagues conclude that "if the quality of the group's solution is of considerable importance, it is useful to include a larger number of members, for example seven to twelve, so that many inputs are available to the group making its decisions. If the degree of consensus is of primary importance, it is useful to choose a smaller group, e.g., three to five, so that each member can have his concern considered and discussed."[14]

Participative Decision Making

The participative approach to decision making is one in which subordinates in a particular situation are allowed and encouraged to participate in decisions that will affect them. The participative approach is evident throughout government, where legislative bodies rely on committees and subcommittees to draft legislation and where administrative agencies encourage group participation and often call on coalitions of public managers and citizen groups to develop recommendations on specific problems. In New York State, for example, the energy crunch resulted in the formation of local citizen groups that have had considerable influence on the location of public utility facilities. Controversies have become polarized, and issue-based coalitions have arisen to counter the power companies, especially when environmental issues are involved. Whether participation by larger segments of the citizenry is viewed as positive or negative, one thing is clear—the trend, in the New York area and elsewhere, is toward greater involvement of citizens in government decisions that affect them.

Decision-making Techniques

In making decisions, public managers like to think of themselves as rational decision makers. The decision maker does not have a high degree of control over the decision-making situation, especially within the realm of public decisions; however, current emphasis on official conduct that is in the public interest admonishes public managers to be rational in their decision making. Public managers' responsibility depends on rationality, and decision makers can act responsibly only if their actions are based on actual and fully developed information and alternatives. And ethical responsibility can exist only where there is a sufficient cognitive base. Essentially, the rational model incorporates the following:

- *Identifying the problem,* or articulating a pervasive or priority problem.
- *Developing* facts and information relevant to the problem.
- *Evaluating and prioritizing* alternative viable solutions to the stated problem.
- *Choosing a course of action* that will satisfactorily solve the problem—at this juncture the decision maker faces several basic considerations such as:
    - —*Consequences.* High risk or high cost decisions obviously deserve longer and more careful deliberation.
    - —*Time constraints.* Deadlines have to be met, but a snap decision can have dire consequences and good judgment may dictate that "no decision is better than a wrong decision."
    - —*Nature of the problem.* The source of the problem, its complexity, impact, and the decision maker's familiarity with it—all have a bearing on how it is handled.
    - —*Availability of delegation.* When competent resources (personnel) for delegation are available, problems can often be referred to them for action.
    - —*Report of action.* The recipient of the report and those affected by the consequences have a bearing on the decision maker's actions.
- *Implementing,* or translating the decision into action calls for gaining the support of those responsible for implementation, programming to ensure efficiency and effectiveness, and follow-up procedures to get feedback from implementors of the decision, for example, program managers.
- *Evaluating feedback,* or a continuous process to detect deviations from objectives and to make necessary changes in the program, or even in the objectives themselves.

Writers in the field of public decision making have criticized the rational model as being impractical. They claim that it contains inherent limitations, for instance, in the amount of information that the decision maker has at hand for any given problem; and that the myriad problems confronting the public manager permit only partial attention to each problem.

Many of those who reject the rational approach subscribe to the strategy of "disjointed incrementalism" or "muddling through" espoused by economist Charles E. Lindblom, or the "mixed scanning" approach advanced by sociologist Amitai Etzioni.

Disjointed incrementalism or muddling through, Lindblom asserts, considers the limited perceptive abilities of decision makers and reduces the disadvantage of having to process excessive amounts of information.[33] The steps in this approach can be summarized as follows:

- The manager analyzes only values and policies which differ marginally from existing policies.
- A drastically limited means-ends analysis is undertaken on only a few alternatives, ignoring their possible consequences and values.
- A succession of limited comparisons continually redefines the problem and achieves incremental changes. Thus, decision makers analyze past sequences of policy steps to acquire knowledge for further steps and to rectify past errors.

The muddling-through approach is designed to correct immediate public problems rather than to promote future social goals.

The *mixed-scanning approach* advanced by Etzioni provides a specific procedure for information gathering called scanning, a strategy for the allocation of resources, and guidelines for the relationships between the two.[21] This approach focuses on problems similar to those that occurred previously and on those which might deserve attention if they arose unexpectedly. Mixed scanning combines various levels of scanning and provides criteria for situations requiring emphasis at one level or another. In this approach managers make fundamental decisions by exploring in an overview fashion the main alternatives they consider to be relevant to the goals, and they also make incremental decisions within the context of the fundamental ones.

Perhaps the ideal approach to problem solving in public policymaking would incorporate mixed scanning and disjointed incrementalism with rational thinking. However, the serious-minded public manager would do well to master the techniques inherent in the rational approach. Then, the application of more intuitive approaches will serve to strengthen the decision.

A Brief Case Study—To Illustrate—To Ponder

The Plan That Lost the War

In the early stages of World War II, an armament company that was a key factor in Germany's war machine had an urgent need for a quart of alcohol to complete a technical project. In order to receive the alcohol from a local supplier the company was required to follow purchasing procedures.

Thus, it requested a requisition slip from the Reich Monopoly Bureau, but the company was referred to the Economic Group who would issue a certificate of urgent need. The matter was referred to the Regional Office which, after six weeks of feverish activity, announced that the request had been approved and forwarded to the Reich Monopoly Bureau for final action. Finally, eight weeks after the initial request, the requisition approved "for technical purposes only" was issued and a company messenger was sent to pick up the alcohol. But on his arrival the messenger was informed that a certificate first had to be obtained from the Food Rationing Board, a Division of the Agriculture Department. When frustrated company officials inquired, the Food Rationing Board informed them it could license alcohol for drinking purposes only and not for manufacturing or technical uses. So, after more than two months, the company abandoned all hope of ever receiving its urgently needed alcohol.

1. How could the planning process have been improved to deliver urgent supplies promptly?
2. What decision could have avoided this fiasco?
3. Redesign the requisition procedure so that urgent requisitions can be handled expeditiously.

CHAPTER 6

Preparing the Resources: Organizing

The organizing function establishes a formal structure of authority or chain of command, delegates authority to accomplish the organization's mission, and provides leadership to support the mission. Public organizations today operate in an era of change—as new officials are elected they influence policy, shifts in the economy impact positively or negatively on the organizations, different special interest groups influence programs, and so on. Consequently, the public manager is constantly involved in anticipating and responding to continuous change.

Implementing Plans Through Organizing

Organizations are designed to carry out the plans that will achieve their objectives. When structuring an organization, managers should proceed as follows:

- Understand the *objectives* and their priorities.
- Identify the *functions* that need to be performed.
- *Group* similar or related activities into departments or units.
- Assign a group or grouping to a *manager* with the appropriate authority to manage it.
- Provide for *coordination* vertically and horizontally throughout the structure.

Finally, the organization must be *designed* so that (1) everyone in it knows his or her specific duties and responsibilities and how they relate to those of other members; (2) assignments are clearly understood; and (3) a communications network facilitates the accomplishment of organization objectives.

Writers on the subject of organizational design have identified a continuum of organizational design patterns. At one extreme is the *mechanistic* pattern that incorporates the traditional pyramidal structure. In this type of organization, all elements are highly structured to attain machine-like efficiency—tasks are highly detailed, communication is formalized, and decision making is centralized at the top. At the other extreme of the continuum is the *organic* pattern. It is an open design where roles are ambiguously defined and constantly changing. Decision making is decentralized and interactions among organizational units are flexible and informal; work groups may even be autonomous. Michael B. McCaskey writing in the *California Management Review* suggests that organizations be designed according to the task and the type of people involved.[36] The mechanistic pattern is most suited to stable, unchanging environments and a staff that prefers certainty, whereas the organic pattern is most suited to an unstable, uncertain environment and people tolerant of ambiguity.

The organizing function is based on a number of concepts, often referred to as principles of management. Those most applicable to the public manager as an organizer are discussed in the following pages.

Span of Control

The concept known as the *span of control* is based on the premise that there is a limit to the number of people a manager can effectively direct. As the number of individuals reporting to a manager increases arithmetically, the number of personal relationships increases geometrically. Thus, with one person reporting to a manager there will be two relationships. But, if one additional person is added, the number of relationships increases by four—from two to six! Since the manager must work with people and their relationships rather than with people as raw numbers, the number of persons that can be effectively managed by one supervisor becomes limited.

Although writers in this field have attempted to identify a specific number that constitutes the most efficient span of control, empirical evidence indicates that the effectiveness of the span depends on a variety of factors. Essentially, a combination of the complexity, variety, and proximity of the tasks being supervised affects the width of the most effective span of control.

Highly complex or technical work obviously requires closer supervision than does simple, basic work. Hence, complex tasks would tend to limit the span. A laboratory manager directing the efforts of serologists, virologists, and biological technicians might have only five or six people in the unit (because of the variety and complexity of the work), whereas an office manager might be able to supervise the work of 15 to 20 accounting clerks who perform basic work that is similar in nature. Finally, when the people being supervised are geographically dispersed, this factor places a constraint on the manager's capacity to direct the work. Conversely, close proximity to the work performed improves control.

Studies also have shown that such factors as the quality of training, the extent and pace of change in the work environment, adequacy of delegation of authority, and degree of objectivity in evaluating performance are additional determinants in the effective span of control.

Unity of Command

Soon after Moses led his people out of captivity, he sat to judge them. Seeing that Moses was not able to listen to all of these people by himself, Jethro, his father-in-law, gave him needed advice. The Bible (*Exodus* 18:25–26) describes Moses' action:

"And Moses chose able men out of all Israel, and made them heads over the people, rulers of thousands, rulers of hundreds, rulers of fifties, and rulers of tens.

"And they judged the people at all seasons: the hard cases they brought unto Moses, but every small matter they judged themselves."

Thanks to Jethro's advice Moses organized a hierarchy with a *chain of command* that freed Moses of "small matters" and permitted him to be more accessible to his constituency on the hard cases. Each of the rulers, or managers, had increasingly greater authority the higher their rank in the organizations. Rulers over thousands might compare with a colonel or an agency division director; rulers over hundreds, a major or department manager; rulers over fifties, a captain or unit manager; and rulers over tens, a lieutenant or first-line supervisor.

Implicit in Moses' organization is the principle of unity of command: for any given assignment an employee reports to only one manager. The logic behind this principle of organizing is that by answering to only one boss there should be better understanding and coordination of the assignment. As desirable as the unity of command principle may be, it is often violated, especially as bureaucracies grow in size and complexity.

Delegation

Through delegation, managers are able to accomplish more because persons lower in the hierarchy are given authority to accomplish specific assignments. Successful managers generally exhibit the ability and willingness to delegate authority. Managers' approach to delegation includes the following:

- *Competence.* They assess the employee's ability to carry out the assignment.
- *Parity.* They delegate authority commensurate with responsibility.
- *Clarity.* They make sure instructions are clear and that the employee understands the assignment.
- *Expectations.* They ensure acceptance of conditions for completion of assignment.
- *Accountability.* They make the employee accountable for results.
- *Control.* They provide for regular, periodic review of accomplishments to verify that the assignment is carried out properly and to correct ineffective performance.
- *Reward.* They evaluate results and provide for a system of rewards that will encourage effort.

Authority versus responsibility: Authority, *not* responsibility is delegated. A manager is given the responsibility for carrying out an assignment and is held accountable for the results. Theoretically, the manager has been given enough authority to complete the assignment. But how many times have you heard someone complain "Oh, I sure do have a lot of responsibility around here, but they never seem to give me any authority to get the job done!"? This kind of problem stems from the confusion with the terms *authority* and *responsibility.* Perhaps if public managers understand the difference they can be more effective at delegating.

Authority is a right. It may be the right to hire and fire or the right to expend specified sums of monies, and so on. The source of that right is usually some higher authority such as a manager's boss. In this case the manager's authority is a function of his or her position in the organization. Authority flows or is delegated from the top of the organization to the bottom. Theoretically, the higher the position in the organization, the more authority it carries. This type of authority is considered formal authority. But to be viable, such authority must be accepted by those under the command of the person exercising authority. Logically, if subordinates do not accept the authority of their boss, that authority becomes meaningless. This points up the necessity for public managers to gain the respect (acceptance) of their employees. Responsibility is accountability for the attainment of objectives; it is the obligation to exercise authority properly, efficiently, and effectively. Public managers often are given responsibility that far outweighs the authority necessary to carry it out. According to the *parity principle,* any manager must delegate authority that is commensurate with the responsibility.

Line-Staff Relationships

As organizations grow in size and complexity the need for specialists becomes evident. Staff units are formed to support, advise, control, and provide services for line activities.

Line is distinguished from staff essentially by the nature of authority relationships. Line authority is a relationship in which the manager exercises direct supervision over employees—the authority relationship is in direct lines or steps. The nature of the staff relationship is advisory. In other words, the line has *direct* authority to carry out the organization's objectives, while the staff supports the line's efforts; staff is auxiliary to the principal operations. Under the concept that authority relationships determine whether a department or unit is line or staff, it is often difficult to categorize organizational units as purely line or staff. However, departments that predominantly advise, for example, personnel, are viewed as staff departments, whereas those that directly carry out the organization's mission, such as police in a public safety agency, are considered line.

How staff gets its power: The most obvious source of staff authority is direct delegation from the line. But why do some staff people seem to have more power or authority than others? Because those who have earned this power have exhibited distinctive competence and have gained the reputation for providing the line organization with the advice and service it needs.

As staff people gain the confidence of the line organization as a result of quality performance, they usually are granted more and more authority. Frequent contact with line managers develops in staff people an ability to sense or even to anticipate areas of need that they can accommodate. A knowledge of line people, coupled with willingness to help and accessibility when needed, creates an environment conducive to the development of confidence. By providing practical solutions to line problems, and presenting them in such a fashion that the line manager can accept or reject the proposal without further study (this is the *doctrine of completed staff work*), the influence or power of the staff is greatly enhanced.

Winning respect and gaining esteem through expertise and reputation is an additional source of power. This status results from the person's credentials—such as a law degree, a Ph.D. in chemistry, or a Master of Public Administration—and demonstrated expertise in his or her specialty. As a result of the staff person's particular area of knowledge, the line might delegate authority to that person to make decisions or take actions in a particular area. This *functional authority* is a prime source of power for staff people. The highly complex nature of personnel problems has increased the influence of those who have demonstrated expertise in the area of human resource management. Knowledgeable personnel professionals have been give wide functional authority to develop affirmative action plans, train public managers, negotiate agreements with unions, conduct team-building programs through the organization, and so forth.

Other Forms of Organization

Although line-staff type organizations are the predominant form in government, others are evident.

The *matrix* form of organization pulls together project groups in a temporary organization to accomplish a specific purpose. Individuals are assigned from functional departments of the traditional line-staff organization. Project personnel are under the authority of the project manager until the completion of the project, at which time they usually return to their original departments. NASA operated under the matrix form of organization to manage the Apollo and Saturn projects.

Other organizational structures found occasionally in government are based on functions performed by various units of an agency and/or by clientele served.

Organization Charting

Charts are graphic representations of the organization structure at a given point in time. They show authority relationships as well as channels of communications. Charts are a useful tool for organizing because they depict departmental and unit relationships. Potential organizational conflicts and inefficiencies often can be circumvented by charting the relationships before the structure is made operational.

The chart also is useful for planning the organization. It describes the location of various elements or units in the structure and can be useful in locating or relocating units within the organization. The drawback of organization charts is that they are diagrams. They oversimplify, whereas the real organization is a complex of formal and informal relationships that rarely operate as depicted in the chart. Furthermore, the chart represents a static picture whereas the organization is dynamic; the relationships and organizational units are constantly changing. But despite these weaknesses, an updated organization chart is a useful planning and development tool.

Organizational Restructuring.

Restructuring is now viewed by public managers at all levels as key to making government responsive and accountable. However, few are naive enough to believe that a restructure alone will accomplish this goal. Restructuring is an evolutionary process, not a panacea. It requires careful analysis and understanding of the problem, a reshaping of attitudes and practices, a substantial commitment of resources, and a resolve on the part of the change agents to see it completed.

A congressional bipartisan study committee proposed to the 95th Congress a thorough overhaul of the committee structure including: a reduction of the number of standing committees to 15 from the existing 31 and a reshaping of some committees. For example, the Interior Committee would absorb the Aeronautical and Space Sciences Committee and all related transportation committees; the Public Works Committee would be transformed into a committee on environment and public works.

Early in his term President Jimmy Carter received limited approval from Congress to restructure the executive branch. He started with a reorganization of the office of the president and then directed his efforts toward eliminating a large number of the existing 1,300-plus federal boards and advisory committees. Through the initiation of zero-base budgeting he required each organizational unit to review its functions annually to ascertain whether or not it should be retained.

President Ronald Reagan reversed the Carter initiatives by cutting back on the size and number of government organizations and focused his reorganization efforts on disengaging government from the economy. President Reagan's actions demonstrated a philosophy on the role of government that was almost the antithesis of President Carter's.

This phenomenon of changing directions is even more prevalent in state and local organizations. Such changes can become intense at the local level because of the existence of multiple government jurisdictions, for example, schools, hospitals, and other activities are usually separate from the general city and county government. In addition, the national and state governments directly administer many programs within most urban areas.

Leadership

Effective organizations depend on strong leaders to run them. While many leaders are not managers, a key ability of the successful manager is leadership. Public managers must exercise leadership skills in getting the organization with its employees to function at its best. Let us see how this important skill affects employee behavior and how formalized leadership programs operate.

Leadership Style

Various theories of leadership effectiveness suggest that there is a relationship between leadership style and effectiveness. Researchers have identified a continuum of styles, but essentially they fall into three categories: autocratic, laissez-faire, and democratic. The primary distinction among these styles is where the decision-making function rests. The *autocratic* leader makes decisions for the group; the *laissez-faire* leader allows the group to make the decisions; and the *democratic* leader guides and encourages the group to make decisions. Recent studies suggest that a variety of styles can be effective, but they depend on the group and the circumstances of the particular situation. However, the increased educational level of public employees and public pressures for accountability of government agencies imply a mandate to involve people in the decision-making process, or a *participative* approach to leadership.

Using the Participative Approach Successfully

Agencies reporting success with the participative approach generally employ the following guidelines—

1. *Define objectives clearly.* Employees involved in decision making should know the group's goals. For instance, if a group is a clerical unit, its goals could be stated in terms of a certain number of units of production per unit of time, with a designated quality index. The employees then might decide how to accomplish the output given the resources of the group.
2. *Provide a system of rewards.* Especially with clerical situations, economic rewards must be tied to outcomes. If the clerical unit employees recognize that their efforts yield tangible rewards, naturally they will strive for optimum productivity. Other situations are not so clear-cut. The drug enforcement agents who developed an innovative education program for high school students received a special merit pay increase. The reward need

not always be economic, but must be a clearly defined outcome of the participative effort.

3. *Make groups accountable.* Agencies that have experienced success with a participative style suggest that decision-making groups be held accountable for their actions. For example, when a grievance review board composed of union and management members rendered a decision on a grievance, each member of the board accepted the answer as if he or she had made it alone. And in the same vein, the group established reasonable time limits within which it agreed to operate. This self-imposed pressure ensures that problems are not stalled in endless debate and never reach an action stage.
4. *Ensure a receptive attitude on the part of top management.* Unless all key executives are convinced of the merits of participative leadership, efforts to involve employees are destined to failure. Lip service alone will not do. The hierarchy must be receptive to suggestions and recommendations from below. Willingness to adopt reasonable proposals is vital to the success of participative leadership. Most employee groups are limited to making recommendations. But group members become frustrated when their recommendations are not followed. By the same token, there must be two-way communication; all recommendations should be listened to at all levels of management, and higher management's opinions should be fed back to the employee.
5. *Introduce gradually.* Organizations cannot expect to move from autocratic management to participative management overnight. Although executives may be convinced of the validity of this modern style, the transition should occur gradually. A change to participative leadership will certainly be met with skepticism by those who had to function under the former style, and hard-nosed managers will resent having to reverse their approach; they will probably be totally incapable of performing the turnabout. Consequently, the participative style should be introduced gradually, preferably through training of both operative employees and managers.

Applied Leadership

Organizations have devised formal leadership programs to elicit and maintain high levels of employee commitment and organizational efficiency. Such programs have been labeled *organizational development* (OD), and they attempt to bring about organizational change and efficiency by involving employees in problem solving and planning. OD depends on the support of employees who understand how the manager wants to change. It is a continuous and overall effort that increases organizational efficiency by integrating individual desires for growth with organizational goals. Managers systematically plan and implement change by sharing power. Specifically, OD locates problem solving as close to the grass roots as possible, builds trust and creates harmony through collaboration, encourages employees' self-direction and self-regulation, and introduces a system to reward the attainment of individual and organization goals.

Formal processes are implemented in OD to create social conditions that encourage employee contributions to organizational objectives. Such methods include:

- Team-building activities, such as intra-agency problem-solving meetings
- Intergroup sessions to discuss changes or to work out common concerns
- Action research involving data gathering
- Corrective action and feedback
- Training programs, such as laboratory (sensitivity) training
- Development of specific skills such as decision making or development of positive attitudes
- Feedback on survey responses
- Activities to resolve problems or provide training

Several years ago, the city of Dallas, Texas, implemented an OD system. Initially, it conducted a dialogue between management and employees to gain both commitment to and involvement in the program. The city used a written instrument to measure participants' perceptions of how their departments looked the previous year, the organization's present state, and a realistic assessment of future expectations. Next, it involved management and supervisory personnel in an intensive four-day seminar on personal and organizational development that focused on team building and behavioral skills. Then questionnaires and interviews were used to collect data about the organization. The information gained from this process formed the basis of a report to management covering problem areas and their causes and making recommendations for change. Finally, OD teams of employee representatives from major job classifications and selected first-line supervisors developed an action plan that identified problem areas and recommended cost-effective strategies to improve operations. Essential to the process was the involvement of the organization's human resources.

As we mentioned earlier, organizational development is a tool for planning and implementing change. "Nothing is so constant as change" is a saying that is particularly apropos of public organizations. New laws and regulations become the impetus for additional or restructured organizations. As new administrations are elected and new appointments of agency heads are made, organizational change is the consequence. Even if organizations are not restructured, they must change to respond to new public policies and programs; economic developments (usually in the form of budget cuts); special interest group demands; economic, political and environmental crises (such as a major earthquake); technological changes (such as new equipment and different processes), and so on. Thus, public managers, as leaders, are challenged to manage change as an integral part of their job.

Managing Change

Because most people resist change, public managers face a difficult task. One reason for resistance is fear of the unknown. Employees are unsure of how change will affect their jobs; the uncertainty of the change causes them not to know what to expect; and they fear that they will not be able to handle the change. In addition, employees may feel less secure in their jobs because of the perceived economic impact of the change. People naturally feel more comfortable doing it the "old" way, so they say, "We've always done it this way, why change?" Changes cause inconvenience. Finally, employees develop personal relationships with their peers, and their threatened disruption by transfers, layoffs, and similar changes cause resistance.

Managers can do a number of things to enhance the acceptance of change. The key is to *involve* employees. When the affected people are involved in the change process right from the beginning, they are more likely to accept and even to actively support the change. In this regard, the organizational development process discussed earlier in this chapter is particularly relevant. *Building trust* wins the confidence of the employees who must support changes. When *contemplated changes* are *discussed* with employees, they are more likely to be receptive. However, discussion means that they should be told in detail what the changes will be and how these changes will affect their lives. Furthermore, managers should give the employees an opportunity to ask questions and should answer each question as completely as possible. The *changes should be reasonable*; however, managers responsible for implementing changes imposed by other areas may need to influence modifications in change proposals that are not reasonable. Often, the originator of a change may not be aware of the problems and can be persuaded to alter an unreasonable proposal to make it more palatable.

When implementing change, managers should avoid threats and should not attempt to coerce employees into submitting to the change. This negative approach will only break down whatever trust has been built, and it will heighten resistance. When change is introduced to the organization, the *time* and *place* should be considered. Implementing change during a holiday season or vacation period is not wise. The manager's sensitivity to his or her people and basic common sense also come into play when scheduling a change. Where to make the change also has a bearing on change management. Efforts should be made to minimize disruption of work flow, efficient work groups, or ongoing projects, and to maximize the impact of the change on the achievement of the organization's mission.

A Brief Case Study—to Illustrate—to Ponder

Reorganization of the State's Department of Health and Human Services—A Model for Change?

The Department of Health and Human Services (DHHS) is the state's largest agency. It spends over three billion dollars a year from revenues received from several federal programs, counties, and clients (in the form of fees). The department employs about 28,000 persons, serves over one million clients, and contracts with more than 30,000 individuals and agencies annually.

A panel of the National Academy of Public Administration (NAPA) identified the basic need for DHHS reorganization:

> The client, not the government, had the responsibility to identify and marshal available resources, trudging from office to office, waiting on many queues, filling out innumerable eligibility forms, challenging or appealing many decisions. Each citizen grappled alone with many bureaucracies to coordinate related services offered by state and local, public and private agencies.
>
> Repeated attempts have been made in various parts of the country to deal with this chaotic situation. It has been easier to diagnose the problem than to solve it. In the State, the solution—or, rather the problem—before 1989 consisted of nine separate bureaucracies encompassing more than 70 separately funded programs, each designed to meet specific federal regulations and funding requirements. Each bureaucracy operated independently with many of the same clients, providers, and community agencies; each was subject to coordination, in the community and state, only or principally by the departmental secretary.

To address these needs, the state legislature in 1989 passed the Health and Human Services Act. The Act moved all program line authority to 11 integrated district offices. This integration of a wide range of social, health, and human services administered by the same governmental unit was expected to include these elements at the local level:

1. The common location of the staff of related services close to a large number of current and prospective clients.
2. The delegation of authority to a local administrator to supervise and coordinate these services.
3. A common intake system for new clients.
4. Case management to ensure that related services to an individual or family with multiple problems are provided, coordinated, and recorded.

The NAPA panel concluded that "the State reorganization was the most significant current effort by any state to consolidate the administration of social services and decentralize their management." But the reorganization also had its management crises. The most serious were a breakdown in voucher payments, the loss of accurate and current data on the number of employees working in each classification and on the allocations and expenditures of programs in each district. Additional problems resulted from new and complex financial reporting requirements; new computer systems being introduced; continuing pressures to answer complaints; and high turnover in key management positions. It was evident that mission attainment under reorganization would take a dedicated effort of competent DHHS managers if the legislative intent were to be operational with the five-year time frame.

1. Identify the principles of organizing that are involved here.
2. Draw an organization chart of the reorganized DHHS.
3. What specific changes are being implemented by DHHS?
4. If you were the leader of the reorganized DHHS, how would you go about instituting the changes?

CHAPTER 7

Managing Human Resources: Staffing

The staffing function involves activities related to the management of human resources in the organization. Government serves its citizens through the skills and dedication of the people who work for it. Thus, the success of public managers depends to a large degree on the effectiveness of the people who work for them. For many managers, human resource management is the most difficult, yet rewarding, part of their jobs. This role of the public manager calls for personal knowledge about what motivates people, ingenuity, and human resources skills.

Personal expertise alone will not suffice in managing for performance effectiveness in government agencies. Regulations and laws have considerable influence on a manager's handling of people. In addition, the sheer size of government and the changing nature of its work force complicates the situation, with the result that public managers face challenges today that their predecessors did not even envision. The public sector employs more than 16 million people today. Their values, attitudes, and aspirations are different from previous generations of employees. This new breed of young, highly educated persons is seeking an individual identity within a mass society. They are challenging the ingenuity of public managers to address societal problems.

Human Resource Management Defined

For the purposes of our discussion in this chapter we might define human resource management as *the process of supporting the accomplishment of the agency's objectives by acquiring human re-*

sources, integrating employees into the organization (agency), developing employee potential, and maintaining the work force.

Acquiring includes anticipating the human resource needs of an agency and employing the people necessary to staff it. Employment encompasses recruiting needed employees, including filling from within, screening applicants for employment, selecting the most suitable candidates, and placing newly hired employees in appropriate job vacancies or training programs.

Integrating employees consists of making them part of the organizational team through counseling activities and interviews to learn about their backgrounds, aspirations, work experiences, and any problems in adjusting to work life.

Developing includes all activities for the education, training, appraisal, and planning of careers to prepare employees for present or future assignments, thereby enhancing their value to the agency. Training and educational activities develop skills, improve behavior, and provide information necessary for more effective performance. Performance appraisal informs employees of their progress and aids them in correcting deviations from established performance standards. Career planning combines agency needs with personal aspirations to ensure that individual talent is optimally utilized.

Maintaining involves compensation and benefits programs that reward people's accomplishments. This activity serves to maintain an efficient and effective work force, to retain valuable talent in government service, and to sustain and improve the favorable working environment within the agency.

This chapter discusses the concepts and techniques associated with each of these activities, including the influence of personnel and regulations, and shows how the public manager can employ them to enhance the effectiveness of human resources.

Human Resource Regulations – the Civil Service Reform Act

The basic law governing personnel practices in the federal government is the Civil Service Reform Act, Public Law 95–454 (S. 2640). Since many states and municipalities either have patterned or will pattern their personnel systems after this Act, it is appropriate to summarize its provisions here.

The Act was designed to improve government efficiency and to balance management authority with employee protection. It became effective in 1978 and includes such major features as incentives and rewards based on performance, independent and equitable appeals process, protections against abuse of the merit system, and specific changes in federal labor relations.

Basic merit principles that govern all personnel practices in the federal government are included in the law. These require

- recruitment from all segments of society.
- fair and equitable treatment without regard to politics, race, color, religion, national origin, sex, marital status, age, or handicapping condition.
- equal pay for equal work with incentives for excellent performance.
- high standards of integrity, conduct, and concern for public interest.
- efficient and effective use of the work force.
- retention, correction, or separation depending on continued performance.
- effective education and training.
- protection of employees from arbitrary action.
- protection of employees against reprisal for lawful disclosure of information, or whistle-blowing.

Prohibited practices are defined by the law. They include discriminating against an employee or applicant, using preferential treatment, or taking an improper personnel action.

New performance appraisal procedures have been instituted that call for each agency to develop and implement its own system.

Adverse actions, such as removals, suspensions for over 14 days, and reductions in pay or grade, may be appealed to the Merit Systems Protection Board (MSPB), an independent agency that hears and decides employee appeals and orders corrective action when appropriate. The Special Counsel to the MSPB has authority to protect whistle-blowers.

Discrimination complaints can be heard by the MSPB, but the Equal Employment Opportunity Commission (EEOC) also can be involved. In addition, the EEOC approves targets and timetables on agencies' equal employment goals and affirmative action plans.

New *grade and pay retention* provisions make it possible for employees to retain their grades for two years and to avoid taking considerable cuts in salary as a result of downgrading actions for which they are not responsible.

Supervisors and managers are required to serve a trial period before their appointments become final. And a merit pay system (for GS-13 through GS-15 employees) recognizes performance, for example, cost efficiency; timeliness of performance; and improvements in efficiency, productivity, and quality of work or service.

A *Senior Executive Service*, consisting of high-level managers in the executive branch, was designed to attract and keep top managers, to use their abilities productively, and to pay them according to their performance.

The *Office of Personnel Management* (OPM) has responsibilities, including central examining and employment operations, development of personnel management policy and regulations, personnel investigations, personnel program evaluation, and executive development and training. OPM also administers the retirement and insurance programs for federal employees and exercises management leadership in affirmative action and labor relations.

Acquiring Human Resources

Public managers often become annoyed at the length of time it takes to fill a position. Planning for people needs can help reduce that time; several aspects of planning that can help include the following:

- Anticipate vacancies and start recruiting well in advance.
- Know the steps that must be accomplished, including budget and ceiling approval, and stay abreast of the paperwork.
- Prepare written position descriptions and qualification requirements, and understand the classification standards that are used to establish the series, title, and salary grade of each position.
- Adhere to a realistic timetable.
- Allocate the necessary time for review of applications and interviews.

Job analysis is performed to determine the criteria for successful performance so that selection methods such as exams and interviews can be valid. The analysis identifies and describes distinguishing characteristics of a job and the requirements for its performance. Agencies use observation, interviews, questionnaires, and studies to gain data for the analysis. Essentially, the process of job analysis consists of three basic elements: (1) identifying the jobs, for example, designating the classifications needed to carry out the agency's mission; (2) determining the specific content of the job; and (3) preparing a written job description. Generally, the agency has a job analyst or personnel specialist who performs the analysis; thus a detailed description of the job-analysis procedure is not relevant for this discussion.

Selection Methods

Whether selecting from within or from the outside, principles of open competition apply. Merit system regulations call for work force composition that is representative of society; selection and promotion based on relative knowledge, skills, and abilities; and the use of open competition to assure equal opportunity. As a direct result of the Civil Service Reform Act, agencies, on request, are now receiving delegation of authority to perform direct recruitment and examining with Office of Personnel Management oversight.

Examinations

As part of the hiring process, applicants are usually examined using one of two methods: assembled or unassembled exams. *Assembled* exams are written performance tests. *Unassembled* exams generate ratings of experience, education, training, and other job-related achievements described by the applicant. Examinations can be a combination of the assembled and unassembled types. The federal government's Uniform Guidelines on Selection Procedures, applicable to public-and private-sector employers, mandate that any requirements established for positions being filled be necessary for successful job performance, and that any tests based on such requirements do distinguish between potentially successful and potentially unsuccessful candidates.

Hiring From Outside the Agency

Many methods are used to attract talent. These include: announcements, recruiting bulletins, consolidated job listings, or similar notices to invite interested persons to apply. Many agencies develop their own recruiting literature, and they regularly visit college campuses to recruit candidates. Most agencies attempt to locate a pool of applicants who are representative of the citizens they serve. Toward this end, they take a multifaceted approach to recruiting using such sources as employee referrals; advertising campaigns; speakers at high schools, colleges, and universities; labor organizations; professional groups; and special interest groups.

The *employment application* is essential to the examining process. It provides biographical information, employment experience data, and other essentials that help the employing agency make a more objective selection decision. In addition, employment applications designed to provide quick and systematic information help to plan the employment interview and are a source of information for personnel records if the applicant is hired.

Processing Applications

Agencies usually maintain registers that include the names of qualified candidates for positions where there are anticipated vacancies. It seems most practical for the manager to screen these registers whenever there is an impending vacancy. This, of course, does not preclude the initiation of recruiting efforts, but it can save time and expense when an acceptable candidate appears on the register.

Once the applicants for a position are identified, the examining office screens them for minimum qualifications and applies qualification standards to determine who is eligible. Candidates are then ranked on their relative qualifications based on education, training, experience, and scores of evaluation instruments. Usually the individual or agency making the hiring decision will also make an evaluation of the unassembled examinations. In federal agencies, eligible applicants with veteran preference receive additional points on their ratings. Those listed as "best" among the eligible candidates are *certified* by the examining office based on *selective* and/or *quality ranking* factors. A selective factor would be the knowledge, skill, or ability to do the job. For an auditor, for example, this would be knowledge of cost accounting. A quality ranking factor would be skill, knowledge, or ability that is desirable, but not essential to the job, such as knowledge of computer programming for the auditor. Some candidates, however, are certified based on scores derived from general aptitude tests, education, or experience.

Selection

In selecting from outside the agency, the "rule of three" applies. Under most merit systems managers may select one of the top three available candidates who have been certified. Sometimes an agency may determine that none of the top three referred on the certificate are acceptable because of lack of experience, poor interview results, conflict of interest, lack of availability, unsuitability for the agency or the job, or other relevant factors. Managers must be able to substantiate such objections should appeal or discrimination complaints be lodged.

Excepted service jobs may be exempted from competitive service, but they do not necessarily waive exam requirements. Excepted agencies, for example, the Tennessee Valley Authority, have their own merit systems that require applicants to demonstrate that they have the basic qualifications required to do the job.

Hiring From Within

Internal selection or promotion from within the agency allows greater flexibility than hiring from the outside. Candidates are already employed, so the agency has performance information in addition to the data gathered for the initial employment. Consequently, candidates for internal selection are usually ranked as "best qualified," "well qualified," and "qualified." A maximum number of candidates who can be considered for each vacancy is established in the agency merit promotion plan, but the number may vary considerably from one agency to another. The promotion plans are often subject to negotiation when employee organizations are recognized as an appropriate bargaining agent of the employees.

Affirmative Action

The Civil Service Reform Act makes clear the obligation of all government agencies to ensure that all personnel actions are made on a nondiscriminatory basis. At all levels of government the federal Equal Employment Opportunity Commission is empowered to bring civil actions against agencies that discriminate in their personnel practices. Whenever selection procedures screen out candidates of a particular minority group or sex, selection devices should be investigated. To ensure fairness in selection, agencies should validate their selection devices and base their selection requirements on rational, relevant job analysis.

In order to comply with the Act, agencies must prepare affirmative action plans. Affirmative action stresses *objective* employment practices. It means achieving representative bureaucracy through open employment systems that include goals and special efforts to recruit and hire, and make provisions for upward mobility of minorities and women.

Integrating Employees Into the Organization

Once employees are selected and assigned, they must be made a part of the organization. Public managers use personnel records for evaluating and controlling personnel activities, and for gaining insight into the backgrounds, capabilities, and aspirations of employees. Then, through interviews and counseling sessions, these managers can help individual employees become viable members of the working team.

Personnel Records

Records are a primary source of data for evaluating and controlling personnel activities; they are also a basis for reports and research on human resources. Personnel records provide facts for a number of uses, such as reports to regulatory agencies (for example records can classify applicants and employees according to sex, race, and religion for the EEOC); reports within the agency on the effectiveness of personnel activities; controls on operating problems (such as absenteeism) and problem situations (for example, grievances); and surveys of wages and personnel practices. Computers have facilitated record-keeping of personnel information. Human resource data banks store a vast amount of data that can be retrieved quickly and simply in the form of a variety of reports.

Interviewing/Counseling

Public managers have numerous occasions to conduct personnel interviews. Interview skills are important in selecting employees, orienting new candidates, teaching or coaching subordinates to improve their job performance, counseling people on their personnel problems, or resolving disputes. An understanding of interviewing is essential to effective management, and special programs on the techniques of interviewing usually are included in supervisory training sessions. Some discussion of the counseling interview, however, is appropriate here because it is basic to integrating employees into the organization.

Employee counseling usually involves a nondirective approach in which the interview is guided by how the interviewee sees the situation. The interviewer asks an open-ended question like, "Tell me about yourself," and listens carefully. The nondirective interview encourages expression of feelings, opinions, and ideas and permits interviewees to emphasize what they feel is relevant and important. The interviewer makes comments or asks questions to stimulate thinking and facial expression. A typical question might be, "How do you feel about your work in government?" Or a comment such as, "You seem to feel that your work is causing you stress," would be an example of a nondirective approach. This approach is most appropriate in counseling because individuals often are in the best position to solve their own problems by gaining greater insight into them. The nondirective approach helps people accept their problems and gain a better understanding of themselves—of both their strengths and weaknesses.

At one time or another all employees have problems; although many are work-connected, some are not. Managers often have no choice about counseling. They cannot escape dealing with the problems that employees bring to them, even if they wish to. Therefore, the public manager's role in counseling requires a sensitivity to employees' needs and an approachable attitude that encourages employees to consult the manager about problems. Also, public managers should be alert for signs that employees are experiencing difficulties. Frequently, managers find that these problems are best referred to a specialist who is experienced in diagnosing a specific difficulty and in working with the employee toward recovery.

Developing Employee Potential

In order to have employees function effectively in the organization, public managers find they must ensure that proper attitudes are instilled, appropriate skills are taught, and necessary information is provided. Enlightened managers emphasize the continuous development of all people within their jurisdiction.

Human Resource Development

Human resource effectiveness depends to a large degree on developing the capabilities of employees. Rapid change in all aspects of government, from technology to social interaction, demands constant efforts to keep employees informed of new policies, techniques, and developments within the agency and the government service. Considering the varied composition of the work force, public managers face a real challenge and responsibility in developing the full potential of every employee. Various federal and state statutes require ongoing in-service, interagency, and nongovernment training programs. The Government Employees Training Act (GETA) enacted in 1958 essentially allows agencies to provide whatever training is necessary to develop the skills, knowledge, and abilities that will best qualify their employees for the performance of official duties. The Office of Personnel Management, as the training arm for the federal government, carries out the provisions of federal laws and executive orders on training. But the OPM also provides guidance and training services for state and local agencies primarily through the programs established under the Inter-Governmental Personnel Act of 1970.

The training/development process is depicted by exhibit 7-1. The basic elements of the model include identifying training/development needs through data analysis, selecting and writing training objectives, conducting instruction, and evaluating training effectiveness.

EXHIBIT 7-1. **Model of the Training/Development Process**

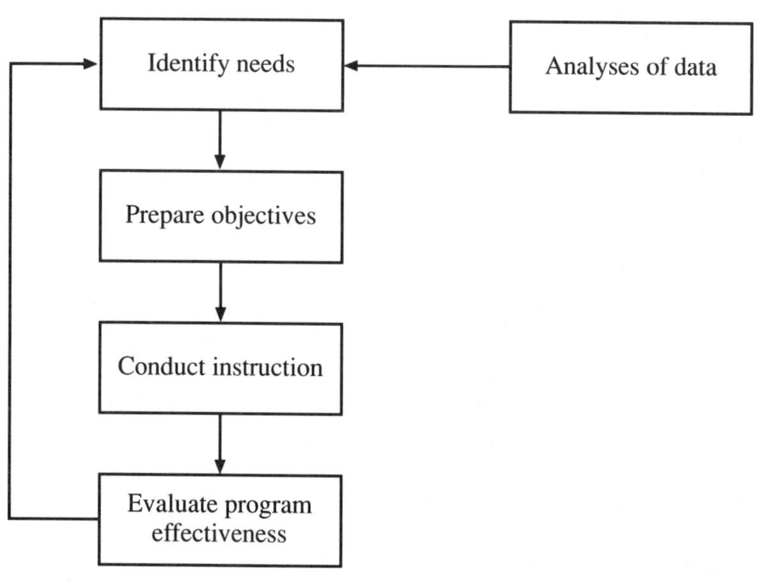

Identifying training/development needs: Job needs data are collected by observation, interviews, surveys, and analyses of records and reports. Governmental agencies use the following methods to analyze training needs—

- *Analysis of management reports* may indicate low efficiency, poor attitudes, high costs.
- *Analysis of personnel reports* may show problems with grievances, turnover, attendance, or communications.
- *Discussion with supervisors* who are closest to the problems that training can overcome may indicate deficiencies in specific employee skills.
- *Review of position descriptions* may be used to ascertain if employees know how to perform all necessary details of the job.
- *Surveys of employee attitudes* may pinpoint problem areas from the employee's view of the work environment.
- *Analysis of planned organizational changes* provides lead time for training. For example, if payroll will be handled by electronic data processing, payroll clerks can be retrained in keypunch operation, computer programming, and related fields.

- Exit interviews with personnel who are leaving the organization can uncover existing or potential problem areas.

A primary consideration in determining training needs is to establish whether training can correct problems. Often training is not necessary, and simply telling people what is expected and letting them know how well they are doing will have a greater impact.

Selecting and writing training objectives: Objectives provide the basis for planning a training program. They delineate the knowledge required in each subject area and guide training specialists in selecting appropriate teaching methods. Managers can then evaluate training effectiveness against these objectives. The following criteria are guideposts in defining objectives:

- Training objectives and agency goals must be compatible.
- Objectives must be realistic.
- Objectives must be clearly stated in writing.
- Results must be measurable and verifiable.

At the same time objectives are selected, the basis for evaluating effectiveness of training should be established—criterion measures need to be determined and methods for implementing them planned. There also should be plans for developing course outlines and lesson plans, selecting and sequencing course content, developing training aids and handout materials, and arranging for instructors and training facilities. In many government agencies, full-time training specialists are responsible for planning and implementing the programs; however, all managers should be aware of the role of the training specialists.

Conducting instruction: The training content and the manner in which it is presented are key to the reception and retention of the material by participants. Instructors must not only thoroughly understand the material they present, but also must be well-versed in the fundamentals of teaching. Technique also affects the impact of teaching. Studies have shown that instruction can be more effective when participants are involved through action-oriented techniques such as role-play, case analyses, simulation exercises, in-basket exercises, projects, and group discussions. However, the lecture method can also be effective, particularly when theoretical information or a variety of details are to be imparted. In developing managers outside the classroom, public agencies have found such techniques as coaching, counseling, job rotation assignments, special projects, and "assistant-to" positions particularly useful.

Course content should address itself to the stated training objectives. The state of Pennsylvania, for example, designed a program that was intended to offer an integrated approach to the development of state and local personnel. Teaching methods, such as seminars and lectures, varied according to the type of personnel and the nature of the jurisdiction, (for example, state or city, large or small). The program combined management theory, program analysis methodology and program technologies, and issues. At the highest levels of the largest jurisdictions the focus was on system-wide issues in the areas of health services, welfare, and the administration of justice. At the more technical levels, emphasis was on state-of-the-art in substantive issues such as new technologies for solid-waste disposal.

Evaluating training systems: The effectiveness of a training program is determined by measuring results against objectives. The most scientific means of accomplishing this is by selecting a control group similar to the group being trained. Both groups are administered tests before and after training. Ideally, the training group shows the greater improvement in test scores, indicating that the training was effective. However, this procedure can often be too expensive and time-consuming for smaller agencies, so alternative methods are used. It is advisable to measure training results at several points: during and immediately following instruction, to determine the level of the participant's understanding of the subject; shortly after the training—one to two weeks—to examine the effect on the trainee's attitudes, behavior, and skills; and six months to a year later, to determine how much of the training has been retained and applied on the job. This type of evaluation can be accomplished in a number of ways. Performance tests and questionnaires or opinion surveys are formal methods. On an informal basis, questioning by the instructor, observations by outside consultants, and discussions with individual students can prove useful.

Management and Executive Development

Training has relevance for all classifications within the agency, including executives. Since government agencies at all levels stress the importance of a "succession of competent managers," the subject of executive and management development warrants some attention. The Civil Service Reform Act established the federal Senior Executive Service (SES), which serves as a model for executive development programs throughout government. The development features of SES include:

1. A climate within each agency conducive to executive growth.
2. Individual Development Plans that focus on enhancing managerial skills, correcting deficiencies identified in performance

evaluations, and preparing for future assignments. The plans include these features:
   - Developmental assignments
   - Attendance at seminars and conferences
   - Formal education and training
3. The Federal Executive Institute—an interagency development center operated by OPM.
4. Sabbaticals for study or work experience outside the government.
5. Annual summary ratings of the executive's performance.

The Senior Executive Service (SES) began in 1979 as a separate personnel system for individuals in managerial, supervisory, and other policy-making jobs equivalent to GS-16 through Executive Level IV. The Office of Personnel Management determines the number of SES positions in each agency, and incumbents in these positions may choose to enter the SES. The number of SES positions are limited (about 8,500), so that those who choose to enter the service must meet specific qualification requirements, and those who seek career appointments (versus noncareer or limited terms) must compete for a position. Career executives in the service who perform well become eligible for rewards. Each year 50 percent of them may be given a lump-sum bonus of up to 20 percent of base salary; up to 5 percent of SES executives may receive the rank of Meritorious Executive, which carries a cash award; and the Distinguished Executive rank (1 percent) has a higher cash award.

Performance Appraisal

The Civil Service Reform Act places considerable emphasis on the evaluation of employee performance. It mandates that each agency develop its own appraisal system, suitable to the peculiar conditions of the agency. Thus, there is no "best" system, but there are certain elements that each should contain.

Critical elements and performance standards: Any component of an employee's job that is so important that below-standard performance for that component requires remedial action (including denial of a within-grade increase or even reduction in grade level) is a critical element. A performance standard is the explicit (measured) level of achievement (quantity, quality, timeliness) established for the duties and responsibilities of a position or positions. Performance standards should be objective, job related, and clearly communicated; managers are encouraged to elicit employee participation in their development.

Performance appraisal discussion: Discussions of appraisal results are crucial to the success of the system. They serve to keep employees informed of their accomplishments relative to management's expectations, enable the timely correction of unacceptable performance, allow for recognition of exemplary performance, provide for documentation of performance, and avoid unpleasant surprises to employees who may have a different perception of their performance.

Unacceptable performance—appropriate action: When an employee fails to meet established standards in one or more critical areas of a position, he or she may be reassigned, reduced in grade, or removed. However, the employee must first be given an opportunity to correct the unacceptable performance. The manager's approach is the key to the success of performance appraisal. To make it work properly, the following factors are essential:

Good communication. This entails a mutual understanding of performance standards, an acceptance of all concerned of the purposes and procedures of the system, and continuous feedback on the employee's accomplishments. The appraisal process includes coaching and counseling throughout the year prior to the official appraisal interview.

Adequate training. All managers associated with the appraisal system must understand its importance and how it works, and they must know the techniques of evaluating performance and of conducting the appraisal interview.

System evaluation. To ensure that the system is working as intended, continuous checks need to be made. Someone in authority can see if appraisals are actually being completed on a timely basis, and if appraisal interviews are being conducted, see that the employee understands what was supposed to have been communicated.

Investing time and effort. Job analyses, establishment of performance standards, completion of the appraisal forms, interviews, and reviews require considerable time and effort. But it is a worthwhile task for managers in terms of the improved performance and employee development that result.

Compensation Management

Pay plans attempt to provide rewards commensurate with an employee's contributions, although compensation rarely accomplishes this goal in practice. Such an objective assumes that there is complete economic freedom throughout the organization to disseminate rewards; this situation never occurs because pay rewards are contingent on factors beyond the control of individual managers. Agencies cannot provide tangible remunerative benefits when budget appropriations are not adequate, despite employees' achievements for the organization. The individual manager can, however, attempt to make sure the available monetary resources are allocated on an equitable basis and provide an incentive for maximum employee performance.

Equity in compensation is another difficult area. Employees generally compare their work and pay to similar classifications in other public and private organizations. Employees usually are satisfied with their pay when it compares favorably with that of employees whom they perceive as holding similar jobs.

Government agencies generally use the prevailing wage to establish rates within their organizations. Since the 1970 enactment of the Federal Pay Comparability Act, most government agencies have attempted to maintain comparability with pay rates in the private sector. The job-matching process is difficult because of the variety of pay schedules among government agencies, for example, most have fixed rate ranges, such as the federal GS schedule, that vary in the width of the ranges and in the nature of the schedule. In addition to the prevailing wage practice, many states and municipalities have attempted to retain a relationship of parity between certain classifications—between police and firefighters, or between administrators and supervisors.

Job evaluation: The pay relationships among classifications can be maintained equitably through systems of job evaluation. An example of a system that is becoming increasingly popular among government agencies is the Factor Evaluation System (FES), approved by the OPM for implementation for nonsupervisory positions. Using a position description as a departure point, each job is assigned numerical points for each of nine factors. Each factor contains levels with varying point values. The total points for all factors translate into the pay grade for the position. These same factors are used to evaluate all positions in the system:

- Factor 1. *Knowledge required by the position.* This factor measures the nature and extent of information or facts that the worker must understand to do acceptable work.
- Factor 2. *Supervisory controls.* This factor covers the nature and extent of direct or indirect controls exercised by the supervisor, the employee's responsibility, and the review of completed work.
- Factor 3. *Guidelines.* This factor covers the nature of guidelines and the judgment needed to apply these guidelines.
- Factor 4. *Complexity.* This factor covers the nature and variety of tasks, steps, processes, methods, or activities in the work

performed, and the degree to which the employee must vary the work, discern interrelationships and deviations, or develop new techniques, criteria, or information.

- Factor 5. *Scope and effect.* This factor covers the purpose of the assignment and the effect of work products both inside and outside the organization.
- Factor 6. *Personal contacts.* This factor includes face-to-face contacts and telephone and radio dialogue with persons not in the supervisory chain.
- Factor 7. *Purpose of contacts.* This factor covers the range of contacts from factual exhanges of information to situations involving significant or controversial issues and differing viewpoints, goals, or objectives.
- Factor 8. *Physical demands.* This factor covers the physical requirements of the work assignment. (For example, climbing, lifting, pushing, balancing, stooping, kneeling, crouching, crawling, or reaching.)
- Factor 9. *Work environment.* This factor considers the risks, discomforts, or unpleasantness that may be imposed upon employees by various physical surroundings or situations.

FES provides a rational basis for assigning salary ranges to positions. Theoretically, merit plays a major role in determining how rapidly an employee progresses within a salary range. One of the most perplexing issues in personnel management is that of linking employee performance to salary administration. Enlightened public managers attempt to avoid automatic pay increases and reward those whose salaries are above the midpoint of the range only when their performance is superior.

Benefits

As a rule, employee benefits appear to be more generous in public agencies than among private employers. Paid leave and retirement benefits in particular are usually relatively higher in government than in private organizations. There is a good reason why this phenomenon exists. Government agencies historically have heeded the admonition to set an example. In times of economic inflation, they endeavor to keep labor costs to a minimum so as not to contribute to the trend. Benefits are considered noninflationary because they do not increase employee purchasing power. Yet agencies must compete with the private sector for talent. Added benefits make *total* compensation appear attractive to employment candidates and are considered a stabilizing influence on employment. Employees realize that benefits improve with longer service and tend to remain in government service to accrue benefits and preserve their "investment."

Benefits represent supplements to pay that are either financial in nature or that protect employees against financial loss. Protection-type benefits include life insurance, accident and sickness plans, and hospital-medical-surgical and major medical plans. In general, their inclusion in a benefits package is fairly standard among government agencies, but the provisions of the plans vary widely as to limits of coverage and specific provisions.

Time off with pay has become popular among government service employees. The amount and forms of leave time vary among agencies, but generally agencies pay employees for holidays, vacations, sick leave, and personal leave. Many agencies have experimented with flexible work hours to enable employees to arrange their schedules for greater personal convenience without interfering with efficient operations. In June 1980, the city of Los Angeles became the first city to put all its municipal employees on "flex-time." Its primary motive was to enhance productivity while reducing air pollution and saving energy. Experiments with four-day workweeks have had mixed results, although there have been numerous reports that the appeal of a longer weekend has attracted employee interest. The state of Oregon, for instance, polled its employees and found that 68 percent favored a 4/40 (four 10-hour days) schedule.

Retirement plans are becoming more flexible, and the trend is toward less stringent age and service requirements. Vesting provisions are also becoming more liberal, and many agencies permit employees to transfer benefits to other agencies if they relocate within the system.

Other benefits that are offered by some agencies include:

- Tuition refund plans that underwrite a portion of educational expenses for approved programs, usually courses that directly relate to present or future work.
- Thrift or savings plans, sometimes with matching contributions by the agency. An additional benefit can be realized when savings plans incorporate a tax-sheltered annuity. Kansas City, Missouri, was one of the first municipalities to institute such a benefit through a "Deferred Compensation" program. It was designed as a long-term savings plan, using before-tax income to supplement the regular retirement program.
- Suggestion systems that stimulate money-saving improvements from employees and reward them when the ideas are adopted.

A host of employee services are offered through government employers. Activities that can be supported by, and provide benefits to, employees include: employee clubs, recreation programs, athletic teams, social events, cultural activities, counseling services, credit unions, and communications programs that provide employee newspapers, bulletin boards, and reading racks.

The Union as a Factor in Staffing

The manner in which public managers handle their employees' dealings with union representatives can materially affect the staffing function. Harmonious labor/management relationships have been found to enhance the efficiency and effectiveness of the agency. Keeping the union informed about plans that may affect employees and treating union representatives with respect improves a cooperative union-management relationship.

Often public managers represent the agency at the bargaining table either in the role of spokesperson or as an adviser to the management negotiating team--collecting and analyzing data, evaluating proposals, forming counter proposals, and observing labor strategies.

Collective Bargaining Law

Executive Orders

Although federal employees had the right to join unions as early as 1912 (Lloyd/LaFollette Act), and Philadelphia municipal employees have had bargaining rights since 1939, the initial pervasive regulation of union-management relations appeared in the form of a series of executive orders. The first, Executive Order (EO) 10988, signed by President John F. Kennedy in 1962, granted federal employees the right to form or join labor organizations. It was amended by President Richard Nixon's EO 11491 in 1969 and EO 11616 in 1971. These orders essentially required that agencies meet and confer in good faith on personnel policies, practices, and matters affecting working conditions with representatives of labor organizations that had been accorded exclusive recognition. Specific matters, such as pay, budgets, mission, technology, or assignment of personnel were excluded.

Amendments contained in President Gerald Ford's EO 11838 in 1975 were designed to expand the scope of union-management activities. Most significantly EO 11838 focused on consolidation of bargaining units, scope or range of bargaining negotiations, and grievance and arbitration procedures.

Civil Service Reform Act: These executive orders were expanded and translated into law through the Civil Service Reform Act of 1978. The Act reaffirms the basic rights of federal employees to form, to join, and to assist labor organizations (or to refrain from these activities). It explicitly prohibits strikes or similar actions that interfere with the operation of the government.

To obtain exclusive recognition, a labor organization (certified as the sole representative of all the employees in the unit) must show by petition that 30 percent of the employees in the unit want an election, and a majority of the employees who vote must elect that organization. An *appropriate bargaining unit* is a grouping of employees who share a community of interest and who will promote effective labor-management dealings and efficient agency operations. The appropriate unit is determined by the Federal Labor Relations Authority. When a labor organization is certified as the exclusive bargaining representative, it is obliged to represent all employees in the unit fairly, whether they are union members or not.

The Act requires that agencies meet with the exclusive representatives of their employees and negotiate in good faith on conditions of employment—personnel policies and practices and general working conditions—with the expectation of signing a collective bargaining agreement. The law, however, reserves certain rights exclusively to management, thus excluding them from the bargaining process. These rights include: pay, mission, budget, organization, number of employees, internal security, and whether vacancies will be filled from inside or outside the agency. The impact of these matters on employees and the procedures for implementing them are negotiated. Management has the exclusive right to promote employees, but the collective bargaining agreement may spell out how employees are to be ranked and certified.

Collective bargaining agreements must contain a simple procedure for the settlement of grievances arising under the contract. Most matters are resolved through the negotiated grievance procedure, but in adverse action cases, an employee can choose either the grievance procedure (if it covers the matter) or the statutory procedure. The Act specifies that negotiated grievance procedures must provide for binding arbitration if the steps of the grievance procedure fail to yield a satisfactory resolution.

The Act also lists unfair labor practices (ULP) by both unions and management. For instance, the law prohibits management from

- discriminating against union members.
- refusing to negotiate in good faith.

By the same token union officials may be cited for a ULP if they

- cause an agency to discriminate against employees in exercising their rights.
- call or participate in a strike.

- take reprisal against a union member to hinder work performance.

The Act is administered by the Federal Labor Relations Authority (FLRA), which determines appropriate bargaining units, oversees representation elections, resolves questions on ULP, and decides appeals from arbitration awards. When an agency reaches deadlock with its union, the parties may seek assistance and opinion from the Federal Service Impasses Panel. In such cases, the Federal Mediation and Conciliation Service (FMCS) often steps in to mediate. While the Impasses Panel is advisory and quasi-judicial in nature, the FMCS attempts to bring the deadlocked parties together. The two agencies complement each other. The Office of Personnel Management provides policy guidance and technical advice to agencies concerning labor-management relations.

It should be obvious from the foregoing summary of the Civil Service Reform Act that it is the most definitive regulation on labor-management relations to date. It clarifies the roles and responsibilities of the parties and expands the rights of employees covered by collective bargaining agreements.

State bargaining laws: The wide variety of state collective bargaining statutes precludes any meaningful analysis within the confines of this chapter. However, state bargaining laws generally cover: (1) rights to organize and bargain collectively, (2) determination of appropriate bargaining units, (3) scope of bargaining, (4) resolution of collective bargaining impasses, (5) strike prohibitions, and (6) union security agreements.

More than half the states have enacted collective bargaining legislation. At least 37 states have enacted comprehensive legislation covering state or municipal employees; 10 have statutes covering teachers; 10 have legislation covering firemen and/or policemen; and several others have laws covering only health care facilities, or transit authorities, or special districts. Only 9 states have no legislative or executive authorization for public sector bargaining.

Legislation governs the conduct of the bargaining relationship and the issues involved. Those basic to most contracts are discussed here.

Labor relations issues: Traditionally, union bargaining demands have centered around economic issues such as wages, hours, and benefits. But more recently employee representatives have pressed for discussion of promotional and educational opportunities, standards of conduct and performance, rights of employees in disciplinary matters, and changes in civil service regulations or labor legislation. The air traffic controllers' struggle for recognition by the

Federal Aviation Administration (FAA) is a case in point. Repeated refusal of the FAA to grant the Professional Air Traffic Controllers Organization (PATCO) exclusive recognition (PATCO represented 5,000 controllers nationwide) resulted in retaliatory slowdowns and sickouts. Following extended court and Labor Department hearings, PATCO was accorded exclusive recognition. As a representative of the Air Traffic Controllers, it influenced legislation (PL 92–297, 1972) that provided for appeal rights and entitlement to receive second career training and/or retirement when a controller is removed from active control duties. (PATCO was disbanded as a result of its 1981 strike.)

The right to strike: As demonstrated by the 1981 air traffic controllers dispute, the dominant issue in public sector relations is whether public employees should be allowed to strike. The question has been tested repeatedly in courts that have held that there is no constitutional right to strike. Legal decisions have consistently reasoned that public employees have a higher obligation to provide uninterrupted functioning of the government in order to ensure public health, safety, and welfare. Nevertheless, the record shows numerous incidents of open defiance by public unions that engage in strikes or other forms of job action.

Such militancy has led critics of public sector collective bargaining to argue that this practice is incompatible with merit systems. To support their position they make these points:

- Negotiated seniority arrangements are incompatible with qualifications or merit as the basis for selection or promotion.
- Collective economic bargaining disrupts the internal consistency of pay relationships.
- Union security arrangements, providing for a union or agency shop, often preclude the selection of otherwise qualified outside candidates.

Based on these arguments, critics feel that collective bargaining in government is not in the public interest.

On the other hand, the Civil Service Reform Act asserts that labor organization and collective bargaining in the civil service are in the public interest, and that its provisions are directed toward maintaining labor relations harmony.

New York City's special tripartite Board of Collective Bargaining serves as an example of an effort to maximize public interest while recognizing the importance of peaceful resolution of bargaining issues. The board, which was created under the New York State Taylor Law, is composed of neutrals and representatives of management and labor. It functions to oversee labor relations between the city and its public unions. The tripartite board is reported to be as successful a method as any in a situation where the law prohibits strikes by public employees. As a result of this prohibition, public employees in New York City still feel they have no say despite the board's existence.

Regardless of efforts to maintain harmony, unions argue that the only legitimate bargaining process includes the right to strike in the event of an impasse. They contend that it has traditionally been accorded legal status in the private sector, and that the ban on strikes in the public service creates an economic imbalance to the disadvantage of working people.

From a political standpoint, opponents of the strike in public employment contend that allowing unions this right would reverse the balance of power. But it should be noted that eight states grant public employees at least a limited right to strike. Moreover, unions have political weapons other than the strike at their disposal. They can exert political pressure through block votes and financial contributions and thereby accumulate bargaining power. Also, outside the bargaining area, they can circumvent negotiations by influencing public officials who are often sensitive to the political power of unions.

A Brief Case to Study—to Illustrate—to Ponder

Recommendations of the Quality of Work Life Team

Martin County had instituted a Quality of Work Life (QWL) program several years ago and, generally speaking, it seemed to be working well. Teams composed of managers and employees (they were members of the County Government Employees Union) had been trained to study and diagnose problem areas and make recommendations to the county commissioners.

Acting on the conclusions of a state senate report on the effectiveness of county government in the state, the QWL team decided to review the county's human resource activities. After an exhaustive 18-month study the team came up with the following observations and recommendations:

- Minorities and women were underutilized in management positions, so outreach programs should be instituted immediately to increase the applicant pool. Employment testing should be abandoned and minorities and women should be awarded an additional five points on their total merit selection score.

- Compensation for all job classifications in Martin County should be compared with results of a national private-and public-sector compensation survey conducted by the county.
- The supervisory training course should no longer be evaluated using participant opinion. Rather, new pre-tests and post-tests should use questions developed from course content.
- A random drug/alcohol testing program should be initiated. Those who test positive should be given the option of entering the county's employee assistance program for rehabilitation.
- Employee attitude surveys should be administered annually and the results shared with the union's bargaining committee.

The QWL team's recommendations were reviewed by the county commissioners who rejected them out of hand as being "too ambitious."

1. What impact would each of these recommendations have on the various human resource functions?
2. Are QWL teams appropriate for reviewing human resource activities? What alternative methods might be used to evaluate the staffing function?
3. Was it a good idea for Martin County to involve the union in the study? What are the pros and cons of involving the union?
4. Why do you suppose the Commissioners rejected the recommendations?

CHAPTER 8

Moving Toward Results: Directing

In the directing function, public managers communicate policies, expectations, and regulations to their employees; they resolve conflicts that may arise between and among individuals and groups; and they maintain discipline, so that planned results can be achieved.

Communication

Communication is the means of exchanging information, ideas, feelings, and attitudes among people within an organization to coordinate activities and channel personnel toward common objectives. Day-to-day supervision of employees requires continuous, effective communication. The decisions resulting from planning are translated into action through proper communication. And the policies, programs, and procedures needed to direct the efforts of human resources call for accurate communication so that these can be effectively implemented. Public managers play a key role in seeing that employees are kept informed of policy changes and relevant developments in the organization. This section will cover the principles of effective communication and the specific methods for getting information to employees and soliciting their inputs and responses.

Principles of Effective Communication

Effective communication depends on the sending of a clear message, the consideration of a receiver's reaction to the message, as well as on the basic principles of the process. The following principles incorporate techniques that can help make communication effective.

Feedback: The single most important aspect of communication is feedback. It is the reaction from those receiving a message that can be used by the sender to evaluate the message. In one-way communication, which lacks feedback, senders have little assurance that their message was received, and receivers can place little reliance on its validity.

In the military, a standing joke is that enlisted men have the last word—"Yes, sir." Orders are a form of one-way communication; troops are conditioned to respond without hesitation to the orders of their commander—an absolute necessity in battle. But to make one-way communication work, a lot of two-way communication—and a fair amount of discipline—goes into the training of troops. In some settings employees are disinclined to obey orders barked at them. Without dialogue, there is little hope that an intended action will result. Feedback not only confirms for senders that information is accurately received, but it also makes receivers confident that their action or behavior is correct.

A number of techniques will elicit feedback. By observing facial expressions in face-to-face communication, communicators can determine whether receivers are paying attention and whether they understand the information being conveyed. Asking recipients to repeat or summarize a message ensures that it was received correctly and reinforces it. Also, having receivers demonstrate the application of a message (instructions) guarantees that the communication was understood.

Simplicity: A good rule of communication is to keep it simple. Simplicity aids understanding. Muddled, obscure, and complex communication usually results in misunderstandings and a failure to respond as intended. Recipients of confusing or complex messages rarely respond enthusiastically. Articulate messages are clear, relevant, and appropriate to a situation and particularly to those receiving them. When receivers clearly understand a message as it was sent, it is usually because it was simple.

Multimedia: The more senses a message appeals to, the more likely it is to be received and acted on. Oral media combined with written methods have proven more effective than either used alone. When a message can be heard, seen, and experienced (through touch or smell for example), the impact is even greater.

Sensitivity: Sensitivity to the feelings and reactions of others certainly enhances communication effectiveness. When communicators empathize—put themselves in other people's places—they can understand them better and are more likely to be understood in return. Especially today, when employees are of diverse backgrounds, values, cultures, and feelings, communicators' sensitivity to the world of the receivers is critical.

The increased number of women at work has given rise to a sensitivity to statements that might offend them. Communication barriers are formed between a male employee and the modern woman who has been sensitized to respond negatively to what she may interpret as a sexist statement. Remarks that stereotype women—that imply a female's appearance is more important than her credentials, or imply subservience—are likely to be ill-received. Hence the statement, "That's a good job for a woman" or "Take your coat off so I can see what you look like" (to a job applicant) would be considered sexist or in poor taste.

Listening: An important part of feedback is listening. In fact, without it, there can be no feedback. But most people are poor listeners, even though they are often good talkers. After several weeks of negotiations, union and management representatives had worked out the *terms* of a new contract for city employees. But the two sides could not agree on the *language* of the contract. Union representatives claimed that it was intended to humiliate the union, while management insisted that they refused to be a party to a face-saving whitewash of labor. After another week of fruitless argument, the parties declared an impasse. Perhaps the differences could have been narrowed, if not resolved, had each party made more of an effort to listen to the basis for the other side's demands.

Listening skills can be sharpened. Good listeners conscientiously encourage other people to talk. They ask questions and probe for answers. And people respond eagerly, because they know they're being heard. Good listeners affirm their interest and understanding by restating the speakers' feelings. They might say, "You seem to feel strongly about . . ." or "You think this will happen if . . . ." Furthermore, they exercise patience. Rather than talk to fill a moment of silence, they may pause to give someone else a chance to say something. Finally, skillful listeners hear with a third ear. That is, they not only do hear the words that are spoken, but they understand the connotations, feelings, and emotions being expressed. Listening is indeed an art; it must be carefully nurtured.

Arbitrators of union-management grievances are paid to listen. The parties (labor union representatives and management representatives) present oral arguments. Not only do these representatives debate an issue, but witnesses tell (they testify to) facts about the case. The arbitrators' job is to form an opinion about which side is right. Because eye movement and body language often say more than the words spoken, a witness who looks at the floor when answering a critical question will lose credibility. Voice inflection, too, may give meaning to what is being said. Words spoken loudly might be a reflection of the witness's anger or short temper, while the same words spoken calmly could have a different meaning. Through many years of *listening* to grievances, arbitrators develop an ability to gain an understanding of and a sensitivity for the issues behind the issue.

Communication in Practice

A constant flow of information and feedback up, down, and across an organization can go a long way toward accomplishing objectives. Some of the current vehicles for communicating with employees are outlined below.

Grievance Procedures: Progressive government agencies, whether unionized or not, encourage employees to make known their complaints, questions, or job problems; insist they be given a fair hearing; and give timely answers. Such grievance procedures should also contain some basis for appeal to management levels above employees' immediate superiors. Though the basic approach is similar in all grievance procedures, agencies may title them differently (Speak Up, Open-Door Policy, and Operation Feedback are examples).

One northeastern city utilizes a formal open-door policy that allows employees to appeal complaints as high as they feel they need to. Employees are asked to put their complaints in writing and present them to their supervisor first. The city strives to make a thorough, expeditious, and objective assessment of all complaints, identify their cause, investigate corrective action, and render a prompt answer to the employee.

Meetings with Employees: Employee discussion groups or open meetings, in which employees or their representatives (selected by management) are encouraged to express their problems and concerns, often facilitate upward communication.

Through employee discussion groups (EDGs) department supervisors hold periodic discussions with their employees. Managers and supervisors have been trained to stimulate upward communication so that EDG participants feel free to express their feelings and concerns. Then, monthly or quarterly, representatives from each department are selected to attend a session with higher officials. These representatives express the group's concerns and get a response from the executives. The representatives then report back to their group the results of the meeting. These dialogues between the employees and managers make for an open communication system.

Bulletin Boards: Bulletin boards are an effective means of disseminating announcements and news of an immediate nature. Also, to keep employees informed, organizations post reminders and information concerning plant rules on bulletin boards.

Reading Racks: Racks contain pamphlets of general and personal interest and may occasionally include basic information about an agency. Reading material covering a wide variety of subjects is readily accessible in racks and can provide entertainment during off hours. It can influence employees on a social, political, or economic issue, or inform them about a particular subject.

House Organs: Newspapers and magazines that inform employees about an organization's plans and activities are useful communication channels. House organs also include articles of personal and local interest.

Communication and Conflict

Conflict and differences of opinion arise in healthy, dynamic organizations. As a matter of fact, such differences can aid progress and innovation. But unresolved conflict can impede progress and may prove dysfunctional. Communication plays a key role in making conflict constructive.

Communication-related conflict stems from a variety of sources, including the following:

Ambiguity: Vague and complex communication causes misunderstandings and uncertainties. An ambiguous directive creates conflict when people do not fully understand its meaning and read into it what they want. Clearly, simply written directives that are straightforward in spelling out responsibility minimize the possibility of misunderstandings that lead to conflict.

Perceptual Differences: When one employee perceives that another is out to get him, a conflict can arise. Dissimilar groups (black-white, young-old, line-staff, union-management) often develop misconceptions about each other. Resolution can best be achieved through problem-solving sessions that enable the conflicting parties to see broader opportunities for resolution. Frequently, keeping both groups informed and involved in the organization can stimulate cooperation. Communication training alleviates conflict caused by perceptual differences. This type of training can modify opinions and attitudes that may hinder understanding between the opposing parties.

Role Conflict: Role conflict occurs when there are multiple reporting relationships, especially within large organizations. Role conflict can be prevented by providing policies to those who might become involved in a conflict situation. For instance, if an employee receives orders from multiple sources, the extent of conflict will depend on the degree to which the orders are incompatible. A clear policy can guide the employee in determining which demand should take precedence. If this same policy has also been communicated to the demand-makers, the probability of conflict will be substantially reduced. In addition, managers might hold frequent communication and review meetings with those whose positions are likely to expose them to role conflict.

Supervisor-employee: Supervisor-employee conflicts arise out of many sources—personality clashes, the boss feeling threatened by the employee ("He's out to get my job"), a lack of respect for each other, unclear organizational goals, and many others. Such conflicts can often be overcome through open communication. If the supervisor can make the employee feel he or she wants to help, supports development, recognizes accomplishments, discusses goals and performance standards, gives feedback on how he or she is doing, keeps the employee informed of new developments, and welcomes suggestions and criticism, trust and cooperation are likely to ensue.

Stress and Conflict

Conflict between people or among group members can be caused by the emotional and mental stress that results from the work environment. As with conflict, some stress can be productive, but too much can be detrimental to effective operations.

Since 1936, medical researchers have studied stress and the body's reactions to it. They point out that the body and mind react to stress and mobilize defenses against its continuance. But, if the causes of stress persist or the defenses prove to be inadequate, energy becomes depleted and exhaustion often accompanied by mental or physical breakdown results. Research studies reveal that stress can be the result of environmental factors such as work overload, time pressure, communications (which we discussed earlier), change, lack of career progression; and personal factors such as relationships with peers, supervisors or subordinates; or family problems—children, spouse, finances. Stressors are elements in the environment or are part of one's personal makeup that contribute to the personally experienced stress. An employee's stress experience results from discrepancies between environmental stressors and personal stressors (self-confidence, tolerance of ambiguity, decisiveness, maturity are a few examples). The outcome might be physical (higher blood pressure, increased heart rate), or psychological (job dissatisfaction, anxiety or tension, increased consumption of alcohol or drugs), or organizational (absenteeism, turnover, performance decline). Ultimately, conflict can be both a cause and a result of stress.

Some jobs, due to their nature, contain more environmental stressors than others. Secretary, office manager, and manager administrator are among the most stressful jobs, according to the National Institute for Occupational Safety and Health. Knowing that stress often results from workplace experiences, public managers can take measures to deal with the problem.

The adoption of a stress management program might be beneficial. Stress management programs take various forms—some oriented to preventing stress and others to relieving the symptoms of stress. A model program addressing both prevention and cure might address the following topics:

- Nonwork-related stressors: family and financial problems
- Making decisions about handling stress situations
- Self-report feedback techniques
- Preventive health management: health profiling, nutrition, and exercise
- Stress education: relaxation responses, meditation, biofeedback, autogenics, time management, and so forth

There are also specific measures managers can take to reduce workplace stress:

- Ensuring that people have the skills they need to perform their jobs
- Properly screening employees to avoid job mismatches
- Setting performance goals that have a standard of excellence but that allow employees to succeed
- Rewarding satisfaction and achievement

The physical work environment can be designed for stress reduction. Ergonomics—the science of matching machines to human needs and comfort—contributes significantly to stress reduction. In offices where computer terminals are widely used, for example, an ergonomically sound environment could be enhanced with rotatable display faces, detachable keyboards, brighter display backgrounds, reduction of office illumination (to improve viewing), and adjustable work surfaces with sufficient work space.

Conflict Resolution Methods

Depending on the type of conflict—interpersonal or structural (functional)—the public manager might utilize one or more optional methods. Actually, public managers are more likely to become directly involved in resolving interpersonal conflicts than in structural or organizational ones. In the latter case, third-party intervention is the prevailing method, and disputes between departments or between labor and management are usually resolved in this manner. Interpersonal conflicts, on the other hand, are traditionally resolved by the manager acting as a referee and counselor and leading the conflicting parties to an acceptable solution. In resolving the conflict the object is to emphasize the constructive aspects of the conflict and to expedite resolution. In this regard, all the principles of communication that were discussed earlier in this chapter come into play. The manager's role is to allow the issues to be discussed freely, while minimizing acrimonious debate and emotionalism. The manager acts as a facilitator, helping the participants understand why the conflict exists, assisting them in articulating the underlying issues, and helping them reach a solution. The conflicting parties may confront each other or they may be kept apart. In either case, the manager must avoid interfering with their progress toward resolving the conflict. A problem-solving climate that starts with an attitude that the conflict can be resolved, and that deals with information (facts) more than with emotion, is most conducive to conflict resolution. This is not to say that feelings should not be expressed in the process. But feelings and emotion should not be allowed to stand in the way of discussing the issues and resolving the dispute.

Conflict resolution between organizations, particularly between the agency and the union representing its employees, traditionally calls for third party-intervention. In this regard, mediation and arbitration are the predominant forms of attempts to resolve union-management disputes in the public sector.

Undoubtedly, the interests of all concerned are best served when the parties themselves can arrive at a negotiated agreement. However, when impasses are reached, the voluntary or compulsory introduction of neutrals often produces an equitable settlement that might not otherwise transpire.

Mediation: In mediation, an impartial third party attempts to persuade disputing union and management representatives to settle their differences. Mediation is either permitted or required by statute. The Civil Service Reform Act covers federal employees, and about half the states have mediation provisions in their laws. States utilizing mediation either furnish mediators from their staff or arrange ad hoc mediation by private individuals. Mediators may need to instruct the parties in negotiating procedures when it is their first exposure to collective bargaining. By the same token, the parties may have to instruct the mediator in the labor relations, economics, personnel policies, and politics of the public sector when the mediator is unfamiliar with these matters. Mediation is usually the dispute settlement procedure used prior to fact-finding and arbitration because it enables the reduction of disputes and helps to clarify unresolved issues. Mediation is often acceptable to both parties because its aim is to assist the parties in reaching agreement themselves. This method is similar to the one just described for resolving interpersonal conflicts.

Arbitration: Similarly, arbitration utilizes a neutral third party. The arbitrator is generally selected by the parties themselves, and the arbitrator's function may be to find facts about the dispute and render an advisory report or to award a judgment that is binding on both parties. Arbitration can be voluntary, (adopted at the discretion of the parties) or compulsory (automatically imposed by law when an impasse is reached). The New Jersey Employer-Employee Relations Act is an example of a statute that allows disputes to be arbitrated by agreement of the parties. By having the advance consent of the parties rather than being imposed by statute, voluntary arbitration is more acceptable to the parties than compulsory arbitration.

Both "rights" and "interests" issues can be submitted to arbitration. Frank and Edna Asper Elkouri in *How Arbitration Works* distinguish between them as follows: "Disputes as to 'rights' involve the interpretation or application of laws, agreements, or customary practices, whereas disputes as to 'interests' involve the question of what shall be the basic terms and conditions of employment." [20]

For some employers, legislated compulsory interest arbitration is specifically authorized in almost one-half of the states. But this approach is often viewed with disfavor and suspicion. Many believe that by placing final decision-making authority in the hands of persons not accountable to the public, interest arbitration weakens political democracy. These same people believe that there is an absence of definite criteria or standards to govern the arbitrator. The question becomes, does the nonpolitical arbitrator arrive at a better decision than the politicians would through bargaining?

Sometimes arbitration becomes attractive to public officials when it is viewed as an opportunity to escape from the responsibility of making decisions that might be viewed as unpopular.

A case in point involves a county that reached a standstill over wages with the police bargaining unit. Although the county commissioners desired to pay increases for police officers, they were constrained by unavailability of funds. Taxpayers would have been hostile to the tax assessment necessary to increase police pay. When the arbitrator granted the desired increase, it relieved the commissioners who could then place the blame on the arbitrator and not suffer at the polls.

Although there is no magic formula for the adjudication of interest disputes, certain standards do exist and must be considered by the arbitrator in rendering an award or an advisory opinion. The arbitrator is admonished to consider what the parties might have resolved had the bargaining been successfully concluded. In addition, the arbitrator must weigh such matters as the best interests of the public, economic comparisons, existing employment conditions, availability of funds, and precedent.

Public managers should be aware, in the conduct of arbitration proceedings, that public sector arbitrators must consider not only the terms of agreement, but the provisions of statutes and regulations that may apply to the grievance or to the interest issue under consideration. The parties have the responsibility of making the arbitrator aware of the applicable legislation.

The costliness in terms of time delays and money are frequent objectives voiced against arbitration. One successful effort to overcome these disadvantages is found in experiments utilizing expedited arbitration. This approach, most appropriate for discipline cases, employs preselected panels of arbitrators who agree, in advance, to conduct hearings shortly after notification, to render an award promptly (usually within 48 hours), and to accept a low level of compensation.

Grievance mediation: More recently, grievance mediation has been successfully employed as a means to resolve conflicts. Where grievances have been certified for arbitration, a mediator (usually a person who has served as an arbitrator) is called in to mediate the dispute. As a final effort before the issue is submitted to arbitration, the mediator attempts to get the parties to resolve the issue. In the rare cases where mediation fails to resolve the matter, the mediator might issue a bench advisory opinion. As a result of the opinion the parties may decide to settle but, in any event, should the matter be submitted to arbitration, the mediator would not serve as the arbitrator.

Maintaining Discipline

In achieving desired results, the public manager may be faced with employees who fail or refuse to behave as expected. Despite the most conscientious efforts to communicate policy and expectations, some employees are unwilling or unable to comply. Under these circumstances, managers are called on to apply discipline. Disciplinary action is always subject to review by higher authority. When a union is present, disciplinary actions may be appealed through the negotiated grievance procedure. Even where unions are not present, disciplinary action is subject to review by appeal panels or trial boards. In the federal service, the Merit Systems Protection Board (MSPB) handles appeals of employees on disciplinary or adverse action.

Basic Concepts of Discipline

If management's philosophy is that the purpose of discipline is to correct rather than punish, positive results are more likely. In the corrective approach to discipline, managers counsel employees to determine the reasons for failure to comply with a rule, to explain the reasons for failure to comply with a rule, to explain the reasons for the rule, and to reach an understanding regarding expectations of the employee's future behavior. Punishment is used only as a last resort.

Counseling by itself does not constitute a disciplinary action. Agencies that have been successful with the corrective approach also have rules with appropriate penalties, and they consistently enforce them through a system of progressive discipline. Many personnel policy manuals and/or union-management agreements specifically mention types of discipline, and the offenses for which punishment may be invoked. Infractions that merit corrective action can be categorized as follows:

- Unacceptable performance—failure to perform acceptably in one or more critical elements of the job.
- Personal misconduct—rule violations such as unreliability; insubordination; dishonesty or disloyalty, such as unauthorized releasing of classified information.
- Violation of the bargaining agreement.

The list of penalties usually designates corrective action commensurate with the infraction. If the penalty the agency imposes is too harsh or does not fit the circumstances, arbitrators or appeal tribunals may modify or reverse the agency's action. Even more frequently, arbitrators reverse penalties for rule infractions because of inconsistent enforcement. Given similar circumstances, violators must be handled similarly. When one employee is reprimanded for habitual tardiness while a second employee with a comparable work record is discharged for the same violation, management is not consistently administering discipline.

Corrective Discipline

Consistent, impartial, and humane discipline is facilitated by a system of progressive discipline. Under such a system, employees are first cautioned or reinstructed through counseling for lesser offenses. Repeated or more serious derelictions result in penalties of increasing severity, such as:

- Oral cautions with a notation in the employee's record.
- Written reprimand.
- Short suspension—three days to one month, or lateral reassignment. (Note: In the federal government, there are no appeal rights to the MSPB for suspensions of 14 days or less.)
- Reduction in grade or withholding of merit increase.
- Suspension—30 days to six months, with loss of seniority.
- Discharge—the most severe penalty.

This philosophy of discipline is best illustrated by the *hot stove rule*, as follows:

- The burn is *immediate.* There is no doubt about cause and effect.
- There was a *warning.* If the stove is red hot, people know what will happen if they touch it.
- The discipline is *consistent.* Everyone who touches the stove is burned.
- The discipline is *impersonal.* People are burned not because of who they are, but because they touch the stove.

Perhaps the following guidelines that arbitrators use in rendering decisions in discipline cases will be helpful to managers of human resources. A manager should be able to answer all of the following questions in the affirmative before administering a disciplinary action:

- Did the employee violate a rule?
- Did the employee know the rule?
- Was the employee properly warned, cautioned, or reinstructed?
- Did the employee have a fair hearing?
- Will the punishment be (a) consistent with past action? (b) fair and equitable in light of the circumstances? (c) administered within a reasonable time?

In the unionized agency as well as in those regulated by a merit system, employees may appeal adverse actions through either a formal appeals procedure or a grievance procedure. Grievance and appeals procedures serve to provide a fair hearing of employee complaints; they also minimize potential disputes and preserve harmony between employees and the administration.

A Brief Case Study—to Illustrate—to Ponder

The Case of Jack Weeks

Jack Weeks, 58, with 18 years of satisfactory employment with a state agency requested a leave of absence. On June 18 he asked his supervisor, Frank Jones, for leave from June 26 to June 30 to travel to his son's graduation from college, and the request was granted.

Jack Weeks was one of three systems analysts who performed various functions and replaced any of the state planners who might be absent or on leave. On June 24, one of the planners was given permission to take time off due to the serious illness of his mother. On June 25, the day before Jack Weeks was to leave on his trip, Supervisor Jones asked him if he could cancel his trip and make other arrangements because the department was short of help. In reply, Jack Weeks pointed out that he had firmed up his plans, and he didn't want to disappoint his son at this late date. Furthermore, Weeks pointed out, the supervisor had promised the leave, and should stick by his word. However, Supervisor Jones insisted that Weeks cancel his plans and report for work on June 26, or he would be given a disciplinary penalty. When Jack returned to work on July 1, he was given a seven-day disciplinary suspension.

A grievance was filed and appealed through the steps to the merit system which reduced the penalty to a one-day suspension and ordered Jack Weeks reimbursed for all but one day's lost wages. The review board of the state merit system felt that the leave of absence had not been properly revoked.

1. How did the outcome of this discipline case affect the relationship of Supervisor Jones with his employees?
2. From a communications standpoint, what did Supervisor Jones do wrong? What did Jack Weeks do wrong?
3. If you were Jones' manager, how would you have handled the conflict before it got to the merit system review board?
4. If you were the review board how would you have ruled? What is the reasoning for your award?

CHAPTER 9

Assuring Results: Controlling

Control is vital to all of the functions of the public manager. If public managers had unlimited time and resources, they might have less need for control. In the real world, however, resources are always scarce, and the public manager never has enough time for all that the organization might do. It is in this context of scarcity that thoughtful control becomes essential.

Perhaps the most "different thing" about managing in government (as opposed to business) is whose money is being used, and, how this money is obtained and controlled. For this reason, we devote most of this chapter to budgeting and the budget process.

The Central Role of the Budget

The budget serves a variety of purposes for the public manager. In its most obvious purpose, the budget identifies planned expenditures and anticipated revenues. The budget is also an instrument by which public managers and political officials can monitor activities and expenditures. It is a crucial tool for managerial control. Auditors scrutinize the expenditures of public organizations and report any discrepancies between agency activities and those authorized in their budgets.

From another perspective budgets have much the same purpose as contracts, although they do not necessarily have the same legal implications. A contract is basically an agreement in which persons or organizations promise to carry out certain activities. Other persons or organizations can then base their actions on the expectation that promised activities will be performed. Budgets become expectations both within and without an agency. Within an organization, the budget serves as a form of unofficial contract among the many units that make up the organization. It tells each unit what to expect from other units and serves as a coordinating mechanism. The personnel office, for example, can use budget information to schedule recruitment and training efforts.

The budget also serves as an important unofficial contract between different government organizations and different levels within the same organization. Contemporary government is a complex network of vertical and horizontal interdependencies among public organizations. This becomes quickly evident by looking at almost any function of government. In the area of education, for instance, local school boards, counties, municipalities, states, and the federal government all have a share of the responsibility. Each depends on the actions of the others. Their budgets serve as unofficial contracts with one another, announcing their individual plans and committing their resources. Budgets, then, are vital coordinating mechanisms in both intergovernmental and interorganizational processes.

Political Aspects of Budgeting

The public manager must also recognize the political function served by budgets. The political process is essentially the way power is allocated in our society. It is the struggle and compromise among individuals and groups seeking to impose their preferences and values on others and attempting to have a voice in the way resources are distributed. Since budgets are statements of resource distribution, they become scorecards of the political process. Budgets announce winners and losers in the political arena and describe the compromises that were made along the way.

From the political perspective, budgets assume several additional dimensions for the public manager, both within a public agency and with regard to the broader political system. First, budgets serve as statements of management philosophy, preferences, and priorities. There is no better way to get to know an organization than to look at the way its resources have been allocated and to note the various levels of emphasis and support given to particular types of activities. The priorities of agency management become quite clear when price tags are attached.

Second, budgets form precedents for the way resources will probably be allocated in the future. As previously mentioned, political struggles are usually settled in compromise, and budgets become the symbols of successful compromises. Thus when it is time to prepare new budgets, it is unlikely that the participants in the process will want to reopen old conflicts that have been settled satisfactorily.

Rather, the previous budget will probably be accepted as the base, and the new budget will reflect marginal adjustments. Conflicts and compromises will be a part of these adjustments, and they will become a part of the new base for future budgets. In summary, the public manager's concern for control should begin with a thorough knowledge of the organization's budget. It is far more than a simple statement about how the bills will be paid. It is also crucial that the manager understand the budget process.

The Budget Process

The appropriate place to begin a review of the process is with the budget cycle. It is a fairly consistent sequence throughout all levels of government. The process generally begins when an agency becomes aware of a need or opportunity. There are many ways this can occur. The agency may receive an unusually large number of requests from citizens seeking information or assistance; political officials may suggest that the agency initiate some new service; agency personnel may recommend expansion of current programs. In some cases, media attention will bring needs and opportunities to the attention of public organizations. Whatever the source, the cycle begins with recognition of a need or opportunity and the decision by agency management to include it in the agency's budget request.

The second stage of the budget cycle is normally the responsibility of the chief executive (mayor, governor, president). All agency requests are reviewed and coordinated into a unified plan for the executive branch. If the jurisdiction has a central budget office, it will examine agency requests against three broad criteria: (1) is the request supportive of the administration's philosophy and program goals? (2) is the recommended program the most efficient way to accomplish its objectives? (3) is the requested program of sufficiently high priority to warrant funding under a condition of limited resources? Obviously, many requests fail one or more of these criteria and are reduced or eliminated. Once the budget has been approved by the chief executive, it is presented to the legislative body (city council, legislature, or Congress).

Traditionally, legislative bodies are charged with the approval of budgets. The Constitution makes this clear at the national level, directing that "No money shall be drawn from the Treasury, but in consequence of appropriations made by law." Thus legislatures assume primary responsibility for the third stage of the budget process.

At the national level, the legislative phase of the budget process is highly fragmented. Responsibilities are divided among several committees within both houses of Congress. House and Senate standing committees specialize in various program areas and authorize specific programs and organizations. They recommend to the Congress which programs should be undertaken and which should not. They also recommend funding ceilings for individual programs, but they do *not* have the authority to provide funds. This is the responsibility of the Appropriations Committees of the House and Senate and their specialized subcommittees. The Ways and Means Committee in the House and the Finance Committee in the Senate recommend tax legislation to the Congress and thereby significantly influence the level of public resources that can be considered in the appropriations process. Finally, the Budget Committees of the two houses are charged with the almost impossible task of setting national budget targets and keeping appropriations and revenues in some state of balance.

Once the budget has been approved (and usually modified) by the legislature, the cycle moves into its fourth phase—budget execution by the chief executive and the administrative agencies. It might be argued that this phase is not properly a part of the budget cycle since the executive branch is required to implement a budget as it was written. The executive branch, in fact, exercises considerable discretion in carrying out the programs in the budget. In reality, the execution of the budget by the executive branch may be quite different from that intended by the legislature.

The final stage in the budget cycle is the audit phase in which both the chief executive and the legislature review the accomplishments of agencies and attempt to confirm whether public funds were spent in a legal, efficient, and effective manner. Normally, within the executive branch, agencies conduct internal audits (performed by their own staffs) and report their findings to the agency head. The legislature also conducts audits, using an external auditing organization. On the federal level, such functions are conducted by the Government Accounting Office (GAO), which reports directly to the Congress. At the state level, independent audit bureaus are normally assigned this task. At the local level, audits are generally performed by certified public accounting firms under contract. The results of these audits are used by both the chief executive and the legislature in judging the effectiveness and efficiency of programs, and they influence decisions on future budget cycles.

It may appear from the previous discussion that the budget process is conducted in an orderly, sequential manner with each phase executed in turn. Unfortunately, it is not that simple. Instead, the public manager will be involved in different stages of several budget cycles at all times. While preparing budget requests for next year, he or she will often still be awaiting decision on the upcoming budget. Often the public manager will be attempting to execute the present budget legally and efficiently while hosting auditors reviewing the agency's work for the previous budget year. In the worst case, the manager may still be in the process of answering audit findings from last year's audit.

The complexity of budget cycles is further compounded by different time schedules at various levels of government. The federal government begins its fiscal year on October 1, most states begin their budget years on July 1, and many local governments set their fiscal years to coincide with the calendar year. As noted earlier, the growth of intergovernmental programs in such areas as education, health, social services, and transportation makes it essential that the budget efforts of the various levels of government be coordinated. The different time schedules used by the various levels of government, however, make that almost impossible, and many public managers are forced to base their budget requests on educated guesses of what other branches of government will do. For example, many federal projects require matching funds from the state or local government. The state budget for the year in which a specific program is to be undertaken, however, may not be passed until June, although the federal funds were approved in the previous October. If the state fails to include the required funds, the appropriated federal funds either cannot be spent or must be approved for carryover to the next year through a cumbersome paperwork process. On the other hand, budgeters at the state or local level are often hesitant in, and may be legally prohibited from, asking the legislature for matching funds before the federal funds have been guaranteed.

There is no simple solution for sorting out overlapping cycles, or for dealing with the differing time schedules of various intergovernmental programs. This much should be clear, however, the budgeting process is not something the public manager does once a year. It is a key part of the continuous public management process.

Players and Strategies in the Budget Process

Beyond budget steps and cycles, it is important that the public manager understand the roles that key players perform and the strategies they employ in the budgetary process.

Public agency personnel, including the managers, are generally specialists in their particular program areas. Thus, the U.S. Environmental Protection Agency is heavily staffed with scientists, engineers, and related professionals whose training has been focused on the agency's programs; for example, lawyers who specialize in environmental regulatory law. Agriculture departments at both the state and federal levels are run by agricultural specialists, and so forth. In addition to their sphere of specialization, agency personnel develop close relationships with clientele groups who are interested in the agency's activities. Agency contacts in the legislature generally focus on those committees and subcommittees with responsibility for oversight and funding of the agency. In short, agencies are highly specialized organizations with relatively narrow views of the broader government system.

Agency officials adopt the role of advocates in the budgetary process. It is the agency officials who, knowing their areas intimately and convinced of the merit of their causes, must plead the cases for their programs and clientele before the chief executive and the legislature. It is the public manager's responsibility to promote the importance of his or her agency's work and to make sure that members of the executive office and the legislature are aware of the needs of the agency. Moreover, the public manager does so with the full knowledge that peers in other agencies will be doing the same.

The chief executive and the central budget office play dual roles in the budgeting process. They must select a package of agency programs that will accomplish the administration's purposes, but they also have fiscal responsibilities. They must attempt to improve the overall efficiency of the executive branch and usually must cut some programs to meet fiscal ceilings set by the chief executive. Also, the chief executive and budget office recognize that agencies, as advocates, usually overstate their funding needs. Thus, the executive office must find the excesses in agency requests and eliminate them from the chief executive's budget proposals to the legislature. The detailed work in this area is normally performed by analysts in the central budget office, using general policy guidance from the chief executive. Nevertheless, it is the chief executive who ultimately approves the executive budget proposal and submits it to the legislature.

The legislature encompasses several groups whose actions do not always seem coordinated in the budget process. The standing committees with their high degree of specialization, narrow focus, and clientele contact play a part similar to the advocates' role of the administrative agencies. Essentially, the standing committees merely authorize programs and need not worry about finding and appropriating the monies to support them. On the other hand, the appropriations committees, and more specifically their subcommittees in particular program areas, are concerned about fiscal matters and often become the agencies' adversaries, challenging requests in the chief executive's budget proposal. It is interesting to note, however, that specialized subcommittees of the appropriations committees sometimes become advocates for agencies they see as "under their wing."

Appropriation committee members may view themselves as "protectors of the public purse." Once members feel this duty has been carried out, they try to prevent further reductions. Finally, the budget committees at the national level attempt to get the legislative players together by setting budget and revenue targets for the various committees. The effectiveness of these committees, however, has been limited at best.

In the typical budget process, the major players operate in a fairly consistent pattern, although individual strategies may vary from agency to agency and from year to year. Generally, agencies ask for more than they expect to get and attempt to sell their programs to anyone who will listen. The chief executive, and more specifically the central budget office analysts, usually make harsh cuts in agency requests, knowing that the legislature will probably restore some portion of those reductions. Finally the legislature, acting through its several committees, usually gives the agencies more than the chief executive recommended but less than they originally asked. The budget process is played out year after year.

Broadening Our View of Control

As noted at the start of this chapter, public managers must understand budgets and the budgeting process. This is the single most important aspect of effective control. The public manager controls with—and is controlled by—the budget. With a basic understanding of budgeting as a frame-of-reference, it is important to review key elements in the broader process of controlling. Control is closely tied to the notion of feedback on organizational performance. A very simplified view of this process would involve three elements: (1) establishment of a specific set of standards for organizational performance; (2) measurement of the organization's actual performance against these standards; and (3) corrective actions to improve performance as it relates to the standard and to rectify any deviations that have occurred.

The orientation of control and evaluation is toward improving the performance of the organization. Effectiveness will obviously increase to the extent all organization members have such an orientation. Control and evaluation, like most management functions, can be handled in part by a separate and specialized staff. A much better result is achieved by having all organization members, especially all involved in management, constantly aware and alert to opportunities for improving the organization's efficiency and effectiveness.

A key difficulty of control and evaluation is the potential for widespread antagonism toward controls and toward people who are attempting to administer controls. Organization members who develop this type of negative attitude toward the control and evaluation process can find a variety of successful but devious ways to resist and not comply with the efforts of the managers above them. Some managers themselves, in fact, can become involved in the process of resistance, noncompliance, or "playing the game" as a result of what they view as overcontrol by higher-level administrators. In general, the higher the degree of self-regulation exercised by each member of an organization, the more effective the organization will be in its total goals.

Organizations have very severe difficulties both in stating goals in specific terms and in identifying ways to measure progress toward those goals. Often, organizations have multiple goals, some of which may be in conflict with others. Goal definition and measurement toward goal accomplishment then becomes a very complex balancing process. Changes can be caused both by change within the organization and by activities that occur in the environments surrounding the organization. The organization must adapt to both internal and external changes. Information relevant to such changes must be assembled and put to use in a positive response to such change.

A Systems View of Control

Another helpful perspective on controlling can be derived using the systems approach. In addition to financial resources, considered in our discussion of budgeting, public managers also need other resources. These may include people, physical facilities, raw materials, or information. The quality of each of these various *inputs* is extremely important. As suggested by the adage, "A chain is as strong as its weakest link," these resources are very much interdependent. A focus on inputs can help the public manager understand and deal with the pre-work stage of agency performance.

A second, useful system focus is the *throughput*, or conversion, stage in which the organization changes inputs into outputs. This is essentially the on-going operation of agency. Such things as appraising employee performance, maintenance of equipment, and so forth, are important in the concurrent stage of control.

The third, and final, focus is that of *outputs*. At this stage the manager is concerned with whether or not the finished good or service was provided to the right person at the right time. At the prework and concurrent stages, the concern is usually preventive in nature. When monitoring outputs, the concern tends to be more corrective. The goal is *feedback* that will improve the planning of future work.

Points for the Public Manager to Remember

The general movement in management theory and practice is toward greater participation by members in the controlling process. As organization members become more involved and committed to group goals, it is believed that they contribute more and need less control themselves. This result is, no doubt, linked to organization members' perception that the organization is likewise involved and committed to helping members achieve their own goals.

Management scholar William Newman has provided useful insights in his book *Constructive Control: Design and Use of Control Systems.* Newman notes the failure of many managers to pay adequate attention to organizational evaluation and control. He believes this may be due, inpart, to the punitive and degrading connotations frequently associated with control. Newman sees the need to focus our attitudes and expectations on four significant points[43]:

1. Control is a normal, pervasive, and positive force in the managerial process. Purposeful activity cannot be successful if no control is exercised.
2. Control can be effective only if it is a guide to behavior. The goal is to secure certain actions.
3. Control must be oriented toward the future. It must be geared to respond to both a changing environment and to goals that are possibly subject to change.
4. All human endeavors require control. All organizations have limited resources, and all are concerned with achieving their goals, whatever they may be.

Managerial control is seen by Newman as a series of steps a manager takes to assure that actual performance conforms as closely as possible to the planned performance. Three basic types of control are recognized:

1. Steering control is oriented toward corrective actions before results are known. Course corrections made by navigators are of this type.
2. *"Yes-no"* control is a checkpoint approach, requiring approval before the process continues. The hiring, or employment, process works this way with applicants going through such steps as

application form, testing, interview, and physical examination. Each step is a yes-no decision point controlling organizational entry.

3. *Post-action* control focuses on examination of completed results. Here the goal is to compare results obtained with those desired and to make corrections to improve future results. Employee performance appraisals or health inspections of operating restaurants would fall in this category.

Almost all organizations use a variety of all three types of controls. Usually a balance of independent and interdependent control processes are required. Control, like other public management activities, is a complex and dynamic process.

A Brief Case Study—to Illustrate—to Ponder

Time to Get Tough?

As the City Manager of Exurbia you have become increasingly perplexed over your difficulties in controlling the various city departments. With a current work force of several hundred, located in nine different departments, you know that personal control of everything and everyone is impossible. At the same time, it seems that the department heads prefer not to exercise strong control. They also seem reluctant to give you all the information you need in working with the City Council. For example, a number of complaints about garbage collection and police actions have come to you from council members, even though the respective department heads had the information several days earlier. The department heads seem totally unwilling to give you any negative information about their departments. They also appear to be more concerned about being "one of the boys" in their department than about being the manager—and a member of your team.

At this point you've decided the time has come to lay down the law to the department heads. You want to be firm, but at the same time tactful, and your goal is to secure their cooperation. You do know, however, that one result could be conflict.

1. How can you best approach the department heads in order to achieve cooperative effort?

2. Outline your proposed presentation and analyze the alternative reactions you may get. Also, consider the possibility that your control problems may be the result of your own management style.

3. What kinds of behavior on your part might be contributing to your current problems?

CHAPTER 10

To Achieve Public Purpose: Social Responsibility and Ethics

The late twentieth century has been a difficult time for social responsibility and ethics. Watergate, Irangate, TV ministries, Wall Street, and $500 hammers are some of the phrases that have come to suggest dishonesty, scandal—a general absence of a sense of social responsibility and ethics.

There is no evidence to suggest that persons working in the public sector are more, or less, socially responsible or ethical than the citizenry in general. Indeed, a good argument could be made that government bureaucracies generally mirror the U.S. population. Approximately one in every six employed persons work in the public sector. The variety of tasks they perform reflects the myriad of highly specialized tasks in a modern industrialized society. The importance of socially responsible behavior in the public sector, however, is not a matter of dispute.

Setting the Moral Tone

One of the more important responsibilities of public managers is to set the highest possible moral tone for their organizations. Public office is a public trust and must not be abused for private gain.

It might be said that public managers are ordinary people who are charged with doing extraordinary things. These extraordinary things represent "the public's business" and must be performed with that fact and goal ever in mind. As was noted in Chapter 1, public management is performed to some extent in a fishbowl. The world is watching the actions and the results of those who perform public management duties.

Public Managers' "Power"

In thinking about social responsibility and ethics it is helpful to begin with a review of how or why the actions of public managers are so important. These reasons can be summed up in a single word—*power.* Public managers have power—their activities can and do affect all of the rest of us. Where does this power come from? While the answer may seem obvious, it has a number of parts:

Right to Coerce—Because public managers have the weight of law behind them, they have a monopoly on the legitimate use of force in our society. Though this is most apparent with police and military activities, it is also true of elevator inspection, environmental protection, and food and drug oversight.

Discretion—While public managers may undertake only those things prescribed by law, significant discretionary choices must be made. While the city council may legislate a 35-miles-per-hour speed limit on a particular street, it is ultimately the police chief (and the motorcycle patrolman) who decide the speed at which the motorist will be stopped. Will it be 36 miles per hour or, more likely, 40 or 45 miles per hour? Another example is the manager of public lands who must decide how to balance competing interests in conservation and recreation.

Expertise—Public managers are usually the most highly trained and knowledgeable persons in various governmental functions. Whether it be Social Security, income tax, public roads, or some other area, the involved public managers have:

- A knowledge of the history of the activity—what has and has not been done in the past.
- Access to current information and a continuity of involvement—others generally have only occasional interest in the subject.
- The opportunity, even the requirement, to advise lawmakers and other elected officials—most laws are drafted by public managers and employees.

In addition to these three general sources of power, other elements may be pertinent to particular situations. The nature of an agency's mission, for example, may be important. J. Edgar Hoover in the Federal Bureau of Investigation and Hyman Rickover in the U.S. Navy Submarine Service received great deference, largely because of the perceived importance of their responsibilities. A different kind of example might be the federal-level public manager who has the ability to approve or disapprove grants of money—something that state and local politicians are usually anxious to receive. The opportunity to apportion resources (or other types of rewards) always provides a certain amount of power. Individual charisma and simple access can also add to the power base of a particular manager.

Making Public Managers Socially Responsible

It is sometimes said that national defense is far too important to be left to the military. Certainly health, education, welfare, jobs, and many other activities are crucial parts of the total national defense picture. A logical extension of this pattern of thinking suggests that public purpose is far too important to be left to public managers. Since literally everyone is affected, perhaps many—if not all—should be a part of this picture. As might be expected, we find there are many roles in the process of making public management responsible and responsive to the needs and interests of society:

1. *Law*—As noted previously, public managers are expected to do only what the law provides. Private managers, on the other hand, can generally do as they choose—provided it is not prohibited by law. Obviously, as also noted, the implementation of law often involves interpretation and, at times, even selective enforcement. Even so, the provisions of law serve a major role in ensuring social responsibility in public management.
2. *Chief Executives*—A second major role is played by the president, governor, mayor or other top-level official who exercises hierarchical control over public managers. Executive supervision by an elected general manager is another important force in the social responsibility picture.
3. *Legislative Oversight*—It is important to also remember that legislative bodies play roles beyond passing laws to create public agencies. Some of these additional functions include annual appropriations of budgets, holding public hearings or investigations, requiring periodic reports and casework when an individual legislator responds to a need of an individual citizen (voter).
4. *Two-Party Political Competition*—In our democratic system, the out-of-power party serves the watchdog role. This goes beyond observing actions of the majority party—it includes a continuing concern with all governmental actions, including those of the bureaucracy and its managers.
5. *Consumer, Client, and Interest-Group Activism*—Beyond oversight by politicians, public management actions—and outcomes—are subject to the intense interest of affected persons and groups. Farmers have a special interest in the Depart-

ment of Agriculture; defense contractors, the Pentagon; veterans, the Department of Veterans' Affairs; and so it goes.

6. *Courts*—Another important instrument of social responsibility is the court system. This third branch of government, like the legislative and executive branches, is also much involved in the total picture. Aggrieved individuals and groups can, and frequently do, pursue action or relief with regard to things done—or not done—by public agencies.
7. *Socialization of Public Managers*—One must remember that public managers, and other public employees, are drawn from the society they are asked to serve. As has been pointed out, the governmental administrative apparatus is largely a representative reflection of the broader society. It seems reasonable to presume that this common heritage should contribute to a more socially responsive process of public management.
8. *The Media*—There is a strong "free press" tradition in the United States. The *Federalist Papers* authored by John Jay, Alexander Hamilton, and James Madison helped forge this tradition prior to the approval of the U.S. Constitution. World War II foxhole reporters such as Ernie Pyle, and Bob Woodward and Carl Bernstein's role in Watergate, are but two examples of how this tradition has evolved. Walter Cronkite, a highly-respected television newsman for two decades was seriously seen by many as a good presidential candidate.

Summarizing the Forces

Each of these eight forces plays a very important role in ensuring a socially responsible public process in the United States. Legislators, chief executives, judges, interest groups, newspeople and others all have a legitimate role to play in the total system. It can easily be argued, in fact, that the most central value in the American system of government is this openness. To provide everyone with a role—a stake—in the system is just as important as any goal the system might seek.

In closing our discussion of these eight forces, we must emphatically point out that they rarely are in full agreement. A time of war or national emergency might be the exception. Normally, the picture is one of great confusion and competition. Tobacco farmers, airline pilots, pharmacists, preservationists, gun owners, business entrepreneurs, and the thousands of other groups in our society rarely define social responsibility in exactly the same way. We call this politics.

Central Role of the Public Manager

Within this hurricane-like environment we find the public manager. Beyond avoiding bribes, graft, and other forms of dishonesty, it is not always easy for one to steer the "right" course. Such a course begins with a thorough understanding of—and an appreciation for—all of the forces just discussed. This is the "house" in which the public manager lives.

Strong evidence suggests that the manager's own value system will play a major part in guiding the decisions and actions that set the moral tone for the public agency. While the "public interest" is difficult to precisely define, it must be a major part of the purpose the public manager seeks to serve.

Guidelines for Socially Responsible Behavior

Codes of ethics often delineate the standards of acceptable behavior of managers. An example of such a code is displayed in exhibit 10–1, City Management Code of Ethics. The City Management Association enforces the Code through the executive board on advice of the committee on professional conduct. Although sanctions are limited to admonition, private or public censure, or expulsion from membership, the ethics process reportedly is working well.

In an effort to stimulate professional thought and discussion on the ethical aspects of public administration, the National Academy of Public Administration published in 1974 a set of ethical guidelines for administrators. And Congress issued a Code for Government Service in June of 1980 (PL 96–303) to provide guidelines for the ethical conduct of federal public managers (see exhibit 10–2).

According to some observers, codes can be overly strict. Former President Carter's stringent rules of ethical conduct for high-level appointees were viewed in some circles as detrimental to attracting highly talented prospects. Carter's code barred, for one year, policy-making appointees from representing anyone for pay before their former department or agency. It also required these appointees to divest themselves of holdings likely to be affected by their official acts. Some Cabinet appointees, for example, might have to give up a lifetime of wealth accumulation, a high price to pay for a short stint in service to one's country.

As tight as some codes are, they may not be enough. Often they do not induce the kinds of behavior the public desires of its office-holders. Most of the Watergate offenders were lawyers. This profes-

EXHIBIT 10–1: **City Management Code of Ethics**

The purpose of the International City Management Association is to increase the proficiency of city managers, county managers, and other municipal administrators and to strengthen the quality of urban government through professional management. To further these objectives, certain ethical principles shall govern the conduct of every member of the International City Management Association, who shall:

1. Be dedicated to the concepts of effective and democratic local government by responsible elected officials and believe that professional general management is essential to the achievement of this objective.

2. Affirm the dignity and worth of the services rendered by government and maintain a constructive, creative, and practical attitude toward urban affairs and a deep sense of social responsibility as a trusted public servant.

3. Be dedicated to the highest ideals of honor and integrity in all public and personal relationships in order that the member may merit the respect and confidence of the elected officials, of other officials and employees, and of the public.

4. Recognize that the chief function of local government at all times is to serve the best interests of all of the people.

5. Submit policy proposals to elected officials, provide them with facts and advice on matters of policy as a basis for making decisions and setting community goals, and uphold and implement municipal policies adopted by elected officials.

6. Recognize that elected representatives of the people are entitled to the credit for the establishment of municipal policies; responsibility for policy execution rests with the members.

7. Refrain from participation in the election of the members of the employing legislative body, and from all partisan political activities which would impair performance as a professional administrator.

8. Make it a duty continually to improve the member's professional ability and to develop the competence of associates in the use of management techniques.

9. Keep the community informed on municipal affairs; encourage communication between the citizens and all municipal officers; emphasize friendly and courteous service to the public; and seek to improve the quality and image of public service.

10. Resist any encroachment on professional responsibilities, believing the member should be free to carry out official policies without interference, and handle each problem without discrimination on the basis of principle and justice.

11. Handle all matters of personnel on the basis of merit so that fairness and impartiality govern a member's decisions, pertaining to appointments, pay adjustments, promotions, and discipline.

12. Seek no favor; believe that personal aggrandizement or profit secured by confidential information or by misuse of public time is dishonest.

Note: Reprinted with permission of International City Management Association.

EXHIBIT 10-2. **Code of Ethics for Government Service**

ANY PERSON IN GOVERNMENT SERVICE SHOULD

I. Put loyalty to the highest moral principles and to country above loyalty to persons, party, or Government department.

II. Uphold the Constitution, laws, and regulations of the United States and of all governments therein and never be a party to their evasion.

III. Give a full day's labor for a full day's pay; giving earnest effort and best thought to the performance of duties.

IV. Seek to find and employ more efficient and economical ways of getting tasks accomplished.

V. Never discriminate unfairly by the dispensing of special favors or privileges to anyone, whether for remuneration or not; and never accept, for himself or herself or for family members, favors or benefits under circumstances which might be construed by reasonable persons as influencing the performance of governmental duties.

VI. Make no private promises of any kind binding upon the duties of any office, since a Government employee has no private word which can be binding on public duty.

VII. Engage in no business with the Government, either directly or indirectly, which is inconsistent with the conscientious performance of governmental duties.

VIII. Never use any information gained confidentially in the performance of governmental duties as a means of making private profit.

IX. Expose corruption wherever discovered.

X. Uphold these principles, ever conscious that public office is a public trust.

Authority of Public Law 96-303, unanimously passed by the Congress of the United States on 27 June 1980, and signed into law by the President on 3 July 1980.

sion has one of the most stringent sets of behavior requirements, but they were not a sufficient deterrent to the actions of the Watergate actors, including the President.

Openness is a highly valued quality with regard to the decisions of public managers. Hawaii law, for example, makes it a crime for public officials to hold any type of private meeting without first notifying and inviting the public and the press. Other writers say that this approach is excessive. They claim that sunshine laws carry with them the connotation that people in government are suspect and that citizens ought to take positive measures to see that their wishes are properly executed. According to this view, sunshine laws arouse public suspicion and create doubt about public managers.

Nevertheless, public managers are in positions of public trust where every action is publicly observed. Their ability to inspire respect and confidence depends on the manner in which they fulfill their public trust.

Although there is no single regulator of a public manager's conscience, one's own system of ethical values combined with codes and laws should provide the basis for right action.

A Brief Case Study—to Illustrate—to Ponder

An Ethical Dilemma

The Cranville County Commission had authorized the construction of a $30 million stadium and sports arena in the central part of the county. Commissioner James Konklin heads the Development Committee that accepts bids and contracts with builders. It is the county's policy to accept the low bid unless the bidder is found to be "undesirable or less than qualified." The low bid on the stadium project was from an established local contractor, Thomson Construction, whose president, Harold Thomson, is the brother-in-law of Commissioner Konklin.

When he opened the bids, Konklin was not surprised to see one from Thomson, but he really did not expect it to be the lowest. At this point, Konklin was in a quandary. I know that Harold's company is highly respected and capable, but everyone knows he's a close relative, he thought, as he tapped his pencil nervously. "If the *Evening Herald* ran the story, those editors would crucify me!" he muttered to himself. Yet, he wondered, how can I legitimately award the bid to someone else when Harold is the lowest bidder?

1. In your opinion, would Commissioner Konklin's acceptance of Thomson Construction's bid be unethical? corrupt?
2. What are the ethical considerations here?
3. What would be the drawbacks to Commissioner Konklin's accepting the bid rather than rejecting it?
4. What should Commissioner Konklin do in this case?

CHAPTER 11

To Enhance Personal Skills: Professionalism and Career Development

The chapters to this point have dealt with the public manager's responsibility to others—to the public and to peers, supervisors, and employees. This chapter focuses on the public manager's responsibility to himself or herself.

The public manager has one of the most challenging jobs in existence. The high stakes and constant demands of managing public organizations require dedicated, competent people who are committed to the public welfare.

Government's impact on health care, education, transportation, criminal justice, the environment, and many other areas illustrate the importance of public management to the citizenry. The authors believe that the quality of public managers is the key to effective public service, and for this reason espouse a "professional" approach to public management. Professionalism is an attitude that encourages public managers to attach the highest priority to continuous self-development, to a career orientation, and to competence in each of their managerial roles.

The Professional Perspective

The term *profession* was originally defined by sociologists in terms so strict that only a few occupations, such as medicine and law, qualified. Traditional criteria used by most writers usually has four characteristics:

1. Professionals undergo lengthy training in a body of generalized and systematic knowledge to become an expert in a specialized field.
2. Professionals believe their work contributes significantly to the public welfare.
3. Professions are self-policing in terms of high standards of performance, codes of conduct, and peer control.
4. Professionals are relatively autonomous in exercising their special competence.

Many would argue that this ideal model of professionalism is not applicable to public management. There are numerous limitations to the scientific theory or body of knowledge that comprises public management education. Many public officials have, in fact, had no formal training in the field. What constitutes "proper" training is also unresolved. Finally, there is no peer control over the quality of work performed by its practitioners. Rather, supervisory evaluations are the basis for assessing the performance of public managers. Thus, a strict application of traditional indices of profession would exclude public management.

A Public Management Response

Medicine, law, the clergy, university teaching, dentistry, architecture, and some fields of engineering are generally accepted as professions because they meet the traditional criteria. Even though traditional criteria are not met in any strict sense, it is still important that public managers exhibit such qualities in their behavior. Public managers can adopt a professional perspective that is broad and flexible enough to enable them to maintain a diversity of interests, yet firm and understandable enough to provide a sense of direction, purpose, and unity to the field. The analogy of the medical profession might serve to illustrate this point. Medicine is a profession, but it is also an assortment of professions and specializations. It is science, art, theory, practice, study, and application all rolled into one, and yet not based on a single discipline. Medical doctors must know something of chemistry and biology, but they are neither chemists nor biologists; they must know something of a number of fields and of their application in specific ways.

The academic and intellectual home of public administration, or public management, has historically been the field of political science. To the extent that the public manager deals with public purposes as a government employee in a political environment, he or she should know something of that field. To the extent that the task is to perform managerial duties within a formal organization, the public manager needs to know something of the fields of general management, law, sociology, psychology, and economics. Public managers would also benefit from an understanding of decision sciences that draws on mathematics, systems analysis, and information systems. In essence, public management is an eclectic field where practitioners synthesize knowledge from a number of fields and apply it in performing their managerial tasks.

The Process of Professionalism

A variety of factors are now emerging in American society that influence the professionalization of public managers. The field of public management has become a career occupation and specialized education is considered essential for practitioners. Professional organizations in the general area of administration, such as the American Society for Public Administration, and in more specific areas, such as the International Personnel Management Association and the International City Management Association, emphasize standards of conduct and recognition of excellence in job performance. Accreditation and licensing of practitioners is gaining acceptance in the field, and codes of ethics along with mechanisms for their enforcement are becoming evident. These are the steps in the process of professionalism.

The preponderance of traditional professions in government is an obvious influence on the professionalism of public managers. Research supports the conclusion that a new breed of manager is emerging—the administrator-professional who was hired for technical or professional skills and later moved into administrative positions. A significant number of federal supervisors are in professional occupations, and many federal executives hold professional degrees.

An analysis by the former U.S. Civil Service Commission (now Office of Personnel Management) of federal executive positions in grades GS 16 to 18 indicated that 68 percent of the occupations represented require professional training; thus their incumbents are professionals in the traditional sense. The presence of these professionals in government organizations and their association with other managers is bound to influence those outside the traditional professions to strive for professionalism. It is the authors' belief that as more individual public managers subscribe to standards of professionalism, public management as an occupation will reach a degree of professionalization.

Standards of Professionalism

The Professional Standards and Ethics Committee of the American Society for Public Administration has developed professional standards for public managers. Each of the areas around which standards will be developed are discussed below with particular attention to their application toward professionalizing public managers.

Knowledge and skills: Specialized training in the field of public management would considerably enhance the professional standing of the field. Toward this end, the National Association of Schools of Public Affairs and Administration (NASPAA) in 1974 adopted *Guidelines and Standards for Professional Masters Degree Programs in Public Affairs/Public Administration* for the purpose of fostering a professional focus and approach to Public Management and to build the necessary competencies in public managers to enable them to perform with excellence. The guidelines consist of a matrix of professional competencies including:

- Knowledge
- Skills
- Values
- Behavior

A qualified public manager should be able to apply each of these components to the following subject-matter areas:

- Political, social, and economic context of administration
- Quantitative and nonquantitative analytical tools
- Individual group organizational dynamics
- Policy analysis and administrative/management processes

The content and application of each component to each subject matter area is specified in the guidelines. NASPAA hopes that the application of the standards will consistently and uniformly establish highly relevant training for public management practitioners.

Those occupations that claim professional standing place high value on educational credentials. For example, the International City Management Association reports that among city managers aged 29 and under, 92 percent hold a bachelor's degree and 39 percent have a Master of Public Administration degree. Military officers are selected for a hierarchy of professional schools during their careers: career courses and update around the fifth year of service, command and staff colleges at mid-career, and senior service colleges near their eighteenth year of service.

Performance and behavior: When public managers adopt a professional perspective, they strive to perform their functions with distinctive competence. They display excellence in their behavior. But how can individual performance be assessed? Unfortunately, government performance is invariably measured in terms of inputs (tax dollars spent, number of clients interviewed, and so on) rather than on results achieved. Until valid measures of manager performance can be found and behaviors identified that yield effectiveness, assessment efforts will be difficult.

Personal development and achievement of potential: The individual public manager must assume full responsibility for his or her professional development. Continuous self-development is essential to a successful public service career. This area for professional standards has special meaning for each public manager; a later section of this chapter is devoted to detailed discussion of the activities for individual professional development.

Relationships to law and political processes: The political environment of the public manager where the realities of the situation involve expediencies that are not always completely rational was discussed in Chapter 2. Standards for public management in these areas might be built around a manager's effectiveness in combining the professional with the political aspects of the job in carrying out legislated programs.

Commitment to the needs of the public service: One of the basic criteria of a profession is a service orientation. The notion that professionalism is good for the public because high-quality management invariably produces better service is a well-established precept. It is idealistic to assume that all public managers will be dedicated to serving the public interest, but that attitude is essential to building and maintaining professionalism.

Responsiveness, responsibility, and accountability: How readily does a manager respond to public needs? And how timely is the response? Commensurate with the authority vested in the manager's office is an obligation or responsibility to exercise that authority for the good of the organization and of the public. Public managers are held accountable for the results of their actions both by higher authority within the organization and by their constituencies, that is, other agencies and the public. Managers who are considered professional have to gain the respect of both the public and of higher authority by being responsive to the public's needs, responsible for their actions, and willing to be judged for their performance.

Ethics, conflicts of interest, public disclosure, and confidentiality: As a result of the Civil Service Reform Act, a list of specific competencies was developed for managers who comprised the feeder group for the Senior Executive Service. These competencies are listed in exhibit 11–1, and they might serve as a guide for the development of any manager who wishes to grow professionally.

Professional Self-development

A prerequisite for professionalism is continuous self-development to stay abreast of new developments in the field and to upgrade managerial and technical skills. This section is designed to stimulate the public manager's thinking about career-planning and to provide some ideas for professional self-development.

Career-planning

One of the attributes of a profession is that it is viewed as spanning a lifetime. Thus, professional managers perceive their work in terms of a career. Elmer Staats, former head of the federal General Accounting Office, emphasizes that an individual's career direction is a blend of the person's aspirations and the organization's needs. And the degree of success of a person's career is based on his or her own assessment and *self*-development—not someone else's. Individual managers can and do exercise some control over their destinies by planning their careers. Many public agencies have career paths or ladders through which an individual advances, but even without this formal mechanism the public manager can prepare a plan for his or her own career progression. Unfortunately, so many of us spend our lives working *at* something that we fail to take the time to plan to work *toward* something. The following section presents a strategy for planning a professional career—a "kit of tools" for working toward future career goals.

A Strategy for Professional Career-planning

The authors have taught career-planning to students enrolled in a Master of Public Administration program. As a term project, students are required to prepare a comprehensive and personal career plan; the elements of such a plan, which are displayed in exhibit 11–2, are explained in the following discussion.

EXHIBIT 11-1. **Management and Executive Competencies**

I. *Management Processes* (Competencies relating to the structures, activities, and procedures through which work is accomplished in an organization)

1. Know agency organization, responsibilities, and role.
2. Know and accept the role of manager.
3. Know and accept the role of the executive.
4. Be able to set objectives and evaluate their accomplishment.
5. Be able to make timely decisions and use appropriate decision-making aids.
6. Be able to establish priorities among alternatives.
7. Be able to develop and implement action plans for the accomplishment of program goals.
8. Be able to develop long-range program goals.
9. Be able to organize resources and structure to accomplish program goals.
10. Be able to effectively delegate.
11. Be able to set individual performance standards and appraise performance.
12. Be able to interact with noncareer managers/executives/staff persons.
13. Be able to utilize the basic management support systems in personnel, budget, research and development, EDP/information systems, and procurement.
14. Be able to apply agency personnel policies in key areas such as LMR and EEO.
15. Be able to plan for the adaptation of the organization to a changing environment.

II. *Personal/Interpersonal* (Competencies relating to working with and through people)

16. le to assess own strengths and limitations.
17. Be able to speak clearly and concisely.
18. Be able to write clearly and concisely.
19. Be able to coach and counsel subordinates.
20. Be able to give and receive feedback constructively.
21. Be able to deal with diverse views and ambiguity.
22. Be able to recognize and overcome blocks to communication.
23. Be able to use various leadership styles.
24. Be able to create an organizational climate which results in a motivated work force.
25. Be able to negotiate on a wide variety of issues.

Exhibit 11-1—Continued

III. *Environment* (Competencies relating to the interaction between the organization and the broader arena within which it operates)

26. Understand relevant social and political forces.
27. Be familiar with relevant technological developments.
28. Understand general economic conditions and issues.
29. Be able to consider agency policy/programs within the context of broad national priorities.
30. Understand the relationships among the workings of Congress, the Office of the President, the executive departments and agencies, and the courts.
31. Understand the relationships between career executives and political executives.
32. Understand the purposes and structure of government as an institution in our democratic society.
33. Recognize the special responsibilities of the public trust.
34. Be familiar with the responsibilities of state and local governments.

Setting personal objectives: Career objectives are stated as short-term (typically one year), or long-range (looking ahead five or more years) aspirations. The importance of a thorough exploration of one's values becomes evident at this point. For example, the individual who values a family relationship, but who seeks high pay through an office that requires extensive travel, may want to reassess the trade-offs. Many public managers who are disillusioned with their present situation mention a job change as being their prime objective. Professionals in public service find that they must update their skills periodically to avoid obsolescence. Hence, conflicts and decisions regarding what a person is presently doing and what he or she wants to do are essential first steps in setting personal objectives.

Next, objective-setting requires quantifying the objectives, including a measure of their attainment. Once properly developed, objectives should be reduced to writing. The importance of *written* objectives cannot be overemphasized. By expressing them in writing, one becomes committed to their attainment; individuals with written objectives have a harder time rationalizing a failure to accomplish them and are more inclined to make an effort to ensure their fulfillment. In recognition of the dynamic nature of public service, managers are well-advised to develop alternative objectives and to anticipate contingency plans to meet them.

Individual development planning: Personal objectives are put into action through the individual development plan. The students, or public managers, analyze their own strengths that will help them meet objectives, and they identify shortcomings that might be drawbacks to achieving the objectives. Then they specify what actions they can take to overcome their shortcomings and preserve their strengths. It is recommended that they develop a set of contingency plans. Too often, in developing career plans, individuals chart only one path because they assume their present employers will move them up a career ladder based on superior performance. On the other hand, they may become resigned to being locked into a particular career path. One might employ the following series of steps to set and eventually attain career objectives:

1. Conduct a rigorous analysis of self, career opportunities and career obstacles.
2. Set career objectives.
3. Develop realistic plans.
4. Review progress toward their achievement.

The career planning scheme in exhibit 11–2 parallels these steps.

Finally, there are myriad possible activities that individuals can engage in to enhance their professionalism and improve the chances of attaining their objectives. Representative of such developmental activities are the following:

- *Reading programs.* Regular reading of current articles in management journals, both public and private, will keep the public manager aware of emerging concepts, practices, and techniques in management. In addition, journals and current literature of a technical nature contain information pertinent to one's specialty field, such as information sciences, accounting, and personnel. A perusal of magazines that provide news and general information keeps the public manager up-to-date on current events. Enlightened managers read consistently in all of these areas.
- *Membership in professional associations.* Professional associations offer current literature in the field, seminars for professional development, meetings and conventions for affiliation with peers or other agencies, and a host of career-related ser-

EXHIBIT 11-2. **Model of the Training/Development Process**

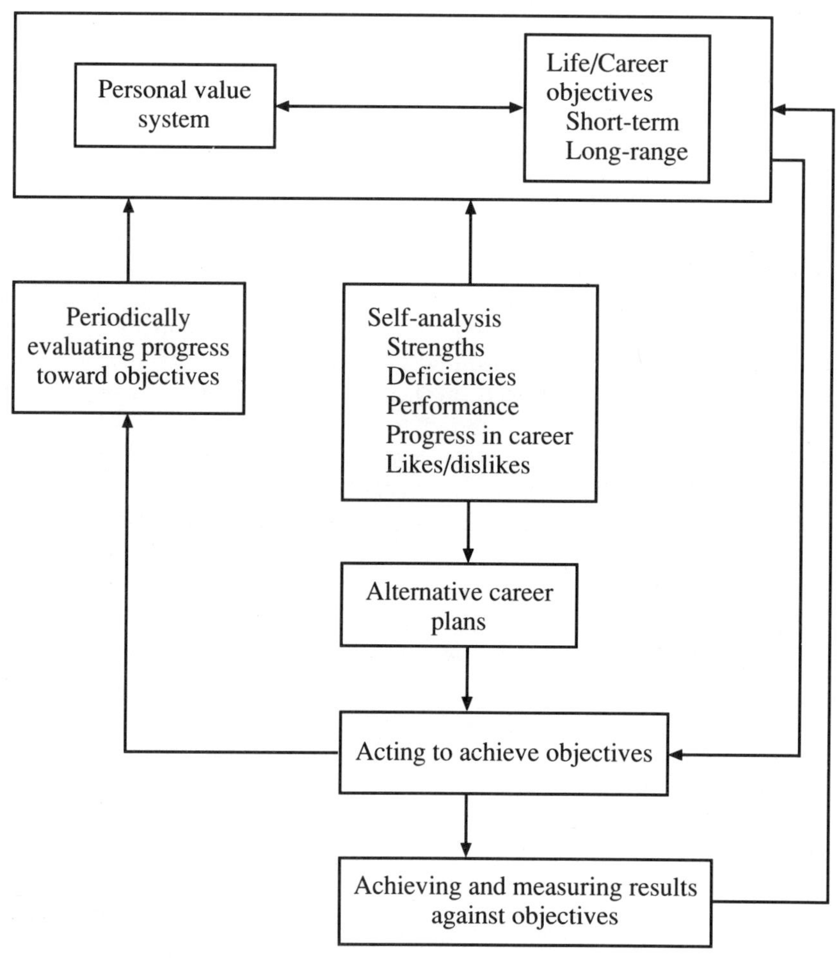

vices. The American Society for Public Administration and the International City Managers Association are broader management-related associations. But there are also professional associations for specific occupational classifications, such as the International Personnel Management Association, the Association of Systems Management, the American Society of Mechanical Engineers.

- *In-service training.* Most government agencies offer, either independently or in conjunction with others, specialized and general management training programs. Many public jurisdictions require minimum training for employees. Public managers should sharpen their managerial and technical skills through both internal and external training opportunities.
- *Professional certification.* Professional advanced degree programs in public management, for example, Master of Governmental Administration and Master of Public Administration, are available in numerous universities throughout the country. Increasing numbers of government jobs are requiring these advanced degrees. Similarly, many states and municipalities are encouraging certification of public managers for the purpose of maintaining their professional competence. The state of Georgia's Certified Public Manager Program is a case in point. Experienced public managers can qualify for certification by completing a series of core courses in state government management; attending professionally relevant elective seminars with at least sixty instructional hours; and successfully completing a comprehensive certification examination.
- *Networking.* This is the function of establishing a personal support system, a network, of individuals a public manager recognizes as having some unique ability or talent he or she might need in the future. Generally, a network includes people from different professions, in different organizations, and from scattered locations. It can prove to be an extremely valuable resource in professional development.
- *Guided experience.* Coaching, counseling, special projects, and job rotational assignments provided by someone in higher authority can offer meaningful growth opportunities for those who aspire to be upwardly mobile. Perhaps this is easier said than done, but the guided experience provided by such a mentor has proven invaluable in numerous public careers.
- *Programs outside the agency.* Seminars, workshops, and special courses are offered through colleges and universities and through governmental agencies. "Seek and ye shall find" is probably an excellent rule of thumb for seeking developmental opportunities.

A Brief Case to Study—to Illustrate—to Ponder

A career is a very personal thing. A career is also something that *each* individual should strive to plan for and manage. It is not a matter that can be delegated. Within the context of information such as that presented in this chapter, one must:

A. Determine career goals.

B. Analyze personal strengths and weaknesses.

C. Analyze surrounding opportunities and threats.

D. Select specific actions that will provide advancement toward chosen goals.

These steps must be pursued in a never-ending cycle as conditions change.

Using this A-B-C-D approach and the material in Chapter 11, develop a plan for *your career* for the next 10 years. Remember—if you don't do it, who will?

APPENDIX A
Cases

Introduction to the Cases

The case studies included in this appendix were selected to complement the cases at the end of each chapter. Each case was designed to address a broad topic covered in a chapter, to reinforce concepts presented, and to relate them to the real world. They were purposely kept brief, so that students or training program participants could read them in class. The subject matter is conducive to lively discussion and debate. The cases also help focus the reader's attention on the text material.

All of the cases are based on real situations. In some, the names of the public agencies are disguised. They take place in a variety of settings, and they depict conditions that are adverse, positive, or a combination of both.

Case 1
Ace Management Company's Challenge

The Ace Management Company is a service organization that seeks opportunities wherever it can find them. The company has just learned that the city of Atlanta has won its bid to host the summer Olympic Games in 1996. A major effort will be required to prepare, market, and collect all of the tickets associated with the various events. Ace has decided to make a proposal to the city that it be given a contract to handle the entire ticket operation.

This committee has been called together to work out the details of this proposal—the organizational, staffing, financial, and other aspects. Top management has found this opportunity in the environment and needs this committee to work through all of the necessary details—"completed staff work" as it is sometimes called in the management textbook. There are obviously many unknown factors at this point. Since neither the committee nor top management knows all of the answers, the group will need to specify any assumptions that are made during the process of developing the proposal.

Case 2

Crisis in Micropolis

In her ten years as the city manager of Micropolis, Betty Kelley has never been under such intense pressure as she now faces. Her suburban bedroom community seems to be in an uproar and all five city council members are in an unpredictable mood. Things are unsettled all over, even in next-door Central City, but Betty knows that her immediate need is to "save her own skin" and to protect her reputation as a good public manager.

Betty recognizes her dilemma as one that is easy to describe but hard to solve. Increasing prices, taxes, and inflation have driven the local citizenry to the point of a tax revolt. The cry for relief is growing louder and election time is getting closer. None of the current council members are interested in retiring from political life, but that prospect seems to be more and more likely.

Betty has analyzed the situation again and again. There is no possibility of further increasing taxes or obtaining other revenue; there was also no way to avoid the increased costs of maintaining the city's current level of public services.

With increased costs a certainty and no possibility of new revenue, Betty calculates her own position to be squarely in the middle. Local citizens are trying to survive an increasingly tight cost-benefit squeeze. Members of the city council are getting ready to fight a cost-vote squeeze. One answer for both groups might be to find a better public manager—to fire Betty and bring in a new face—one, for example, who could bring more business efficiency to running city hall.

With all of this in mind, Betty has been able to think of only one possible solution—turn over one or more of the city services to the private sector. Over the years Micropolis has become the provider of a full range of local government services, such as police and fire protection, water and sewerage, and garbage collection. Maybe the time has come to withdraw from some of these activities. Betty decides to present such a proposal to the council at its next meeting.

As her assistant manager, Betty needs you to prepare a detailed plan immediately. You must determine which local government activity might best be contracted to a private company, prepare the argument for such a change, and anticipate the arguments Betty will hear from whatever opposition might develop. As is so often the case in public management, Betty must have your recommendation by the close of business today. It is now 3:45 p.m. The council meeting is tonight.

Case 3

The Good-Old-Days Are Gone

The X-Bureau is a first-rate public agency that developed a fine reputation under the direction of its first director, John Dunn. Mr. Dunn always insisted on having the final say in all decisions, and he has guided the organization through the years by doing things his way.

Supervisors learned to accept Dunn's management style and became comfortable in their jobs. Many were fond of saying "Nothing ever changes around here." They were never encouraged to be innovative, nor were they ever asked for input about operational decisions. They just came to work and "followed the old man's directions."

As the agency grew over the years, it became increasingly difficult to maintain an efficient operation and stay responsive to the community's needs. John Dunn refused to change his style of management, but he finally retired.

The new director, Mary Jackson, decided to personally administer the agency. One of her first actions was to set up a new unit to study ways to improve procedures and reduce costs. Tom Banks, with degrees in management and engineering, was hired to manage this new activity.

Tom spent the first month getting acquainted with various supervisors and mostly listening. At the end of the month, he called all of the supervisors together and explained that he had plans to reduce costs by 10 percent and make the agency more efficient. Tom told the supervisors that he expected them to actively support his effort since they knew more than anyone about the agency's operation.

After the meeting, Bob Smith was heard saying to one of his fellow supervisors, "I see the honeymoon is over—I guess the good-old days are gone. I wondered how long it would take him to start trying to pick our brains—but it will be a cold day in July before he gets anything out of me!"

1. How could Tom win the support of unit employees?
2. What options other than 10 percent cost reduction might there be for improving efficiency?
3. How could the impact of major change in the agency—that is, a new director and a new unit manager—have been minimized?
4. How can Tom involve his people in fulfilling the mission of his new unit?

Case 4

The Personnel Manager

Art Reilley, a personnel specialist in his state's Department of Transportation, was discussing personnel management with Dorothy Daniel, the personnel manager of the state Department of Education. Ms. Daniel was completing her explanation of her agency's performance appraisal system:

"I think that I can fairly say that ours is the most comprehensive evaluation system in this state. Not only that—it is accepted with enthusiasm by both the raters and the ratees. Every six months we require a formal appraisal of all our managers by their superiors. This formal appraisal, of course, is in addition to the daily coaching we encourage.

"Our form of appraisal has two parts, one of which concerns itself with the traits, abilities, and attributes of the person. This part helps us make decisions concerning promotions, transfers, schooling, and the like. The second part has to do with results—statements of objectives set and attained, projects completed, and so forth.

"After the appraisers complete the form, they must conduct an appraisal interview, taking as long as they need to discuss appraisal results with their employees. Each appraisal is reviewed by the rater's immediate superiors to ensure fairness and accuracy. And here, in personnel, we analyze each form to detect trends and determine how well each manager evaluates."

Jack Harmon, Ms. Daniel's administrative assistant, followed the discussion with interest. When Ms. Daniel paused, Jack made the following statement: "Dorothy, are you sure that we require an appraisal interview? I've been working for you for three years now, and you've never discussed my appraisals with me."

"Jack," said Ms. Daniel, "I am sure you will agree that hasn't been needed. We work together so closely that I am sure you always know how I appraise you."

1. What do you think of this formal performance appraisal system?
2. Why was Jack Harmon never interviewed?
3. What should Art Reilley recommend to his department to ensure that managers conduct appraisals thoroughly?

Case 5

Contract Negotiation in the City of Sunkist, Florida

Under the provisions of the Florida Public Employee Relations Act, a neutral third party called a *special master* is selected jointly by labor and management to hear any unresolved collective bargaining issues and to render an advisory opinion to settle them. Following are the special master's opinions of several issues that were in dispute:

Management Rights/Prevailing Rights

The Union stated that it would be willing to accept the Management Rights clause from the expired agreement if the Prevailing Rights clause were retained. However, the City had proposed a much broader clause that excluded the Prevailing Rights provision. The City stated that it had proposed a clause that would read in essence: "All rights, privileges, and benefits shall remain in writing except as prohibited by the city commission. The Union testified that this wording was unacceptable because there was nothing in writing.

> *Special Master's Opinion:* These management rights existed in the previous agreement by implication; the City has merely made them explicit. Thus, the City's proposed wording of the *Management Rights* clause is accepted. By the same token, the Union's *Prevailing Rights* clause was previously accepted by the City as evidenced by its inclusion in the expired agreement. Absent a strong argument by the City for its exclusion, the Union's request that it be retained is accepted.

Work Hours

The Florida Code, Section 447.301. *Public employees' rights organization and representation,* states:

> (2) Public employees shall have the right to . . . negotiate collectively through a certified bargaining agent with their public employer in the determination of the *terms and conditions* [emphasis added] of their employment

The City proposed to allow the city commission to change work hours as necessary, but the City explained that the commission would hold open hearings before any change would be made. City counsel reported that a new substation would probably be opened in the near future that would create the need to change work hours.

The Union countered that it wanted to be assured that the hours it had negotiated would remain in effect for the duration of the agreement.

> *Special Master's Opinion:* Universally and traditionally, hours of work have been a *basic* issue for inclusion in negotiations of the terms and conditions of employment. The Florida Code is clear in its meaning that

terms and conditions be negotiated or re-negotiated as the case may be. Taking away from this basic right to negotiate hours of work would be tantamount to circumventing the Florida Statutes. Therefore, the clause on *Work Hours* should be retained as worded in the expired Agreement.

Residency Requirement

The expired Agreement extended the residency requirement from the three-mile limit to the electric utility service area (estimated to be approximately 10 miles). The Union fears that the city commission could legislate a new, more stringent requirement that would place a burden on firefighters, who would be required to move back to the City. Union witness Mike McCurdy testified that because of the proximity of family amusement areas to the City, the cost of housing is higher in Sunkist than in outlying areas. He also presented evidence that no other city's fire department employees have a residency requirement. An explicit exemption in the Agreement would prevail over any commission legislation, the Union argued.

> *Special Master's Opinion:* Why raise an issue that has little prospect of becoming a reality? No evidence was presented to indicate that the Commission had passed or intended to pass a new ordinance on residency. It is in the mutual interests of the City and the firefighters to have the Agreement remain essentially in its original form on this issue; no explicit statement regarding exemption from residency requirements should be added. The *Residency Requirement* clause should read:
> "Article -----. Residency Requirements. The City agrees that the Residency Requirements for employees of the Fire Department shall continue to be the service area of the Electric Utility of the City of Sunkist."

1. *Management Rights/Prevailing Rights.* In a collective bargaining agreement, what is the purpose of a management rights clause? How important is it for the City to have the unencumbered right to contract out?
2. *Work Hours.* How important is the City's prerogative to adjust work focus in this case?
3. *Residency Requirement.* Is the residency requirement significant here?
4. If you were city manager, would you accept the arbitrator's opinions here? Why, or why not? How might the city commission affect the outcome of these negotiations?

Case 6

The Problem of the Growing Budget

Suburban City has grown rapidly since its incorporation five years ago. The current population totals 8,000 and projections call for a 50 percent growth rate over the next three years. In voting to incorporate, the citizens had thought they would avoid many of Central City's problems. At the heart of these problems has been a constant tension between the cost of city services and the availability of adequate city income. As a result of its growing size, Suburban City now has its own financial difficulties.

Like many such cities, Suburban City employs a minimum of professional staff. The general philosophy is that elected officials will make all important decisions and clerks, policemen, firemen, truck drivers, and other city employees will be hired as required.

Financial pressures have now increased to the point that the city council knows that something must be done. In their wisdom, the council has made two decisions—first, to research the situation before acting; second, to assign you (their administrative assistant) to do the research. Specifically, your assignment is to investigate this type of growth-related problem, and to develop an overall approach to financial management for Suburban City.

As you undertake your task, remember the need to stick to basic considerations. Suburban City needs a basic design for financing, planning, and controlling government activities. Also, be sure to determine the types of services (costs) usually provided by such cities and the usual sorts of revenue sources.

Case 7

Crown County Public Safety Division: A Professional Police Force

Metropolitan Crown County and the Police Benevolent Association (PBA), the collective bargaining representative of the police, have reached an impasse in their negotiations. The Association is demanding a 10 percent across-the-board pay increase; and the County, claiming unavailability of funds, has proposed a zero increase. A special master was selected by the parties to hear both sides of the issue and propose a settlement. One of the considerations in this case was the professional caliber of the Public Safety Division. Here are excerpts from the special master's report:

On the issues of the high caliber of Public Safety Division (PSD) employees and the fine reputation of the Department, there was unanimous and enthusiastically positive feeling by the county and the PBA. One expert witness testified that the PSD was one of the "best in the country." He substantiated his claim by stating,"Book after book and article after article attests to the professionalism, the excellence, the innovativeness and creativity of this police department. It is a superior agency." The witness also said that the two most authoritative publications on police, *Task Force Report: The Police,* by the President's Commission on Law Enforcement and Administration of Justice, and the National Advisory Commission's *Report on Criminal Justice Standards and Goals* consistently cite the excellent performance of the Crown County PSD. In addition, he noted that the PSD is continually called on to perform services for other communities.

The supervisor of training for the PSD testified that $15,212 is spent to train each recruit. He described what is reputed to be the most comprehensive and innovative police training program in the country.

County officials and PSD employees praising themselves might appear immodest. Yet the department's reputation justifies its pride. Its selectivity—only 5 out of 100 are invited to attend the Academy—the comprehensive and innovative training, insistence on continuous upgrading of credentials—average educational level approaches three years of college and one requirement for promotion to sergeant is a master's degree in criminal justice—and a code of ethics that is even incorporated into the *collective bargaining* agreement help make PSD a *professional* organization.

Crown County should be proud of the caliber of its police department and the reputation it has earned, the special master emphasized. The administration should continue to expend its resources financially and otherwise, to maintain the level of professionalism it has worked so diligently to achieve, he concluded.

1. Should Crown County be willing to pay a premium for a professional police force?

2. If you were a County Commissioner, how would you respond to the special master's opinion?

3. As director of labor relations for the county, how could you counter the association's arguments for the raise without disagreeing with the statement that the PSD was the best?

4. How might the professional attributes of PSD affect the performance of the individual police officer?

Case 8

Updating the Department—Getting the University Involved

State universities, especially land-grant institutions, are giving increased emphasis to their public service role. Declining student enrollments, tight financial resources, and pressures to become more relevant are among the reasons for this trend. New market opportunities and alternative funding sources are being sought.

As a part of his efforts in this direction, Coastal State University's president signed a service contract with the commissioner of the state Department of Human Services. The department saw the contract as an opportunity for assistance in planning and managing its many complex programs. From the university's viewpoint, the contract offered both research opportunities and a new source of financial support. The Department of Human Resources agreed to provide $500,000 each year for the jointly directed Research Center. The center was housed at the department building in the state capitol, about a two-hour drive from the campus at University City. Operation of the Research Center and the total service contract was under the direction of a 10-person steering committee. Five members were designated by the university's Vice President for Research and five were named by the department's Assistant Commissioner for Administration. University and department staff were free to propose any project or idea for possible center support and action.

The contract has now been in effect for 18 months, and the most obvious result is a high level of frustration by everyone involved. There is even talk by both sides that this second year may be the last. Everyone is starting to wonder: How Could Such a Good Idea Go So Wrong?

Case 9

Reorganizing the Burkville City Fire Department

City Background

The city of Burkville is one of several surrounding cities that make up a large metro area in a southeastern state. In the past 10 to 15 years Burkville has experienced tremendous growth. With the rapid growth, new and increasing demands were placed on city government services. The increase in population brought new business establishments and housing developments across the city. The Burkville City Fire Department and attached Emergency Medical Services were forced to adjust to the new demands with additional fire stations, equipment, and personnel. While the fire department required increasing technical sophistication to deal with the variety of new circumstances in fighting fires as well as in emergency medical treatment and associated liability, the department was also experiencing growing pains.

There are eight fire stations located across the city. Each station has three shifts. There is a sergeant and a lieutenant on each shift. A shift consists of 24 hours on and 48 hours off. When the chief first came to the department, the city was a small, rural, farm community with a handful of employees. Today the department has approximately 150 employees. Because of greater personnel demands in recent times, the department has a number of newer and younger employees.

Reorganization

In January 1986 the Burkville city council announced a plan to reorganize the fire department. The new plan was designed to spread responsibility among three deputy chiefs and the assistant chief, with all reporting directly to the fire chief. Before the reorganization, areas of responsibility appear to have been assigned by the fire chief according to the personal strengths and weaknesses of the individuals in the assistant and deputy positions (Exhibit A-1). A battalion chief EMS however was over the EMS operations and also reported directly to the fire chief.

With the new plan (Exhibit A-2), some responsibility areas once held by the assistant, deputy, and battalion chiefs would be reassigned to two new deputy chiefs, thereby alleviating some of the workload. Fire chief Don Nelson in supporting the plan, said, "The increased number of deputy chiefs will allow for a more manageable division of duties."

The plan calls for the assistant chief to head fire prevention, a deputy

---

Note: This case was prepared by an MBA Student at Georgia State University under the direction of Dr. Paul Swiercz.

EXHIBIT A-1. **Original Organization**

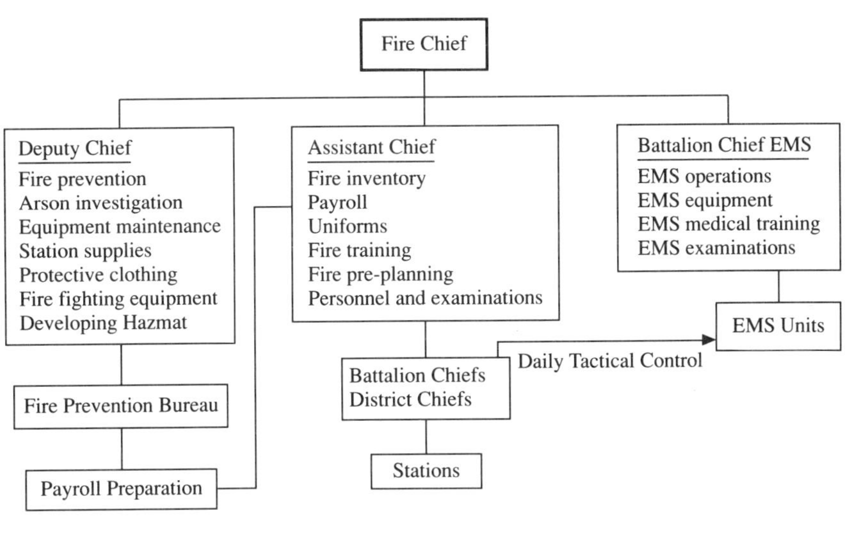

chief over Special Services, one deputy chief for Operations, and another deputy chief over Administration. The battalion chief EMS would only retain EMS field operations but would still report to the fire chief. Fire chief Nelson said, "This is the first major realignment of deputy chief positions and duties in the department's 21-year history."

Along with the establishment of two new deputy chief positions, the reorganization plan also calls for creating two training lieutenants and a training captain.

Richard Marx, a firefighter and spokesman for the Fraternal Order (employees' association) criticized the plan, saying: "The plan does not address problems in the EMS and filling the new positions could result in further disputes before the Civil Service Board or in federal court."

A 14-page report was sent to the Burkville city council from Richard Marx on behalf of the Fraternal Order. The report pointed out weaknesses in the new reorganization plan as well as its failure to address seven main problem areas:

1. Personnel shortages in Fire and EMS line personnel
2. Personnel shortages in the Fire Prevention Bureau
3. The lack of EMS field supervisors
4. The lack of a career ladder for EMS personnel
5. A unified streamlined chain of command
6. The grouping of like functions in one office

EXHIBIT A-2. **Reorganization Plan**

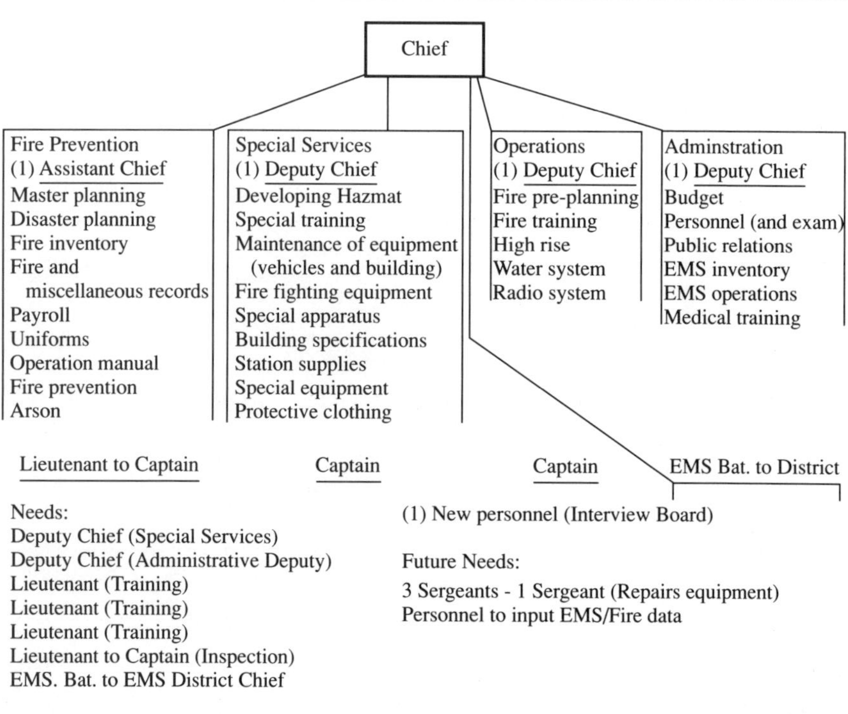

Needs:
Deputy Chief (Special Services)
Deputy Chief (Administrative Deputy)
Lieutenant (Training)
Lieutenant (Training)
Lieutenant (Training)
Lieutenant to Captain (Inspection)
EMS. Bat. to EMS District Chief

(1) New personnel (Interview Board)

Future Needs:

3 Sergeants - 1 Sergeant (Repairs equipment)
Personnel to input EMS/Fire data

7. The inability to promote from within due to promotional litigation in which the department is presently embroiled."

1. What would be the best organizational structure for the fire department given the changed needs of the community and the personnel changes within the department?

2. What activities should be taken to improve the downward or upward communication processes in the fire department?

3. What approach should management take with the Fraternal Order of Burkville Firefighters?

APPENDIX B
Readings

Introduction to the Readings

Many areas of continuing discussion and debate exist in the field of public management. Articles dealing with a few of these have been selected for inclusion in this book. A deliberate decision was made not to include a large number of reprints. Instead, the goal is to provide the reader with a limited number of high quality commentaries on topics that are receiving considerable attention.

Interested readers are encouraged to use the bibliography at the end of this book as a guide for additional reading. Especially useful would be the list of periodicals that address public management issues. Readers new to this field will likely be surprised at the number and complexity of issues under discussion.

The first reading included here is "Comparing Public and Private Management: An Exploratory Essay" by Michael A. Murray. This article first appeared in the *Public Administration Review* (July–August 1975). It provides one writer's analysis of management similarities and differences in the public and private sectors. One of the first writers to address the topic of public and private management differences and similarities was a young scholar by the name of Woodrow Wilson. He later made a name for himself as President of Princeton University, and still later as President of the United States. Wilson's article, "The Study of Administration," was initially published in the *Political Science Quarterly* in June 1887.

To the extent one views public management as being "different," the next question must be, "So what?" The second reading provides one response to this question. Few people (if any) have contributed to the management literature to the extent this author has. Peter Drucker identifies and discusses what he terms "The Seven Deadly Sins of Public Administration." This article, also reprinted from the *Public Administration Review* (March–April 1980), speaks to several issues of continuing concern to the public management community.

Few management books have achieved the prominence of *In Search of Excellence*. This work by Thomas J. Peters and Robert H. Waterman has become well known by the general public as well as by individuals with a specific interest in the field of management. In the third reading, Jed Kee and Roger Black ask the question, "Is Excellence in the Public Sector Possible?" This article, taken from the Spring 1985 issue of *Public Productivity Review*, explores the applicability of Peters and Waterman's ideas to the public sector.

The fourth reading focuses on the topic of marketing. Prior to the publication of this article, marketing was generally not seen as a relevant topic for managers in the public sector. Philip Kotler and Sidney J. Levy helped to put this subject on the agenda of public managers with their "Broadening the Concept of Marketing" in the *Journal of Marketing* (January 1969).

The fifth reading deals with what many public sector observers view as the number one issue of our time—taking public services private. This has been a major "movement" around the world in the 1980s and early 1990s. Indiana University's School of Public and Environmental Affairs devoted the entire Spring 1989 issue of its journal, *Review*, to privatization. Articles dealt with the state of this movement in a number of countries, including Great Britain, Japan, Germany, Thailand, Korea, France, Brazil, Egypt, Hungary, the USSR and Eastern Europe, and the United States. Included here is "Privatization in the United States" by Frances P. Clark.

The sixth, and final, reading recognizes a variation of an old adage—"All work and no play can make a book less fun to read." The reality is that humor, like marketing, is increasingly being recognized as a subject with a legitimate contribution to the field of public management. This article draws from a number of other writings in an attempt to make this point with a light touch of satire. It was first published in *The Bureaucrat: The Magazine for Public Managers* (Winter 1987–88).

The authors of this book would like to express their appreciation to the original sources for permitting them to reprint the six articles in this volume. The authors would also encourage the reader to further consult these journals as well as the others that are included in the bibliography.

Comparing Public and Private Management: An Exploratory Essay

Michael A. Murray

Historically in America two different institutional approaches to management science have developed: one in the private sector and one in the public sector. This dual development, however, has not gone unchallenged. For perhaps two generations scholars and practitioners have realized that management can be viewed as a generic process, with universal implications and with application in any institutional setting—whether a private firm or a public agency. More recently, on the assumption that public and private management have much to share, a new body of literature has developed around the idea of

---

general management. Especially significant, entire new management schools are being founded on the generic model. The historic "separate but equal" doctrine is being challenged by a nascent integrationist movement.

Like the movement in the race area, however, the integrationist policy is not progressing with "due speed." There are many reasons for this. One is the traditional mistrust or misunderstanding between the public and private practitioner. Another is the perceived threat which the merger poses to free-standing schools of business and to schools of public administration. A more significant reason perhaps, is the lack of development of the concept that public and private management have points in common. If one examines the literature, or pages through the brochures of the new schools of management, there is little specific comparative analysis that is discussion of points where public and private management converge or diverge.

The important question then is what are the areas of comparison; and what specifically are the similarities and differences? In short, are public and private management comparable?

I: Substantive Issues: Inherent Conflict or Natural Congruence?

The key substantive issue is whether there is an inherent conflict between the rational, private management model with its criteria of economic efficiency and the political public management model with its criteria of consensus and compromise. Obviously these are idealized types and this perhaps is the first and most important point to be made.

Fact vs. Value: The Context of Decision Making

Although conventional taxonomy divides society into two sectors, public and private, the actual similarities between a business firm and a government organization are increasingly apparent. In any complex organization, "defining purposes and objectives, planning, organizing, selecting managers, managing and motivating people, controlling and measuring results, and using a variety of analytical, problem solving and managerial techniques . . . are essential."[1] The point is that these elements are relevant in any complex organization and are common aspects of a universal or generic management process, whether in the private or public sector.

But are they the same? That is, are similar activities comparable even though the institutional setting differs? In his famous discussion of fact and value, Herbert Simon argued no. Simon argued that the means of administration (the facts) are quite different from the ends (the values). To ignore this central difference, he said, is to ignore the importance of the end or value as the major independent variable. The inference is that the values of the public sector, aimed a consensus, are different than the values of the private sector, aimed at profits. Hence, it is a misrepresentation to say that the value, or the context of the decision, is not important. What is important in the managerial relationship is not the tool, the means, but the context of the decision, the ends. If the context is different, then the values are different, and thus the application and function of the tool is different. In brief, Simon argued that the *process* of management has a value component itself and that fact cannot be separated from value.[2]

Many public administrators cite this argument as evidence of the chasm separating public administration and business administration. But as Norton Long has pointed out, Simon's distinction between fact and value has one fatal flaw. "It does not accord with the facts of administrative life."[3] Though the quest for scientific distinctions has a psychological appeal, it runs the risk of becoming ivory tower escapism.[4] The same can be said of Simon's implication that business and government administration are different. Built on the sandy base of logical positivism, Simon's argument derives from formal distinctions and ignores the *informal* mix between public and private activities. There is another problem with Simon's argument. Even if we accept his distinction between fact and value, the question remains: are the ends of government and business different?

Profits vs. Politics

To ask whether the values of the private sector differ from the objectives of the public sector is to ask a large question and a normative question; a question surrounded by a great deal of controversy. The issues will not be resolved in this paper, but the question remains: Are the differences real or superficial?

To begin, the notion that profits are the sole or main reason for the existence of private business is itself misleading. First of all, profits are an essential requirement for existence; but the focus on profits as the single objective distorts or minimizes other advantageous business activities such as products, services, employment, and all of the "hidden hand" effects of community and social contribution. A second point is that, while profits are a handy measure, benefits and costs do not always lend themselves to a monetary judgment of effectiveness.[5]

On the other hand, to say that profits are never the objective of public sector activities is equally misleading. Government projects are notoriously subject to cost-benefit analysis, and efficiency in government is a by-word of bureaucrats. Once stereotypes are discarded, similarities emerge.

To carry the argument further, however, a distinction made is that the criteria of political decisions are based on objectives of compromise, consensus, and democratic participation, and that these are quite different from the private sector objectives of efficiency, rationality, and profit or product maximization. But this also is an idealized type. As Theodore Levitt argues, "The culture of private bureaucracies is . . . basically the same as that of public bureaucracies. . . ."[6] That is, the desire for personal power and security is the same; responsiveness to outside pressures is the same. In short, once general priorities are established, private and public bureaucracies operate about the same.

Are the Objectives Measurable?

Beyond the abstract question of whether rational man differs from political man, the issue is whether objectives in the public and private areas are capable of comparison. The problem arises because objectives in the private sector often can be reduced to clear, concise, and quantifiable statements. Many public organizations must deal in social intangibles such as the right to privacy, increased political participation, or improving quality of life. Those are difficult to articulate in any clear specific way.

One example of this is the notion of divisible and indivisible services. In the private area goods and services can be purchased on an individual basis. Hence they can be defined and delivered in specific tangible ways. In the public sector many services such as clean air, decent housing, and adequate education are indivisible in the sense that these are communal services which increasingly have to be "purchased" jointly. Hence the problem of individual values has to be stated in the general terms of social choice. Such a conceptualization can only be stated in generalizations.[7]

Which One Is Better: The Normative Issue

Another normative argument is that the modern technologies of business administration are somehow superior to the less systematic and structured tools of the public sector. Indeed the popular disdain toward the public sector is reflected in choice of terms. For example, we often use the term management when referring to private business, but substitute the term administration when talking of public organizations. In part this reflects the acceptance of the private enterprise ethic in our social labels. In part it reflects the less attractive position of the public service in a country where for the past century industrialization was the most exciting thing happening. Recently some of this has changed.

Perhaps because of the Depression, but certainly dating from that point, the myth of the well-managed firm has been challenged. The legend of private efficiency lives in company brochures but is seldom realized in the lives of millions of Americans who fight the daily battle with insurance agencies or auto mechanics or TV repairmen. As early as 1945 the dean of public administration, Paul Appleby, argued that the alleged superiority of business represented a gross over-generalization which did not withstand close analysis.[8] Today we can ask the same kinds of comparative questions as 30 years ago. Is business less corrupt than government? Are public administrators less moral than business executives? Is fiscal management better in the aerospace industry than it is in Health, Education, and Welfare? The point is that what we find overall are more similarities than differences; a blending and mix between public and private. Neither sector has a corner on the morals market.

Government Attitudes vs. Business Attitudes

In the end many of these normative issues are related to questions of attitude. This is a central point in the comparative literature: "that the dissimilarity between government and all other forms of social action is greater than any similarity among those other forms themselves," and that the major difference is one of attitude.[9]

Today we are beginning to question even this attitudinal difference. For example, is it true that former businessmen cannot adjust to the chaotic world of government? The fact is that some can and some cannot, but generalizations do not hold. Likewise, it is inaccurate to say that all public officials are non-materialistic do-gooders who disdain the profit motive. These are obviously stereotypes which do not fit the facts. In short, in a democracy there is a great deal of consensus on values and norms; and attitudes between businessmen and career bureaucrats are not necessarily contradictory. More and more old stereotypes are being challenged. Nonetheless, these attitudinal, normative issues are difficult to resolve. Hence, we turn to more specific criteria for comparison.

II. Procedural Issues: Is Management a Universal Process?

In a procedural context, management might be defined as any activity or behavior concerned mainly with the means for carrying out prescribed ends. Although the ends of the business sector and government agencies might be different, often the means of achieving these ends are quite similar. These common procedural elements or aspects permit academics and practitioners to view management as a universal process.

But is it? We know from Part I that there are important distinctions between public and private values and objectives. Do these substantive differences affect procedural matters as well? Or are we so conditioned to examining the boundaries of things that we miss the thing itself?

The Accountability Factor: The Goldfish Bowl vs. The Closed Board Room

Almost 50 years ago John Dewey said that the line between public and private "is to be drawn on the basis of the extent and scope of the consequences of acts which are so important as to need control. . . ."[10] Consequences which affect only those directly involved in the transaction are private. Consequences which affect others beyond those immediately concerned are public, and need to be regulated.

In this concept of consequence and regulation we find the germ of the procedural difference between public and private management. What

Dewey is saying, and what others have said before and after, is that the key distinction between the public and private sectors is the accountability factor, the degree to which the institution is responsible to others for its actions.

The argument is that the business sector operates in relative, although not complete, autonomy and perhaps secrecy; free of the checks and balances of the public arena. The public sector, on the other hand, is subject to the pressure of the press and to public scrutiny, it operates in a "goldfish bowl."

For example, government's susceptibility to public criticism is sometimes carried to extremes, and at the very least complicates public management and brings into play organizational forms and methods of accountability which explain many of the differences between public and private administration. An example of this is the public corporation. In creating such corporations, government intended to establish businesslike agencies that would permit government institutions to provide services in a modern businesslike manner. But because of the political environment in which public agencies function, guidelines and measures were introduced, aimed mainly at establishing fiscal accountability, which undercut the principal advantages of the corporation device.

This is the point repeated in the literature, that government administration differs from all other administrative work because it is subject to public scrutiny and outcry. Every change in government has to be thought about in terms of the possible public agitation resulting from it.[11]

But in the past quarter century conditions have changed. As Daniel Bell argues, in the postindustrial society every organization is politicized, including the private firm. A specific change is increase in public regulation of the so-called "private firm." The regulation of air and water pollution is only one example; automobile safety and airline schedules are others. In an age of communal pressure and political mobilization even private firms are not dispensed from public scrutiny. The line between public and private has blurred, and today the businessman faces as much public as the public official. Consider the fact that bureaucrats often operate in relative privacy while businessmen squirm under the glare of the public eye.

Evaluation Techniques: Social Good and Fiscal Control

A second comparison concerns the application of evaluation techniques. Simplified, the argument is as follows. In the private sector it is quite easy to go to the bottom line and determine whether the firm or organization is measuring up to its organizational goal. This can be translated very easily in terms of profits and losses.

In the public sector, even though modern, businesslike fiscal control techniques are utilized, they are less easily transferable to public "social good" questions. A good example of this might be the popular pressure to apply cost-benefit analysis to War on Poverty programs. As proponents of the community action program argued, some of the objectives of the War on Poverty were to reverse apathy and powerlessness, the chief characteristics of the poor. This meant designing political mobilization activities to counter-condition long-range and inbred psychological attitudes of shiftlessness and withdrawal; to generate feelings of pride and involvement. Such psychological or intrapsychic reflections of economic disparity are often difficult, if not impossible, to measure in terms of traditional or even modern businesslike techniques. Recall the debate of a few years ago when OEO officials complained that *economic* cost-accounting tools were irrelevant to measuring the long-range *political* goals of the poverty program.

This "bottom line" distinction has other implications. It also means, for example, that government and public agencies do not have the measure of achievement which the business sector enjoys. Without clear standards of government performance often public administration results in sloppy or irrational activities. Things slide along often to the detriment of accountability. The point is that it is very difficult in the public sector to clarify objectives and then to apply the sophisticated, precise tools of profit and loss to measure performance.

A final point, however, is that it is difficult to measure quality in both sectors and that the attempt to apply fiscal control simply represents a first step in developing science in either sector.

Criteria of Decision Making: Rational Man vs. Political Man

Although decision making is the basic operation of management, it has been argued that this operation varies in the public sectors. For example, even though the *formal steps* in decision making are technically the same (definition of problem, outlining options, crystallizing preferred response, allocating resources, etc.), the *criteria* of decision making are different. That is, the logic, or mode of thinking, the movement from point to point, is different. In a word, it is often argued that the technology of decision making varies from private to public areas.

An understanding of the term technology is important here. As used in this paper, the term technology means "not simply a 'machine', but a systematic, disciplined approach to objectives, using a calculus of precision and measurement and a concept of system that are quite at variance with traditional and . . . intuitive modes."[12] The difference may be one of degree but the reality is that the systems approach has triumphed in the private sector while it is viewed with some distrust in the public sector.

There are several reasons for this. One is the fact that a technological conception of a problem limits the focus to those factors that can be expressed quantitatively and which fit certain models.[13] This encroachment of economics into intrinsically political processes is inherently contradictory. The emphasis, automatically, is on neatness and order versus social disorder; technical precision versus confusion and conflict; gestalt theories instead of ad hoc piecemeal fragmentation; efficient management versus "bumbling bureaucracy."[14] In short, the distinction is between the process of management based on criteria of economy, efficiency, and rational results, versus a process of decision making based on ideas of consensus, the broadest social good, and "muddling through."

Another reason why "technology" has been resisted in the public sector is the assumption that governmental problems are basically social in nature. Although many of society's pressing problems have been generated or aggravated by technological change and development (e.g., transportation problems, housing design), the technical solution is not automatically transferable. Referring to a range of social ills, Ida Hoos analogized that "calling upon an engineer to cure them is much like asking an economist to treat a heart ailment because the patient became ill over money matters."[15]

The counterpart is that whether or not technology, and particularly systems analysis, is appropriate to public decisions, it is in fact being applied. Some would say that Bertram Gross' fears about a new breed of technipols have been realized. In this sense, government has accepted business as its model and economics as its decision-making means. Hence, the theoretical differences in modes of public and private criteria may well be moot at this point.

Personnel Systems

In reflecting on comparisons between business and government, Paul H. Appleby argued:

> It is exceedingly difficult clearly to identify the factors which make government different from other activity in society. Yet this difference is a fact and I believe it to be so big a difference that the dissimilarity between government and all other forms of social action is greater than any dissimilarity among those other forms themselves. Without a willingness to recognize this fact, no one can even begin to discuss public affairs to any good profit or serious purpose.[16]

The single most determinative factor that Appleby identified was personnel. One aspect of this difference has to do with recruiting patterns; a second element has to do with socializing processes.

In the private sector candidates theoretically are recruited through formal credentialing systems. In the public sector, recruitment, especially for top-level positions, is often informal, ad hoc, and on a personal (who do you know) basis. At least this is the accepted notion. Realistically, it is difficult to say whether there is more or less nepotism in business than in government. Are appointments in government more or less a function of pull and privilege than in the business world? Obviously, it would be hard to prove the argument one way or the other.

With regard to differences in socialization, a number of points can be made. On the one hand, some observers view background as the critical variable. For example, some businessmen do poorly in government. They come into government service with strong personalities and are unable to adjust to situations which they cannot control. There is a contradiction between the businessman's attitude and government needs. The businessman sees his role as executive, as decision maker. Yet the reasons for bringing him into government may have been simply to coopt his support, to win legitimacy for policies made, or to seek his prestige in order to maintain national unity. These are political as opposed to business reasons.

On the other hand, businessmen have traditionally succeeded in government executive positions, indicating that their skills are transferable. This is likely to continue especially given the current disaffection with the politician image. In fact, businessmen may, because of their supposed neutrality, be in even greater demand. The operational question is the reverse of this: whether ex-government people can shift into the private sector. On this score, there is some evidence that former administration officials are prime candidates for top corporate positions and that public experience is not an undesirable reference.

Planning

Planning is an activity common to both the public and private sectors. Although the term refers generally to the process of uniting ideas with action, it needs to be analyzed in its specific institutional setting.

There are two ways to view planning: as a process of decision making or as a means of control. In terms of process, planning means lateral consultation, sharing of information, discussion of short- and long-term objectives. It implies a participatory process in order to come up with mutually satisfactory goals.

Planning as a means of control refers to a system of gathering information and marshalling available resources in a sequential priority framework in order to maximize agreed-upon objectives.

The advantages and disadvantages of each approach have been discussed elsewhere.[17] The question for this article is whether one mode is used more in business or in public. As in many of the areas discussed, distinctions blur when applied to actual situations. Consider the fact that the vital circumstances surrounding any planning effort are intangible, ad hoc, and uncertain. In both the public sector and the private sector this is evidenced by the first impulse of planners, to "get more, or better, data." Planning is an eclectic science with no distinct theoretical base. As such it is hardly a precise science. It is true that planners seem more common in government circles than in private firms. But this may be simply a matter of labels, i.e., calling the corporate finance officer financial analyst instead of resident planner, or calling the city planner by that title instead of research associate. In either area planning is at best a secondary function, and the point is that in actual situations the process of planning appears to be the same.

The Efficiency Question

Too much has been written on the subject of government waste and business efficiency for this article to dispel any widespread notions. But a few comments are in order.

If one accepts the notion that the business of government is politics (the allocation of authority for a society) and that the goal is not efficiency by resolution of conflict, then it is impossible to say that government is less efficient than business.

There are three important points to be made. First, in terms of efficiency it is difficult to compare the two areas. It is the old apples and oranges problem. Is the Supreme Court less efficient in protecting the first amendment than General Motors is in producing cars? Is Boeing Aircraft more efficient in what it does than TVA is in producing electricity? To go even further, it is difficult to make comparisons within a particular area, public or private. For example, in the so-called private sector, is the *New York Times* more or less efficient in producing news than the Chicago Bears organization is in producing entertainment? The point is obvious: If this quantity efficiency cannot easily be measured within one supposedly similar area, then how are comparisons to be made between different areas?

There is a second point. In government what appears to be inefficiency is sometimes essential to the public purpose of the agency. For example, millions of dollars spent every year on public scrutiny of government activities operates in the public interest, and the net effect is to make the agency more efficient in terms of its central purpose which is political responsiveness.

The third point is that in terms of efficiency the private sector is not without criticism; business has its share of horror stories. The facts emerging from the aerospace industry belie the notion of rational, efficient operations in private industry. Efficiency and waste it seems are more a matter of case-by-case analysis than across-the-board generalizations.

Theoretically similar principles of hierarchic control, comprehensive coordination, the rule of merit, and line of authority apply in both the public and private sectors. A word on each of these is in order.

With regard to the principle of hierarchic control, the theory of the scalar process, or the application of superior-subordinate relationship is honored in every formal organizational chart but seldom in fact. This applies to the private sector myth of "chairman of the board" and to the ceremonial role of the "agency director" in public affairs. In either case the head is often a ceremonial figure with political as opposed to operational duties.

Coordination, a second principle, means the rational allocation of resources to meet needs and depends on two factors: (1) definition of need, and (2) availability of resources. Coordination is, however, a similar process in any operation since it relates to maximization of agency goals.

The rule of merit is protected by informal systems, as well as by formal codes and contracts in both the public and private sectors, but it is violated with equal impunity in either area. The temporary assignment in the civil service has as its counterpart the position of management consultant in private industry.

Another principle is that authority should be commensurate with responsibility. This is the cardinal rule of management and a central objective of public and private practitioners. The fact that it remains a central objective underscores its absence in either area.

Conclusion

1. Substantive Issues: More Blurring Than Bifurcation

The large issue, the central question, is whether public and private management are inherently different. Based on this exploratory survey of the issues, the answer is a cautious no, not at this time. In Daniel Bell's postindustrial society, characterized by a diffusion of goods, there may be a growth of public decision making which so overwhelms the free market as to radically alter the society. As yet this has not happened. The situation that seems to be evolving is a mixture of public-private, government-market decision making with a blurring of the lines rather than a distinct bifurcation of responsibilities. This is reflected in the analysis of the substantive areas like objective setting and evaluation techniques. Few lasting differences were found. For example, the central issue of different value systems seems to be more a difference of degree and emphasis than of substance. Politics conditions judgment in both areas; private decisions transcend immediate application in either sector. Boundaries between public and private activity seem to be blurring. At any rate, in areas such as attitudes and values it will require a good deal more behavioral research to establish the fact of difference as opposed to the sentiment of difference.

2. Procedural Issues: Distinctions Not Differences

As Justice Holmes once remarked to a lawyer making a fine legal point: That's a distinction, but not a difference. The same dictum applies to the survey of procedural areas. For example, in the area of ethics it is true that the public sector conduct is characterized by clear, formal, even legal guidelines (the Constitution, conflict of interest laws, etc.). It is also true that these laws are honored as much in the breach as in the fact. In the private sector, although pressures and constraints may be informal, studies have shown that private executives are extremely sensitive to the appearance of ethical behavior. Some argue that this has led to conformist type mentality in the private sector. At any rate, ethical questions seem to be reemerging as legitimate issues in either sector and where differences exist they are formal and superficial, i.e., legalistic in nature. In actual practice this difference dissipates.

3. Apples and Oranges

A third conclusion has to do with the "apples and oranges" syndrome of comparing unlike objects. On the question of efficiency, for example, it is impossible to match political efficiency with economic efficiency. One must judge one agency's political efficiency with another agency's political efficiency, and so on. It is unfair and illogical to use the efficiency criterion alone and apply it to the public and private sectors.

4. Myths and Sentiments

A fourth conclusion is that some of our most cherished and popular myths do not hold up under cold analysis. For example, is private management superior to public administration in terms of waste management? Not by aerospace industry standards. Is the public sector run more openly and democratically? Not if public sentiment and recent criminal cases against officials is any measure. The view of "big bureaucracy" as a mismanaged monolith is as unrealistic as the view of business as a social rip off. The law of variations tells us that the situation differs as management practice varies—from case to case.

5. The Primacy of Method

The essential issue it seems is not what procedural or substantive distinctions or differences exist, but what *management tools* are applied to problem solving, whether in the public or private sector. The choice of tools and models is the critical intervening variable between the definition of the problem and the crystallization of a policy. With regard to public-private activities it is clear that what may be acceptable in the private sector in the technical sense may be completely unsatisfactory in the public area where social questions cannot be subordinated to technical approaches.

The issue, of course, is only part of a larger question facing a society enamored by systems approaches, and empirical models and quick technological solutions. As suggested above, it may be too late to raise the issue; the public sector already relies on modern technical solutions to a great degree. Ida Hoos has noted:

> The main myths in the business world that most needed exploration and explosion have become doxology in government circles, with critical inquiry tantamount to heresy. Indeed, he who has the temerity to raise questions runs the risk of being considered not only anachronistically and iconoclastically unscientific but probably a bit subverse and un-American as well.[18]

At the risk of being unpatriotic, it is this reckless application of cheap, visible, quantitative solutions to social problems which poses the greatest threat to problem solving and ultimately to harmonious interface between the public and private sectors. As Robert Merton has said:

> The technician sees the nation quite differently from the political man: to the technician, the nation is nothing more than another sphere in which to apply the instruments he has developed. To him, the state is not the expression of the will of the people nor a divine creation nor a creature of class conflict. It is an enterprise providing services that must be made to function *efficiently*.[19]

Or as others have said: data does not automatically solve problems; human beings, with the help of data, are capable of problem solving.

Rather than conceptualizing management in the public sector as an extension of private sector practices and values, this article points toward an increasing convergence in management processes in the public and private sectors. Traditional barriers and distinctive patterns in decision making and goal definition are breaking down. While prevailing ideal-type models stress the uniqueness of public organizations as opposed to private organizations, this article argues that in the postindustrial society, which is emerging in the U.S., the old distinctions are no longer operational. Both in the handling of substantive issues and procedural matters, actual management practices point to a blurring of public and private sectors rather than to a bifurcation. Public and private management procedures, operations, and goals cannot be viewed as separate processes.

Endnotes

1. Fredric H. Gench, "Public Management in America," *AACSB Bulletin*, vol. 9, no. 3 (April 1973), 6.

2. Herbert A. Simon, *Administrative Behavior* (New York: Macmillan, 1949).

3. Norton Long, "Public Policy and Administration: The Goals of Rationality and Responsibility," *Public Administration Review*, vol. 14, no. 1 (Winter 1954), 22.

4. Ibid.

5. Genck, op. cit., 7

6. Theodore Levitt, *The Third Sector* (New York: Amacom, 1973), 28-29.

7. See *The Future of the American Government*, Daniel Pearlman (ed.) (Boston: Houghton Mifflin, 1968), especially foreword by Daniel Bell.

8. Paul H. Appleby, *Big Democracy* (New York: Knopf, 1945), 50–51.

9. Ibid., 1.

10. John Dewey, *The Public and Its Problems* (New York, 1927), 15.

11. Appleby, *Big Democracy.*

12. Daniel Bell, "Trajectory of an Idea," in *Toward the Year 2000*, Daniel Bell (ed.) (Boston: Houghton Mifflin, 1968), 5.

13. Ida R. Hoos, *Systems Analysis in Public Policy: A Critique* (Berkeley: University of California Press, 1972), 26.

14. Ibid., 89.

15. Ibid., 24.

16. Appleby, *Big Democracy*

17. Aaron Wildavsky, *The Politics of the Budgetary Process* (Boston: Little, Brown, 1964), especially chapter 5.

18. Hoos, op. cit., 196.

19. Quoted in Frank Trippet, "The Shape of Things as They Really Are," *Intellectual Digest* (December 1972), 28.

The Deadly Sins in Public Administration

Peter F. Drucker

I

No one can guarantee the performance of a public service program, but we know how to ensure nonperformance with absolute certainty. Commit any two or the following common sins of public administration, and nonperformance will inevitably follow. Indeed, to commit all six, as many public service agencies do, is quite unnecessary and an exercise in overkill.

(1) The first thing to do to make sure that a program will not have results is to have a lofty objective—"health care," for instance, or "to aid the disadvantaged." Such sentiments belong in the preamble. They explain why a specific program or agency is being initiated rather than what the program or agency is meant to accomplish.[1] To use such statements as "objectives" thus makes sure that no effective work will be done. For work is always specific, always mundane, always focused. Yet without work there is nonperformance.

To have a chance at performance, a program needs clear targets, the attainment of which can be measured, appraised, or at least judged. "Health care" is not even a pious intention. Indeed it is, at best, a vague slogan. Even "the best medical care for the sick," the objective of many hospitals in the British National Health Service, is not operational. Rather, it is meaningful to say: "It is our aim to make sure that no patient coming into emergency will go for more than three minutes without being seen by a qualified triage nurse." It is a proper goal to say: "Within three years, our maternity ward is going to be run on a 'zero defects' basis, which means that there will be no 'surprises' in the delivery room and there will not be one case of post-partum puerperal fever on maternity." Similarly, "Promoting the welfare of the American farmer" is electioneering, while "Installing electricity in at least 25 percent of America's farms within the next three years"—the first goal of the New Deal's Rural Electrification Administration, which was, perhaps the most successful public service agency in all our administrative history—was an objective that was specific, measurable, attainable—and attained. It immediately was converted into work, and very shortly thereafter, into performance.

(2) The second strategy guaranteed to produce nonperformance is to try

---

to do several things at once. It is to refuse to establish priorities and to stick to them. Splintering of efforts guarantees non-results. Yet without concentration on a priority, efforts will be splintered, and the more massive the program, the more the splintering effects will produce nonperformance. By contrast, even poorly conceived programs might have results if priorities are set and efforts concentrated.

It is popular nowadays to blame the failure of so many of the programs of Lyndon Johnson's "War on Poverty" on shaky theoretical foundations. Whether poorly conceived or not, quite a few of the Headstart schools had significant results; every one of them, without exception, was a school that decided on one overriding priority—having the children learn to read letters and numbers—despite heavy criticism from Washington and from all kinds of dogmatists.

An even more impressive example is the Tennessee Valley Authority (TVA) in the thirties. Despite tremendous opposition, the bill establishing the TVA only passed Congress because its backers promised a dozen different and mutually antagonistic constituencies: cheap power, cheap fertilizer, flood control, irrigation, navigation, community development and whatnot. TVA's first administrator, Arthur Morgan, a great engineer, then attempted to live up to these promises and to satisfy every one of his constituencies. The only result was an uncontrollably growing bureaucracy, uncontrollably growing expenditures, and a total lack of any performance. Indeed, the TVA in its early years resembled nothing as much as one of those "messes" which we now attack in Washington. Then President Roosevelt removed Morgan and put in a totally unknown young Wisconsin utilities lawyer, David Lilienthal, who immediately—against all advice from all the "pros"—announced his priority: power production. Within a year, the TVA produced results. Lilienthal, by the way, met no opposition, but was universally acclaimed as a saviour.

(3) The third deadly sin of the public administrator is to believe that "fat is beautiful," despite the obvious fact that mass does not do work; brains and muscles do. In fact, overweight inhibits work, and gross overweight totally immobilizes.

One hears a great deal today about the fallacy of "throwing money at problems," but this is not really what we have been doing. We have been throwing manpower at problems, with Vietnam, perhaps being the worst example, and it is even worse to overstaff than to overfund. Today's administrators, whether civilian or military, tend to believe that the best way to tackle a problem is to deploy more and more people against it. The one certain result of having more bodies is greater difficulties in logistics, in personnel management, and in communications. Mass increases weight, but not necessarily competence. Competence requires direction, decision, and strategy rather than manpower.

Overstaffing is not only much harder to correct than understaffing, it makes nonperformance practically certain. For overstaffing always focuses energies on the inside, on "administration" rather than on "results," on the machinery rather than its purpose. It always leads to meetings and memoranda becoming ends in themselves. It immobilizes behind a facade of furious busyness. Harold Ickes, FDR's Secretary of the Interior and one of the New Deal's most accomplished administrators, always asked: "What is the fewest number of people we need to accomplish this purpose?" It is a long time since anyone in Washington (or in the state governments) has asked that question.

(4) "Don't experiment, be dogmatic" is the next—and the next most common—of the administrator's deadly sins. "Whatever you do, do it on a grand scale at the first try. Otherwise, God forbid, you might learn how to do it differently." In technical or product innovation, we sometimes skip the pilot-plant stage, usually to our sorrow. But at least we build a model and put it through wind tunnel tests. In public service, increasingly we start out with a "position"—that is, with a totally untested theory—and go from it immediately to national, if not international, application. The most blatant example may have been the ultrascholastic dogmatism with which we rushed into national programs in the "War on Poverty" that were based on totally speculative, totally untried social science theories, and backed by not one shred of empirical evidence.

However, even if the theories on which a program is based are themselves sound, successful application still demands adaptation, cutting, fitting, trying, balancing. It always demands testing against reality before there is final total commitment. Above all, any new program, no matter how well conceived, will run into the unexpected, whether unexpected "problems" or unexpected "successes." At that point, people are needed who have been through a similar program on a smaller scale, who know whether the unexpected problem is relevant or not, or whether the unexpected success is a fluke or genuine achievement.

Surely one of the main reasons for the success of so many of the New Deal programs was that there had been "small scale" experiments in states and cities earlier—in Wisconsin, for instance, in New York State or in New York City, or in one of the reform administrations in Chicago. The outstanding administrators of the New Deal programs—Frances Perkins at Labor, Harold Ickes at Interior, or Arthur Altmeyer at Social Security—were all alumnae of such earlier small-scale experiments. Similarly, the truly unsuccessful New Deal programs, the WPA for instance, were, without exception, programs that had not first been developed in small-scale experimentation in state or local governments but were initiated as comprehensive, national panaceas.

(5) "Make sure that you cannot learn from experience" is the next prescription for nonperformance in public administration. "Do not think through in advance what you expect; do not then feed back from results to expectations so as to find out not only what you can do well, but also to find out what your weaknesses, your limitations, and your blind spots are."

Every organization, like every individual, does certain things well. They are the things that "come easy to one's hand." Nevertheless, every organization, like every individual, is also prone to typical mistakes, has typical limitations, and has its own blind spots. Unless the organization shapes its own expectations to reflect the accuracy of results, it will not find out what it does well and, thus, not learn to apply its strengths. Moreover, it will not find out what it does poorly and will, thus, have no opportunity to improve or to compensate for its weaknesses or its blind spots. Typically, for instance, certain institutions expect results much too fast and throw in the towel much too soon. A good many of the "War on Poverty" agencies did just that. Also, there are many organizations which wait much too long before they face up to the fact that a program or a policy is unsuccessful—our Vietnam policies, both civilian and military, probably belong here. One can only learn by feedback, and we know that feedback from results always improves performance capacity and effectiveness. Without it, however, the weaknesses, the limitations, the blind spots increasingly dominate. Without learning from results through feedback, any organization, like any individual, must inevitably deteriorate in its capacity to perform. Yet, in most public service institutions such feedback functions are either nonexistent or viewed with casual skepticism. If the results do not conform to expectations, they are all too frequently dismissed as irrelevant, as indications of the obtuseness of clients, as the reactionary obscurantism of the public, or, worst of all, as evidence of the need to "make another study." Most public service institutions, governmental ones as well as nongovernmental ones, are budget-focused, but the budgets measure efforts rather than results. For performance, the budget needs to be paralleled with a statement of expected results—and with systematic feedback from results—on expenditures and on efforts. Otherwise, the agency will, almost immediately, channel more and more of its efforts toward nonresults and will become the prisoner of its own limitations, its weaknesses, and its blind spots rather than the beneficiary of its own strengths.

(6) The last of the administrator's deadly sins is the most damning and the most common: the inability to abandon. It alone guarantees nonperformance, and within a fairly short time.

Traditional political theory, the theory inherited from Aristotle, holds that the tasks of government are grounded in the nature of civil society and, thus, are immutable: defense, justice, law and order. However, very few of the tasks of modern public administration, whether governmental or nongovernmental public service institutions, such as the hospital, the Red Cross, the university, or the Boy Scouts, are of that nature. Almost all of them are manmade rather than grounded in the basic essentials of society, and most of them are of very recent origin to boot. They all, therefore, share a common fate: they must become pointless at some juncture in time. They may become pointless because the need to which they address themselves no longer exists or is no longer urgent. They may become pointless because the old need appears in such a new guise as to make obsolete present design, shape, concerns and policies. The great environmental problem of 1910, for instance—and it was a very real danger—was the horrendous pollution by the horse, with its stench and its liquid and solid wastes, which threatened to bury the cities of that time. If we had been as environmentally conscious then as we are now, we would have saddled ourselves with agencies which only ten years later would have become totally pointless and yet, predictably, ten years later they would have redoubled their efforts, since they would have totally lost sight of their objectives. Moreover, a program may become pointless when it fails to produce results despite all efforts, as do our present American welfare programs. Finally—and most dangerous of all—a program becomes pointless when it achieves its objectives. That we have a "welfare mess" today is, in large measure, a result of our having maintained the welfare programs of the New Deal after they had achieved their objectives around 1940 or 1941. These programs were designed to tackle the problems caused by the temporary unemployment of experienced (and almost entirely white) male heads of families—no wonder that they then malperformed when applied to the totally different problems caused in large measure by the mass movement of black females into the cities 10 or 15 years later.

The basic assumption of public service institutions, governmental or nongovernmental ones alike, is immortality. It is a foolish assumption. It dooms the organization and its programs to non-performance and non-results. The only rational assumption is that every public service program will sooner or later—and usually sooner—outlive its usefulness, at least insofar as its present form, its present objectives, and its present policies are concerned. A public service program that does not conduct itself in contemplation of its own mortality will very soon become incapable of performance. In its original guise it cannot produce results any longer; the objectives have either ceased to matter, have proven unobtainable, or have been attained. Indeed, the more successful a public service agency is, the sooner will it work itself out of the job; then it can only become an impediment to performance, if not an embarrassment.

The public service administrator who wants results and performance will, thus, have to build into his own organization an organized process for abandonment. He will have to learn to ask every few years: "If we did not do this already, would we now, knowing what we know now, go into this?" And if the answer is "no," he better not say "let's make another study" or "let's ask for a bigger budget." He better ask: "How can we stop pouring more effort, more resources, more people into this?"

II

Avoidance of these six "deadly sins" does not, perhaps, guarantee performance and results in the public service organization, but avoiding these six deadly sins is the prerequisite for performance and results. To be sure, there is nothing very recondite about these "do's and don'ts." They are simple, elementary, indeed, obvious. Yet, as everyone in public administration knows, most administrators commit most of these "sins" all the time and, indeed, all of them most of the time.

One reason is plain cowardice. It is "risky" to spell out attainable, concrete, measurable goals—or so the popular wisdom goes. It is also mundane, pedestrian and likely to "turn off" backers or donors. "The world's best medical care" is so much more "sexy" than "every emergency patient will be seen by a qualified triage nurse within three minutes." Furthermore, to set priorities seems even more dangerous—one risks the wrath of the people who do not really care for electric power or fertilizer, but want to protect the little snail darter or the spotted lousewort. Finally, of course, you do not "rank" in the bureaucracy unless you spend a billion dollars and employ an army of clerks—"fat is beautiful."

Perhaps so, but experience does not bear out the common wisdom. The public service administrators who face up to goal-setting, to ordered priorities, and to concentrating their resources (the public service administrators who are willing to ask: "What is the smallest number of people we need to attain our objectives?") may not always be popular, but they are respected, and they rarely have any trouble at all. They may not get as far in their political careers as the ones who put popularity above performance, but, in the end, they are the ones we remember.

III

But perhaps even more important than cowardice as an explanation for the tendency of so much of public administration today to commit itself to policies that can only result in non-performance is the lack of concern with performance in public administration theory.

For a century from the Civil War to 1960 or so, the performance of public service institutions and programs was taken for granted in the United States. It could be taken for granted because earlier administrators somehow knew not to commit the "deadly sins" I have outlined here. As a result, the discipline of public administration—a peculiarly American discipline, by the way—saw no reason to concern itself with performance. It was not a problem. It focused instead on the political process, on how programs come into being. *Who Gets What, When, How?*, the title of Harold Lasswell's 1936 classic on politics, neatly sums up one specific focus of American public administration, with its challenge to traditional political theory. The other focus was procedural: "The orderly conduct of the business of government" an earlier generation called it. It was a necessary concern in an America that had little or no administrative tradition and experience and was suddenly projected into very large public service programs, first in World War I, then in the New Deal, and finally in World War II. We needed work on all phases of what we now call "management": personnel, budgeting, organization, and so on. But these are inside concerns. Now we need hard, systematic work on making public service institutions perform.

As I noted, for a century, from the Civil War until 1960 or so, performance of public service institutions was taken for granted. For the last 20 years, however, malperformance is increasingly being taken for granted. Great programs are still being proposed, are still being debated, and, in some instances, are even still being enacted, but few people expect them to produce results. All we really expect now, whether from a new Department of Education in Washington or from a reorganization of the state government by a new governor who preaches that "small is beautiful," is more expenditure, a bigger budget, and a more ineffectual bureaucracy.

The malperformance of public service institutions may well be a symptom only. The cause may be far more basic: a crisis in the very foundations and assumptions on which rests that proudest achievement of the Modern Age, national administrative government.[2]

But surely the malperformance of the public service institution is in itself a contributing factor to the sickness of government, and a pretty big one. Avoiding the "deadly sins" of public administration may only give symptomatic relief for whatever ails modern government, but at least we know how to do it.

Endnotes

1. On this, see my article, "What Results Should You Expect? A User's Guide to MPO," *Public Administration Review*, Vol. 36, pp. 12–19.

2. I hope eventually to finish a book on this subject, tentatively entitled "Can Government Be Saved?," on which I have been working for ten years or more.

Is Excellence in the Public Sector Possible?

Jed Kee
Roger Black

The purpose of this article is to examine some recent popular ideas about improving organizational performance—pursuing excellence—in the public sector. Our reference point is the "excellence literature"—the current wave of best-selling nonfiction books that focus on organizational life and offer prescriptions for success.[1] We also suggest that the report of the President's Private Sector Survey on Cost Control (Grace Commission) belongs in this literature.[2] Critics of public management implicitly assume that the ideas presented in the "excellence literature," ought to work in government as well as they work in business. The apparent inability to do so must, therefore, be a failure of leadership. If public managers were only to apply these principles and adopt hard-nosed business principles, taxpayers would benefit immensely.

We wonder if this is really so. Glossing over fundamental differences between tax-supported entities and market-supported organizations may do

---

Reprinted with permission from *Public Productivity Review* (Spring 1985), published by the National Center for Public Productivity, John Jay College of Criminal Justice, CUNY, New York, New York.

both sectors a disservice. In many ways, the achievement of excellence in the public sector is much more challenging than in the private sector because of the multiplicity of actors, inherent value conflicts, deliberate and often erratic policy shifts, and intense public scrutiny on how public funds are spent. These special conditions and the tendency of public managers to idealize a "rational model" approach to decision-making militate against the risk-taking, free-wheeling entrepreneurial behavior and values-rich personal charisma that apparently lead to excellence in the private sector.

The Challenge of Public Sector Management

Identifying the Customer

Organizations must pay attention to their customers. Failure of for-profit companies to do so brings the inevitable discipline of the marketplace. Firms either succeed in meeting customer demands or they go out of business. For this reason, companies carefully identify the customers they intend to serve and they spend freely to discover or shape consumer buying habits. The relationship between buyer and seller is voluntary and intimate. Each party knows something about the personal identity of the other. And each understands that the buyer is solely responsible for deciding if the product or service is worth the price.

Not so with public sector organizations. Here, the identity of the buyer is obscure, neither party has a choice, and the responsibility for measuring satisfaction falls on the seller. Obviously, these conditions produce a different kind of relationship between producers and consumers of government services than exists in the private sector. Public agencies must first define their customer. This is difficult to do when those who receive government services and those who pay for them are not always the same people. Obviously, direct recipients, e.g., welfare clients, motorists, recreationists, and high school students, are customers. So are taxpayers who "consume" safe streets, national security, open spaces, a healthy economic climate, consumer protection, an educated citizenry, etc. But taxpayers often fail to see the connection between their personal tax bills and these social benefits.

Elected officials face special challenges. They are in the middle of an ongoing, four-party marketplace that involves themselves, taxpayers, direct consumers, and the career civil service. They have the difficult job of being both buyers and sellers. They are buyers in the sense that they represent people who actually consume or pay for public services; they are sellers in the sense that they direct the agencies which deliver the services. Intuitively, elected officials are sensitive to taxpayers and interest groups. But they incline toward an institutional suspicion of the career establishment. This suspicion presents a complication in developing an effective customer orientation that private sector managers simply don't experience. In the private sector it is in everyone's self interest to focus on the needs of specific customers in specific markets. In the public sector, elected officials rarely see things in the same way professional managers do. Therefore, even to reach agreement on who the customer is demands extraordinary patience, perseverance, commitment, and dialogue between the elected official and public managers.

Good public sector customer relations is the more difficult because customers, whether clients or taxpayers, are usually involuntary. In the abstract, citizens may recognize that tax dollars pay for goods and services which are necessary for an orderly society. But it is very clear that these services are, in no sense, purchased in the same way that a consumer purchases an automobile or a television set. There is, for example, no voluntary market for national defense. Most citizens feel strongly that we need it but none can buy it in amounts that exactly match personal tastes.

Some political economists have suggested that people express a preference for a mix of local services and taxation by their location choices.[3] The mobility of Americans lends some credibility to this concept. However, if it applies at all, it is restricted to local government settings where there is a reasonably clear relationship between the menu of schools, roads, and other local services provided, and the property taxes paid. In any case, in today's high-interest-rate environment, people do not readily choose to relocate just to balance the level of taxation and service consumption. And no one can unilaterally reduce his or her tax payments to avoid support of services not used as one can in the private sector. Therefore, business methods for meeting customer needs may not work or may not be appropriate in the public sector. However, there is much that government managers can do to foster a customer orientation. On a program-by-program basis, professional employees and elected officials should be able to agree on who the customer is. Given this agreement, managers can focus attention on service levels that meet legitimate expectations of specific customers.

Determining Core Values

The "excellence literature" emphasizes the importance of a strong set of central guiding values. We agree with this basic premise. The public sector, however, faces a complexity and multiplicity of values that, in many cases, conflict with one another. To illustrate, a department of natural resources may contain strongly pro-development divisions, and divisions whose missions are inherently contradictory to development (for example, energy extraction vs. environmental protection).

Furthermore, the political process itself creates a diffusion of power and responsibility that makes the articulation of central values very difficult. There are many actors who have a vested interest in not recognizing the value conflicts embodied in a competitor's position. After all, coalitions are difficult enough without insisting that all parties agree on a common set of values. Public managers, therefore, face: client groups demanding a service; special interest groups, representing or opposing client desires; a bureaucracy delivering the service; policy makers establishing guidelines for the service; legislative committees refereeing the contest; the law, itself, placing constraints but rarely charting a clear course; and finally, the taxpayer asserting interests that often counter those of service recipients. The welfare client, for instance, prefers looser eligibility standards; the taxpayer, presumably, tighter standards.

Since the conflicting set of values and actors results in a fuzziness of focus for government managers, it is no wonder that they are attracted by the so-called "rational model" of public administration. Proponents of the model preach that professional public administration is hard-headed rationality; that detached analysis makes for good decisions; and that a professional manager can manage anything. Such archetypical "rational managers," as Robert McNamara, of the Department of Defense and Ford Industries, and Roy Ash, of the Office of Management and Budget and Litton Industries, relied on a series of rational management techniques; including PPBS, performance budgeting, and zero-based budgeting.

Aaron Wildavsky and other political commentators have challenged the applicability of these ideas.[4] However, at an operating level, conventional wisdom and public expectations create a bias towards the rational model that may be greater in government than in business. Governmental institutions tend to be preoccupied with process rather than results. Management accountability and the ideal of a science of public administration are easier to talk about than assessing the product of public schools or the Department of State. Nevertheless, the limitations of the rational model are even greater in the public sector than the private marketplace. Government deals with values and with multidimensional, often intangible, products; such as equality, environment, justice, and quality of life. Furthermore, government exists, in part, to cope with the irrationality of the world in which people carry on from day to day.

The aggressive pursuit of a rational model of public administration is undesirable, not merely because we are unlikely to succeed in applying it, but because movement toward it can actually be counter-productive. We need strict accountability for achieving public value. In practice, we have accountability for mundane mechanics. R. A. Leone, of the Kennedy School of Government, has suggested that a preoccupation with the cost of public services, which he labels "operations fetishism," not only sacrifices public value but also sacrifices economy in government at the same time. At its worst, bureaucratic complexity creates costs today and produces inflexibility that adds cost tomorrow.[5]

In order to avoid these problems of the rational model, excellent public organizations must find a way to manage the ambiguity of values and harness the commitment and energy of staff. Successful attempts to sharpen focus are rare.

A little appreciated but potential untapped reservoir of commitment is the intrinsic value content of public service. Perhaps a majority of public employees work in government because they support the values government seeks to promote. And they subscribe to standards of performance and ethics that their professional peers and colleagues have evolved over time. The commitment to excellence in the attainment of professional success may never be as obvious and measurable in the public sector as it tends to be in the private sector, where the focus on products and markets can be very narrow. But it is a good start. Government is a conglomerate responsible for many goods and services and obligated to serve the entire population. While these factors tend to diffuse attention and dissipate energy, small work units can develop their own driving set of values and develop an organizational capacity and political mandate to succeed.

Most successful organizations have shown a strong sense of continuity in leadership, often with a dominant figure who has either founded or provided the inspiration for the corporate success. In the public sector, however, political swings are built in. Mayors and governors typically turn over every four to eight years and legislators, more often. Even professional appointed administrators expect to move on after four or five years. With new leadership comes new visions and policy changes which can have a fundamental impact on the directions of an organization.

The public sector must rely more on middle management, normally protected from political swings, to provide continuity of central organizational values. In our view, this is a task for which we seldom prepare middle managers. Achieving this continuity begins with a recognition and support of this role of middle management.

Promoting Risk-taking

Autonomy and entrepreneurial risk-taking are nearly impossible in the public sector. Unlike profit-making organizations which can bury mistakes in the overall financial statement, the miscalculations of public sector organizations receive considerable public scrutiny. The media is ever anxious to accentuate government failures, and the opposition party can make such failures rallying cries for a change of administrations.

Governmental budgets, funding approval requirements, purchasing and other controls on the expenditure of public funds further tend to inhibit risk-takers in government. Some even create perverse disincentives. For example, line-item budgeting restricts managerial flexibility to the point of removing managerial accountability; intransigent merit systems make rewarding good people difficult and firing bad people impossible; inflexible promotional practices tend to reward managers on the basis of the number of people managed and size of budget rather than on the success—that they consciously tolerate performance on the safe side of what is possible rather than push toward the theoretical optimum?

Legislation, public scrutiny, and constitutional checks and balances all create legitimate legal and political limitations on the freedom of public managers to act. Yet within the constraints, there is considerable room for experimentation and action. Ad hoc task forces, pilot projects, simplifying decision-making (for example, one-page decision memos), refusing to study a problem to death, are all methods for creating a bias for action. Legislative bodies have a special responsibility to engender a climate that rewards doing. While the Peters and Waterman phrase "ready, fire, aim" may provide an impossible action orientation for the public sector,[6] the notion of "try it, then fix it, don't just study it" might provide an appropriate substitute.

Risk-taking in the public sector is possible, if there is strong support from organizational leadership and a willingness to permit failure (not perpetuate them), an acceptance of diversity in ideas and service delivery mechanisms, and legislators who will give managers some flexibility.

Private Sector/Public Sector Similarities

While the challenges outlined in the preceding paragraphs are many, there are significant similarities between private and public sector organizations that make the "excellence literature" valuable for public managers. Perhaps most important is the belief that an organization's success is tied to its people. Increased productivity ultimately comes from the perspiration and inspiration of workers. This is as true for public sector organizations as it is for private sector companies. A major part of government budgets for pay for the people who do the public's business. They are the teachers in public schools, professors at institutions of higher education, highway patrol troopers, soldiers, social workers, prison guards, engineers, tax collectors, and wildlife officers. Virtually all want to do a good job.

The "excellence literature" observes that people, without regard for where they work, need to succeed, to be winners, to feel that they contribute. There is increasing evidence that successful organizations benefit from a management style which recognizes the value of individuals. It is clear that people today are looking for more than a paycheck from their nine-to-five job. They are less tolerant of doing work that they do not understand and intolerant of co-worker or management incompetence. They are concerned with the financial benefits, or course, but they want work to have meaning. Public sector managers who ignore this fact do so to the detriment of their organization and the public they serve.

Vision Counts

A second area of similarity is the notion that a strong sense of vision can make a difference in employee output. An organization's values and culture really do have an impact on workers' behavior. If they feel better about what they do, they are more likely to work harder. Apparently, a strong culture helps to remove much of the uncertainty of the workplace. It provides easily understood structure and standards, and it gives people a value system to guide their behavior. Vision, in the sense of specific unambiguous goals may be difficult to achieve in a political arena; but vision, in the sense of seeing one's work as part of something intrinsically worthwhile and therefore important, is inherent in most profit sector work.

Many successful profit-making organizations rely on the vision and understanding of people with first-hand knowledge of the business—the lower level rank and file worker. This tends to reinforce the person's importance in the workplace, contributes to greater worker productivity, and provides practical solutions to problems. There is no institutional reason why this insight can't be applied in public organizations. Indeed, there is growing evidence to suggest that it works very well.

Simple Structure, Lean Staff

The "excellence literature" raises doubts about the benefits of economies of scale in organizational structure. In government, as well as private organizations, size often generates complexity. Yet success depends upon the ability to keep things simple. Long standing traditional, public administration concepts tend to perpetuate a hierarchal organization structure in government. Many successful private organizations have shown that this practice may be counter-productive. The successful company makes sure that line managers have the freedom and the resources to do their jobs well. This policy fixes accountability squarely where it belongs.

The concept works in the public sector as well, but its application is much more tenuous. Popular mistrust of government and government officials seem to demand institutional checks and balances that prevent abuse of power but also cloud accountability. To reach excellence, government managers must provide resources to work units that allow them to succeed or fail in their mission; not be overburdened by a corporate staff who tend to reinforce organizational complexity.

Measurement

Finally, successful organizations measure their success. In the private sector, standard profit/loss equations or sales/earning ratios create a natural discipline that is easy to understand. Measurement in the public sector is more difficult. In the absence of reliable, comprehensible performance measures, the public is conditioned to suspect its public servants. Elected officials respond by imposing excessive procedural controls. While not easy, it is possible to measure public agency performance utilizing indicators which are meaningful to top management, to rank and file workers and to the public. Harry P. Hatry[7] and D. Scott Sink *et al.*[8] have offered a number of conceptual and practical ideas about how to do this. However, the focus of accountability in the public sector must shift from process measures to the success of the organization in producing public value.

Top management's insistence that performance be reported and its consistent use of such information is often sufficient to create a market for measurement data. Once created, the demand for performance data can stimulate public servants to overcome the problems of measurement. Success in doing so, over time, will create the conditions of trust that permit flexibility and creativity.

Conclusions

If we were to draw the most important lessons for the public manager from the excellence literature, it would be that good management, whether in the private sector or in the public sector, means the articulation of values and reliance on people to achieve those values.

Public managers must define the public purposes which their organizations serve. Within evident constraints, managers can articulate their vision and obtain the political mandate and capacity to produce the desired public value.

Endnotes

1. See, for example, Thomas J. Peters, and Robert H. Waterman, Jr. *In Search of Excellence: Lessons from America's Best Run Companies*, (New York: Harper & Row, 1982); Craig R. Hickman and Michael A. Silva, *Creating Excellence: Managing Corporate Culture, Strategy, and Change in the New Age*, (New York: New American Library, 1984); Rosabeth Moss Kanter, *The Changemasters: Innovation for Productivity in the American Corporation*. (New York: Simon & Schuster, 1983); Terrence E. Deal and Allan A. Kennedy, *Corporate Cultures: The Rights and Rituals of Corporate Life*, (Reading, Mass.: Addison Wesley, 1982); John Naisbitt, *Megatrends* (New York: Warner Books, 1982); Alan Toffler, *The Third Wave*, (New York: Bantam Books.)

2. J. Peter Grace, *War on Waste, President's Private Sector Survey on Cost Control*, (New York: Macmillan, 1984).

3. See, for example, Charles M. Tiebout, "A Pure Theory of Local Expenditures," *Journal of Political Economy*, LXIV (October 1956, 416–24).

4. Aaron Wildavsky, *The Politics of the Budgetary Process* (Boston: Little, Brown, 1964).

5. Robert A. Leone, Unpublished lecture notes, Kennedy School of Government, 1984.

6. Peters and Waterman, *In Search of Excellence*, 155.

7. Harry P. Hatry, "Performance Measurement Principles and Techniques: An Overview for Local Government," *Public Productivity Review*, IV (December 1980, 312–39).

8. Sandra J. DeVries, D. Scott Sink, and Thomas C. Tuttle, "Productivity Measurement and Evaluation: What is Available?" *National Productivity Review*, Ill, No. 3, 265–87.

Broadening the Concept of Marketing

Philip Kotler
Sidney J. Levy

The term "marketing" connotes to most people a function peculiar to business firms. Marketing is seen as the task of finding and stimulating buyers for the firm's output. It involves product development, pricing, distribution, and communication; and in the more progressive firms, continuous attention to the changing needs of customers and the development of new products, with product modifications and services to meet these needs. But whether marketing is viewed in the old sense of "pushing" prod-

Reprinted with permssion from *Journal of Marketing*, vol. 33 (January 1969), published by the American Marketing Association.

ucts or in the new sense of "customer satisfaction engineering," it is almost always viewed and discussed as a business activity.

It is the authors' contention that marketing is a pervasive societal activity that goes considerably beyond the selling of toothpaste, soap, and steel. Political contests remind us that candidates are marketed as well as soap; student recruitment by colleges reminds us that higher education is marketed; and fund raising reminds us that "causes" are marketed. Yet these areas of marketing are typically ignored by the student of marketing. Or they are treated cursorily as public relations or publicity activities. No attempt is made to incorporate these phenomena in the body proper of marketing thought and theory. No attempt is made to redefine the meaning of product development, pricing, distribution, and communication in these newer contexts to see if they have a useful meaning. No attempt is made to examine whether the principles of "good" marketing in traditional product areas are transferable to the marketing of services, persons, and ideas.

The authors see a great opportunity for marketing people to expand their thinking and to apply their skills to an increasingly interesting range of social activity. The challenge depends on the attention given to it; marketing will either take on a broader social meaning or remain a narrowly defined business activity.

The Rise of Organizational Marketing

One of the most striking trends in the United States is the increasing amount of society's work being performed by organizations other than business firms. As a society moves beyond the stage where shortages of food, clothing, and shelter are the major problems, it begins to organize to meet other social needs that formerly had been put aside. Business enterprises remain a dominant type of organization, but other types of organizations gain in conspicuousness and in influence. Many of these organizations become enormous and require the same rarefied management skills as traditional business organizations. Managing the United Auto Workers, Defense Department, Ford Foundation, World Bank, Catholic Church, and University of California has become every bit as challenging as managing Procter and Gamble, General Motors, and General Electric. These nonbusiness organizations have an increasing range of influence, affect as many livelihoods, and occupy as much media prominence as major business firms.

All of these organizations perform the classic business functions. Every organization must perform a financial function insofar as money must be raised, managed, and budgeted according to sound business principles. Every organization must perform a production function in that it must conceive of the best way of arranging inputs to produce the outputs of the organization. Every organization must perform a personnel function in that people must be hired, trained, assigned, and promoted in the course of the organization's work. Every organization must perform a purchasing function in that it must acquire materials in an efficient way through comparing and selecting sources of supply.

When we come to the marketing function, it is also clear that every organization performs marketing-like activities whether or not they are recognized as such. Several examples can be given.

The police department of a major U.S. city, concerned with the poor image it has among an important segment of its population, developed a campaign to "win friends and influence people." One highlight of this campaign is a "visit your police station" day in which tours are conducted to show citizens the daily operations of the police department, including the crime laboratories, police lineups, and cells. The police department also sends officers to speak at public schools and carries out a number of other activities to improve its community relations.

Most museum directors interpret their primary responsibility as "the proper preservation of an artistic heritage for posterity."[1] As a result, for many people museums are cold marble mausoleums that house miles of relics that soon give way to yawns and tired feet. Although museum attendance in the United States advances each year, a large number of citizens are uninterested in museums. Is this difference due to failure in the manner of presenting what museums have to offer? This nagging question led the new director of the Metropolitan Museum of Art to broaden the museum's appeal through sponsoring contemporary art shows and "happenings." His marketing philosophy of museum management led to substantial increases in the Met's attendance.

The public school system in Oklahoma City sorely needed more public support and funds to prevent a deterioration of facilities and exodus of teachers. It recently resorted to television programming to dramatize the work the public schools were doing to fight the high school dropout problem, to develop new teaching techniques, and to enrich the children. Although an expensive medium, television quickly reached large numbers of parents whose response and interest were tremendous.

Nations also resort to international marketing campaigns to get across important points about themselves to the citizens of other countries. The junta of Greek colonels who seized power in Greece in 1967 found the international publicity surrounding their cause to be extremely unfavorable and potentially disruptive of international recognition. They hired a major New York public relations firm and soon full-page newspaper ads appeared carrying the headline "Greece Was Saved From Communism," detailing in small print why the takeover was necessary for the stability of Greece and the world.[2]

An anti-cigarette group in Canada is trying to press the Canadian legislature to ban cigarettes on the grounds that they are harmful to health. There is widespread support for this cause but the organization's funds are limited, particularly measured against the huge advertising resources of the cigarette industry. The group's problem is to find effective ways to make a little money go along way in persuading influential legislators of the need for discouraging cigarette consumption. This group has come up with several ideas for marketing anti-smoking to Canadians, including television spots, a paperback book featuring pictures of cancer and heart disease patients, and legal research on company liability for the smoker's loss of health.

What concepts are common to these and many other possible illustrations of organizational marketing? All of these organizations are concerned about their "product" in the eyes of certain "consumers" and are seeking to find "tools" for furthering their acceptance. Let us consider each of these concepts in general organizational terms.

Products

Every organization produces a "product" of at least one of the following types:

Physical products. "Product" first brings to mind everyday items like soap, clothes, and food, and extends to cover millions of *tangible* items that have a market value and are available for purchase.

Services. Services are *intangible* goods that are subject to market transaction such as tours, insurance, consultation, hairdos, and banking.

Persons. Personal marketing is an endemic *human* activity, from the employee trying to impress his boss to the statesman trying to win the support of the public. With the advent of mass communications, the marketing of persons has been turned over to professionals. Hollywood stars have their press agents, political candidates their advertising agencies, and so on.

Organizations. Many organizations spend a great deal of time marketing themselves. The Republican Party has invested considerable thought and resources in trying to develop a modern look. The American Medical Association decided recently that it needed to launch a campaign to improve the image of the American doctor.[3] Many charitable organizations and universities see selling their *organization* as their primary responsibility.

Ideas. Many organizations are mainly in the business of selling *ideas* to the larger society. Population organizations are trying to sell the idea of birth control, and the Women's Christian Temperance Union is still trying to sell the idea of prohibition.

Thus the "product" can take many forms, and this is the first crucial point in the case for broadening the concept of marketing.

Consumers

The second crucial point is that organizations must deal with many groups that are interested in their products and can make a difference in its success. It is vitally important to the organization's success that it be sensitive to, serve, and satisfy these groups. One set of groups can be called the *suppliers. Suppliers* are those who provide the management group with the inputs necessary to perform its work and develop its product effectively. Suppliers include employees, vendors of the materials, banks, advertising agencies, and consultants.

The other set of groups are the *consumers* of the organization's product, of which four subgroups can be distinguished. The *clients* are those who are the immediate consumers of the organization's product. The clients of a business firm are its buyers and potential buyers; of a service organization, those receiving the services, such as the needy (from the Salvation Army) or the sick (from County Hospital); and of a protective or a primary organization, the members themselves. The second group is the *trustees* or *directors*, those who are vested with the legal authority and responsibility for the organization, oversee the management, and enjoy a variety of benefits from the "product." The third group is the active *publics* that take a specific interest in the organization. For a business firm, the active publics include consumer rating groups, governmental agencies, and pressure groups of various kinds. For a university, the active publics include alumni and friends of the university, foundations, and city fathers. Finally, the fourth consumer group is the *general public*. These are all the people who might develop attitudes toward the organization that might affect its conduct in some way. Organizational marketing concerns the programs designed by management to create satisfactions and favorable attitudes in the organization's four consuming groups: clients, trustees, active publics, and general public.

Marketing Tools

Students of business firms spend much time studying the various tools under the firm's control that affect product acceptance: product improvement, pricing, distribution, and communication. All of these tools have counterpart applications to nonbusiness organizational activity.

Nonbusiness organizations to various degrees engage in product improvement, especially when they recognize the competition they face from other organizations. Thus, over the years churches have added a host of nonreligious activities to their basic religious activities to satisfy members seeking other bases of human fellowship. Universities keep updating their curricula and adding new student services in an attempt to make the educational experience relevant to the students. Where they have failed to do this, students have sometimes organized their own courses and publications, or have expressed their dissatisfaction in organized protest. Government agencies such as license bureaus, police forces, and taxing bodies are often not responsive to the public because of monopoly status; but even here citizens have shown an increasing readiness to protest mediocre services, and more alert bureaucracies have shown a growing interest in reading the user's needs and developing the required product services.

All organizations face the problem of pricing their products and services so that they cover costs. Churches charge dues, universities charge tuition, governmental agencies charge fees, fund-raising organizations send out bills. Very often specific product charges are not sufficient to meet the organization's budget, and it must rely on gifts and surcharges to make up the difference. Opinions vary as to how much the users should be charged for the individual services and how much should be made up through general collection. If the university increases its tuition, it will have to face losing some students and putting more students on scholarship. If the hospital raises its charges to cover rising costs and additional services, it may provoke a reaction from the community. All organizations face complex pricing issues although not all of them understand good pricing practice.

Distribution is a central concern to the manufacturer seeking to make his goods conveniently accessible to buyers. Distribution also can be an important marketing decision area for nonbusiness organizations. A city's public library has to consider the best means of making its books available to the public. Should it establish one large library with an extensive collection of books, or several neighborhood branch libraries with duplication of books? Should it use bookmobiles that bring the books to the customers instead of relying exclusively on the customers coming to the books? Should it distribute through school libraries? Similarly, the police department of a city must think through the problem of distributing its protective services efficiently through the community. It has to determine how much protective service to allocate to different neighborhoods; the respective merits of squad cars, motorcycles, and foot patrolmen; and the positioning of emergency phones.

Customer communication is an essential activity of all organizations although many nonmarketing organizations often fail to accord it the importance it deserves. Managements of many organizations think they have fully met their communication responsibilities by setting up advertising and/or public relations departments. They fail to realize that *everything about an organization talks.* Customers form impressions of an organization from its physical facilities, employees, officers, stationery, and a hundred other company surrogates. Only when this is appreciated do the members of the organization recognize that they all are in marketing, whatever else they do. With this understanding they can assess realistically the impact of their activities on the consumers.

Concepts for Effective Marketing Management in Nonbusiness Organizations

Although all organizations have products, markets, and marketing tools, the art and science of effective marketing management have reached their highest state of development in the business type of organization. Business organizations depend on customer goodwill for survival and have generally learned how to sense and cater to their needs effectively. As other types of organizations recognize their marketing roles, they will turn increasingly to the body of marketing principles worked out by business organizations and adapt them to their own situations.

What are the main principles of effective marketing management as they appear in most forward-looking business organizations? Nine concepts stand out as crucial in guiding the marketing effort of a business organization.

Generic Product Definition

Business organizations have increasingly recognized the value of placing a broad definition on their products, one that emphasizes the basic customer need(s) being served. A modern soap company recognizes that its basic product is cleaning, not soap; a cosmetics company sees its basic product as beauty or hope, not lipsticks and makeup; a publishing company sees it basic product as information, not books.

The same need for a broader definition of its business is incumbent upon nonbusiness organizations if they are to survive and grow. Churches at one time tended to define their product narrowly as that of producing religious services for members. Recently, most churchmen have decided that their basic product is human fellowship. There was a time when educators said that their product was the three R's. They try to serve the social, emotional, and political needs of young people in addition to intellectual needs.

Target Groups Definition

A generic product definition usually results in defining a very wide market, and it is then necessary for the organization, because of limited resources, to limit its product offering to certain clearly defined groups within the market. Although the generic product of an automobile company is transportation, the company typically sticks to cars, trucks, and buses, and stays away from bicycles, airplanes, and steamships. Furthermore, the manufacturer does not produce every size and shape of car but concentrates on producing a few major types to satisfy certain substantial and specific parts of the market.

In the same way, nonbusiness organizations have to define their target groups carefully. For example, in Chicago the YMCA defines its target groups as men, women, and children who want recreational opportunities and are willing to pay $20 or more a year for them. The Chicago Boys Club, on the other hand, defines its target group as poorer boys within the city boundaries who are in want of recreational facilities and can pay $1 a year.

Differentiated Marketing

When a business organization sets out to serve more than one target group, it will be maximally effective by differentiating its product offerings and communications. This is also true for nonbusiness organizations. Fund-raising organizations have recognized the advantage of treating clients, trustees, and various publics in different ways. These groups require differentiated appeals and frequency of solicitation. Labor unions find that they must address different messages to different parties rather than one message to all parties. To the company they may seem unyielding, to the conciliator they may appear willing to compromise, and to the public they seek to appear economically exploited.

Customer Behavior Analysis

Business organizations are increasingly recognizing that customer needs and behavior are not obvious without formal research and analysis; they cannot rely on impressionistic evidence. Soap companies spend hundreds of thousands of dollars each year researching how Mrs. Housewife feels about her laundry; how, when, and where she does her laundry; and what she desires of a detergent.

Fund raising illustrates how an industry has benefited by replacing stereotypes of donors with studies of why people contribute to causes. Fund raisers have learned that people give because they are getting something. Many give to community chests to relieve a sense of fear that they may be struck by a disease whose cure has not yet been found. Some give to feel pride. Fund raisers have stressed the importance of identifying the motives operating in the marketplace of givers as a basis for planning drives.

Differential Advantages

In considering different ways of reaching target groups, an organization is advised to think in terms of seeking a differential advantage. It should consider what elements in its reputation or resources can be exploited to create a special value in the minds of its potential customers. In the same way Zenith has built a reputation for quality and International Harvester a reputation for service, a nonbusiness organization should base its case on some dramatic value that competitive organizations lack. The small island of Nassau can compete against Miami for the tourist trade by advertising the greater dependability of its weather; the Heart Association can compete for funds against the Cancer Society by advertising the amazing strides made in heart research.

Multiple Marketing Tool

The modern business firm relies on a multitude of tools to sell its product, including product improvement, consumer and dealer advertising, salesman incentive programs, sales promotions, contests, multiple-size offerings, and so forth. Likewise nonbusiness organizations also can reach their audiences in a variety of ways. A church can sustain the interest of its members through discussion groups, newsletters, news releases, campaign drives, annual reports, and retreats. Its "salesmen" include the religious head, the board members, and the present members in terms of attracting potential members. Its advertising includes announcements of weddings, births and deaths, religious pronouncements, and newsworthy developments.

Integrated Marketing Planning

The multiplicity of available marketing tools suggests that desirability of overall coordination so that these tools do not work at cross purposes. Over time, business firms have placed under a marketing vice president activities that were previously managed in a semi-autonomous fashion, such as sales, advertising, and marketing research. Nonbusiness organizations typically have not integrated their marketing activities. Thus, no single officer in the typical university is given total responsibility for studying the needs and attitudes of clients, trustees, and publics, and undertaking the necessary product development and communication programs to serve these groups. The university administration instead includes a variety of "marketing" positions such as dean of students, director of alumni affairs, director of public relations, and director of development; coordination is often poor.

Continuous Marketing Feedback

Business organizations gather continuous information about changes in the environment and about their own performance. They use their salesmen, research department, specialized research services, and other means to check on the movement of goods, actions of competitors, and feelings of customers to make sure they are progressing along satisfactory lines. Nonbusiness organizations typically are more casual about collecting vital information on how they are doing and what is happening in the marketplace. Universities have been caught off guard by underestimating the magnitude of student grievance and unrest, and so have major cities underestimated the degree to which they were failing to meet the needs of important minority constituencies.

Marketing Audit

Change is a fact of life, although it may proceed almost invisibly on a day-to-day basis. Over a long stretch of time it might be so fundamental as to threaten organizations that have not provided for periodic reexaminations of their purposes. Organizations can grow set in their ways and unresponsive to new opportunities or problems. Some great American companies are no longer with us because they did not change definitions of their businesses, and their products lost relevance in a changing world. Political parties become unresponsive after they enjoy power for a while and every so often experience a major upset. Many union leaders grow insensitive to new needs and problems until one day they find themselves out of office. For an organization to remain viable, its management must provide for periodic audits of its objectives, resources, and opportunities. It must reexamine its basic business, target groups, differential advantage, communication channels, and messages in the light of current trends and needs. It might recognize when change is needed and make it before it is too late.

Is Organizational Marketing a Socially Useful Activity?

Modern marketing has two different meanings in the minds of people who use the term. One meaning of marketing conjures up the terms selling, influencing, persuading. Marketing is seen as a huge and increasingly dangerous technology, making it possible to sell persons on buying things, propositions, and causes they either do not want or which are bad for them. This was the indictment in Vance Packard's *Hidden Persuaders* and numerous other social criticisms, with the net effect that a large number of persons think of marketing as immoral or entirely self-seeking in its fundamental premises. They can be counted on to resist the idea of organizational marketing as so much "Madison Avenue."

The other meaning of marketing unfortunately is weaker in the public mind; it is the concept of sensitively *serving and satisfying human needs.* This was the great contribution of the marketing concept that was promulgated in the 1950s, and that concept now counts many business firms as its practitioners. The marketing concept holds that the problem of all business firms in an age of abundance is to develop customer loyalties and satisfaction, and the key to this problem is to focus on the customer's needs.[4] Perhaps the short-run problem of business firms is to sell people on buying the existing products, but the long-run problem is clearly to create the products that people need. By this recognition that effective marketing requires a consumer orientation instead of a product orientation, marketing has taken a new lease on life and tied its economic activity to a higher social purpose.

It is this second side of marketing that provides a useful concept for all organizations. All organizations are formed to serve the interest of particular groups: hospitals serve the sick, schools serve the students, governments serve the citizens, and labor unions serve the members. In the course of evolving, many organizations lose sight of their original mandate, grow hard, and become self-serving. The bureaucratic mentality begins to dominate the original service mentality. Hospitals may become perfunctory in their handling of patients, schools treat their students as nuisances, city bureaucrats behave like petty tyrants toward the citizens, and labor unions try to run instead of serve their members. All of these actions tend to build frustration in the consuming groups. As a result some withdraw meekly from these organizations, accept frustration as part of their condition, and find their satisfactions elsewhere. This used to be the common reaction of ghetto Negroes and college students in the face of indifferent city and university bureaucracies. But new possibilities have arisen, and now the same consumers refuse to withdraw so readily. Organized dissent and protest are seen to be an answer, and many organizations thinking of themselves as responsible have been stunned into recognizing that they have lost touch with their constituencies. They had grown unresponsive.

Where does marketing fit into this picture? Marketing is that function of the organization that can keep in constant touch with the organization's consumers, read their needs, develop "products" that meet these needs, and build a program of communications to express the organization's purposes. Certainly selling and influencing will be large parts of organizational marketing; but, properly seen, selling follows rather than precedes the organization's drive to create products to satisfy its consumers.

Conclusion

It has been argued here that the modern marketing concept serves very naturally to describe an important facet of all organizational activity. All organizations must develop appropriate products to serve their sundry consuming groups and must use modern tools of communication to reach their consuming publics. The business heritage of marketing provides a useful set of concepts for guiding all organizations.

The choice facing those who manage nonbusiness organizations is not whether to market or not to market, for no organization can avoid marketing. The choice is whether to do it well or poorly, and on this necessity the case for organizational marketing is basically founded.

Endnotes

1. This is the view of Sherman Lee, director of the Cleveland Museum, quoted in *Newsweek*, Vol. 71 (April 1, 1968), 55.

2. "PR for the Colonels," *Newsweek*, Vol. 71 (March 18, 1968), 70.

3. "Doctors Try an Image Transplant," *Business Week*, No. 2025 (June 22, 1968), 64.

4. Theodore Levitt, "Marketing Myopia," *Harvard Business Review*, Vol. 38 (July–August, 1960), 45–56.

Privatization in the United States

Frances P. Clark

Introduction

Privatization is a worldwide phenomenon which has gained major attention in the last decade. Based on the belief that private enterpreneurship and private markets can operate services more effectively and efficiently than

Reprinted with permission from the *SPEA Review* (Spring 1989) vol. 10, no. 2, published by the School of Public and Environmental Affairs, Indiana University, Indianapolis, IN 46223.

can governments, it has struck a responsive cord in developed and developing countries alike. Few countries have escaped its influence—even Eastern block countries and China are experimenting with it.

While privatization has been public policy in the United States for much of this decade, 1987–1988 may be its pivotal period. During these two years the federal government sold its 85% share of Conrail, the nation's freight rail system, for almost $1.9 billion; loans with a face value of $7.9 billion were sold or prepaid by borrowers yielding $5.6 billion in gross proceeds; approximately 140,000 low-income families received housing assistance through vouchers allowing them to subsidize their rents in the private market; a Presidential Commission on Privatization was established to recommend privatization opportunities; and an Office of Privatization was established within the Office of Management and Budget to develop strategies for implementation of the President's privatization program. During the same period, state and local governments continued to contract out services. Contracting for jails and prisons and other infrastructure projects were the hottest issues.

Over and above these privatization successes, the 1987–1988 time frame is important because, for the first time in the United States, privatization made its way into the popular culture. "Privatization" is now in the dictionary, and mentioned as background in novels and TV shows. Media coverage increased significantly. Before 1987, it was rare for a newspaper or a popular magazine to carry an article on privatization. Now at least one article appears daily in a major newspaper or journal, and frequently four to five a day. The popular press is particularly adept at ferreting out the general public interests, and is, therefore, a good barometer of that interest. The current level of coverage indicates that the taxpayer or the average citizen is becoming more interested in privatization—an essential ingredient for major progress.

This discussion will provide an overview of the current status of privatization in the United States and recent events at the federal, state, and local government levels.

Characteristics of Privatization in the United States

Privatization Is Broader Than Divestiture or Sale of Assets

In many countries, privatization is essentially denationalization of major industries run by the government. In these cases, privatization is synonymous with divestiture or the sale of government-owned assets to the private sector. Indeed, asset sales is the image that is conjured up by the public, even in the U.S., when privatization is mentioned.

However, in the United States, privatization is not just asset sales. In the United States, asset sales are not the only, or even the principal, form of privatization. Unlike Britain or France, the United States, never aggressively nationalized commercial enterprises. What commercial-like enterprises are owned by the government have been governmental since inception or generally are believed to be unable to survive in a competitive market. Examples of enterprises which have been governmental since inception include the Tennessee Valley Authority and Bonneville Power (large electrical power enterprises) and uranium enrichment. Amtrak, the government-financed passenger rail service, and the Postal Service are typical of entities with are perceived unable to survive in a competitive market. Enterprises performing these functions are viewed as inherently governmental throughout the world. Beyond these few major enterprises, what remains are several similar entities producing limited services or products for narrow markets (helium production, the National Technical Information Service, Alaska Power Marketing Administration) or the government's vast portfolio of loan assets.

The remainder of the government is comprised of a vast array of service-oriented programs that are more amenable to vouchers or to contracting than they are to divestiture. Vouchers are used to provide cash or the equivalent to program beneficiaries so that they can acquire the service themselves from private providers. Examples of vouchers or voucher-like programs are food stamps instead of food, housing vouchers instead of public housing, Medicare instead of government doctors and hospitals, and student loans instead of Federal universities. In the United States, most of the income transfer and social welfare programs that are amenable to being operated through vouchers are already in this form, and few opportunities remain.

This leaves contracting out as the privatization technique most applicable to the remaining government programs which are not suitable for divestiture or vouchers. These are often discretionary programs, operated by professional and clerical workers possessing the same skills found in the private sector. What is of unique value, however, is the *franchise* or *contract* that such programs implicitly have with the government. In many instances, this franchise or contract can be put out for bid to other private providers without any diminution in the quality or reliability of the service.

Privatization Is At All Levels of Government

Privatization is not just a phenomenon of the federal government, but rather it is occurring simultaneously at *all* levels of government. It is neither a top-down nor bottom-up type of movement. Each level of government—state, local, or federal—is exploring and learning as it goes, learning from the other levels of government in the process. Each level has different reasons for pursuing privatization, different forms of privatization, and different degrees of success. As the problems differ, the uses of the private sector to solve them also differ.

At the state and local government level, privatization is characterized by contracting out and infrastructure proposals with few asset sales. It is viewed very much as a tool to solve practical problems—increased service, decreased costs, replacement of existing service.

At the federal level privatization consists of all types of privatization—

asset sales, contracting out, vouchers, and deregulation. It is also more caught up in the ideological debate on the "proper role of government." With time, however, the federal government is slowly shifting to using privatization as a public policy tool.

Active Debate Among All Participants

In the United States, taxpayers, unions, employees, business communities, legislatures, and government entities are all active participants in the privatization debate. It is not an orderly debate, and progress is frequently characterized by two steps forward and one step back. Sides are continually shifting. Unions, employees, taxpayers, legislators—all of these people have active roles and they are constantly changing sides. More and more, traditional opponents of privatization are finding themselves on the other side of the argument. Just recently, for example, a non-government union proposed organizing employee buy-outs of government activities. Privatization is both a Republican and a Democratic party phenomenon. At the federal level it is currently a Republican effort but contracting out has its antecedents in the prior Democratic administrations. Deregulation was first championed by the Democratic Carter Administration. At the state and local level many liberal democrats have led the way for privatization. It cannot be characterized either as a liberal or conservative movement. It varies by location and, particularly, by the type of activity being proposed for privatization.

Privatization at the State and Local Government Level

In many respects privatization in the United States has been led by state and local governments. Officials there have turned to privatization to satisfy real and practical problems—problems of taxpayers demanding increases in services without comparable increases in taxes.

Contracting Out

Privatization at the state and local level has occurred in two principal forms—contracting out and infrastructure development—more the former than the latter. Touche Ross, a national accounting firm, conducted a survey of state and local governments in 1987, sending questionnaires to 5,700 city and county officials. The response rate was approximately 20%. Nearly 80% of the respondents indicated that privatization represented a primary potential tool for providing local government services and facilities in the next decade. About the same number had used privatization before or planned to use it in the future. The survey results indicate that state and local governments contract out a wide variety of community services—building maintenance services, airport operation and maintenance, day care facilities, data processing, vehicle maintenance, towing of vehicles, parking meter collection, and sanitation collection. Specific examples include:

- Newark, New Jersey, contracts out its sewer cleaning, computer services, snow removal, street sweeping, and tree and stump removal;
- Phoenix, Arizona, one of the leaders in contracting out at the local level, contracts out building and grounds maintenance, municipal parking lots, security, storage of towed cars, and similar functions.
- Los Angeles county has an aggressive contracting out program accomplished with minimal adverse effect to county employees who were holding those jobs when the private sector assumed control. The country contracts out motor vehicle operation and repair, building and grounds maintenance, custodial services, and security guard service.

About 98% of the people who responded to the Touche Ross survey had engaged in some kind of contracting out in their community and the contracts had reduced costs. About four-fifths of the people had received positive cost savings and indicated that they were going to continue to pursue contracting out. The cost saving at the state and local government level is in the order of 10%–40%. (This is consistent with similar experience at the federal level which averages about 30% savings.)

Infrastructure privatization

The second area in which state and local governments are increasingly active is infrastructure privatization. In the United States today there has been a revival in infrastructure interest, largely because existing roads, bridges, buildings, waste water treatment plants, and prisons are in great need of repair or renovation. In addition, the demand for new infrastructure, especially in urban areas, is increasing at a rapid rate. The recently published report to the President by the National Council on Public Works Improvement, *Fragile Foundations: A Report on America's Public Works*, estimates that $90 billion, a doubling of our current infrastructure, will be needed annually to address these needs. Capital investment resources of the magnitude needed to repair existing infrastructure and to satisfy needs for new infrastructure are beyond the reach of all levels of government, particularly in light of other competing needs. But as state and local governments are coming to realize, the private sector represents an untapped source for new capital as well as managerial and development expertise. As a consequence, they are increasingly turning to the private sector to provide these kinds of services. Approximately one-third of the governments using privatization surveyed by Touche Ross have turned to the private sector to build (or buy) and operate capital facilities for the government. Nearly 40% expect to arrange this kind of privatization in the next two years. The range of facilities that have been and can be privatized is broad. In the last five years, local governments have privatized roads, bridges, tunnels, wastewater treatment plants, municipal buildings and garages, and prisons. In the next two years, they expect to continue this trend. Privatization of stadiums, municipal buildings and garages, and correctional facilities is expected to increase substantially. Touche Ross estimates that nearly $3 billion worth of facilities will be privatized by its survey respondents over the next two years.

Examples of current or recently completed major private infrastructure projects include the approved Dulles Toll Road Extension in northern Virginia, the proposed Chicago-Kansas City Toll Road, a $2.2 billion, 400-mile private tollway project intended to stimulate development along a corridor in Illinois and Missouri, and the recently completed Fargo North Dakota-Moorhead Minnesota Bridge. The last is the first private toll bridge in 40 years. The private owners have the primary responsibility for setting toll rates, managing revenues, controlling expenses, and marketing.

Kentucky and other states are using the private sector to accommodate the overcrowding in prisons and the increase in prisoner population by building prisons with private sector capital and leasing them to the local community. In many cases the prisons will be maintained and operated by the private sector firm, and then turned over to the local government at the end of the contract period. For example, the U.S. Corrections Corporation was hired to house state inmates in the town of St. Mary, Kentucky. The company built the facility in a record nine-month period and operates it in accordance with American Correctional Association standards. According to Kentucky governor, Martha Lane Collins, the state avoided costs of some $10 million by contracting with the company. The Corrections Corporation of America (CCA), one of the nation's largest private corrections companies, was awarded two contracts for secure, pre-release facilities in Cleveland, Ohio, and Venus, Texas. CCA also recently obtained a contract to operate a facility in France. Another large firm, the Wachenhut Corporation, received awards for two similar facilities—one in Bridgeport, Texas, and the other in the Austin-San Antonio corridor. Prison privatization has advanced to the point that the city of Ault, Colorado, is building a prison on spec as a measure of its faith in the burgeoning private sector opportunities and for purposes of local economic development and jobs. When completed it plans to lease the prison to the local and state prison authorities.

Another indication of state and local government interest in privatization can be found in the recent activities of state legislatures. Currently, eight to ten state legislatures have ongoing privatization proposals or studies. The State of Virginia, for example, recently passed legislation to allow for the construction and operation of private toll roads. The Governor of Indiana asked the legislature to consider private sector operation of many typical municipal services including prisons, waste water treatment plants, etc., and a legislative study group recently recommended privatization of at least one prison. Finally, a bill passed the Georgia State Senate to form a joint legislative committee to study the desirability of contracting out government services and to identify government activities that compete with private enterprise.

Privatization at the Federal Level

At the federal level, the 1987 and 1988 period has been very important as well. Successful privatization initiatives range from cases simply improving operational efficiency to cases that will have profound effects on the way the federal government runs vital programs. For example:

- The federal government's 85% share of Conrail, our national freight rail service, was sold for almost $1.9 billion. It is the country's largest public offering to date.
- A *loan asset sales* program, established as part of the Administration's program to improve the management of its $234 billion portfolio of direct loans, was started in 1987. Loans with a face value of $7.9 billion were sold or prepaid by borrowers yielding $5.6 billion dollars in gross proceeds. The sales produced significant management improvements in addition to their contribution to deficit reduction. Additionally, the federal government's administrative costs will decrease over time as the private sector assumes the service and collection responsibilities for the loans. At the same time, federal agencies are adopting private sector standards and operating procedures, thereby upgrading their systems to accommodate the information demands of the market.
- Under the *housing voucher program*, 140,000 low-income families in the United States received housing assistance. The Administration has requested funding for another 127,500 vouchers in 1989. These vouchers are provided directly to low-income households to subsidize their rents in the private market. They are not tied to particular units, but are portable and independent of the actual rent for a given unit. Households thus have a much wider range of housing choices and stronger incentives to shop around. The voucher also moves the Federal government out of new construction and its overlay of multiple subsidies, which cost two to three times as much as vouchers cost to provide housing to needy households.
- *Tenant management of public housing projects* are improving living conditions, reducing operating costs, and increasing resident involvement in decisions about their immediate environment. A recent study found that the tenant managers at Kenilworth-Parkside in Washington, D.C. had increased rent collection by 77% and cut administrative costs by 60% since the experiment began. The same study estimated the net benefit to the city at $4.5 million from 1982 through 1991, including savings from lower Federal operating subsidies to the project, increased tax collections, and reduced welfare dependency and crime. These types of tenant management efforts are the first step toward conversion of a project to cooperative ownership.
- Since 1981, the federal government has saved $700 million a year and eliminated over 70,000 staff years through its *contracting out program*. This has been accomplished without loss of quality or

service. For example, the National Oceanic and Atmospheric Administration's (NOAA) Climatic Data Center employed 114 personnel to provide automated data processing, archival and technical support at a cost of $2.7 million per year. A cost competition between the government and the private sector resulted in an award to a private contractor for $2 million per year, a savings of $700,000 per year of $3.4 million over the five-year contract period.

In addition to these successes, the Administration embarked on a major effort in 1987 to accelerate privatization at the federal level. This new effort consists of four major thrusts:

- First, an *Office of Privatization*, headed by an Associate Director, was created within the Office of Management and Budget to develop strategies for the implementation of the President's privatization program and to provide leadership and coordination for privatization efforts. The Office acts as a clearinghouse for the Administration's privatization efforts. The Office has surfaced and advanced the privatization debate on a mature rational basis, trying to eliminate the emotionalism surrounding privatization. Its goal is to focus on public policy problems and determine if privatization can be used as a tool for solving those problems. In this way the fears and emotionalism that surround privatization can be minimized, and the public can be educated at the same time.
- Second, as part of his Economic Bill of Rights, President Reagan created a *Presidential Commission on Privatization*. This twelve-member, bipartisan Commission reviewed and recommended the appropriate division of responsibilities between the federal government and the private sector, as well as recommended implementation priorities and strategies. The Commission issued its final report in March, 1988. The President endorsed its recommendations in principle, and specific implementing plans and legislation are now being developed.

  The Commission recommended a phased or gradual approach to privatization, recognizing that the extreme options in privatization at this stage of its evolution in the United States probably would not be accepted by the general public. For example, for the postal service, they have recommended achieving increased efficiencies in the current system through contracting out; turning over unprofitable areas in the postal service to the private sector (for example the delivery of mail in the rural areas); as well as eliminating private express statutes which give the postal service monopoly status. Their approach was similar in air traffic control. Again with the public's concern of safety, they did not recommend an immediate turnover of the complete air traffic control system to the private sector. Rather, they recommended increased contracting out of services at airports, turning over some of the air traffic control functions and some of the smaller more rural air traffic control systems—a very incremental approach to privatizing the function. Most of their recommendations used privatization as a tool for improving services and reducing cost.

- Third, the President issued *Executive Order 12615* on contracting out which reinforces the government's policy of reliance on the private sector for the provision of commercial goods and services. The Executive Order requires agencies to designate senior officials to coordinate privatization efforts and meet aggressive goals to study activities for performance by the private sector. Agencies are provided an incentive to meet their goals by taking out the anticipated savings from the budget in advance. They are also provided with incentives to minimize the effect on the employees by encouraging employee equity participation programs, providing incentives to the employees for participating in the process. The Office of Personnel Management is also required to revamp personnel policies and regulations to give government managers the flexibility to organize in the most efficient manner and to reduce adverse effects of contracting out on employees.
- Finally, as a consequence of the above initiatives, a *Fiscal Year 1989 Privatization Plan*, consisting of a number of new privatization efforts to improve the services provided by the government, was developed. A three-tier approach was used. For those functions where there is anecdotal evidence that indicated privatization would be beneficial, but where there was a significant amount of emotionalism, comprehensive studies are to be performed. Three studies are to be performed—on the postal service, uranium enrichment, and air traffic control. The studies are to provide definitive information on which to base any decisions to go forward in privatization.

  The second tier consists of a series of pilot projects. Projects were chosen where a body of previous privatization experience exists at either the state and local government level or in similar functions at the federal level. Functions which were easily severable, allowing tests on a portion which could then be applied to the whole were also selected. These pilots will provide the opportunity to test privatization techniques before making major programmatic changes. They will also demonstrate the benefits of privatization while allowing fine-tuning of implementation strategies. Typical examples of pilot projects include (1) prisons; (2) Federal Prison Industries, Inc.; (3) commercial cargo inspection; (4) military commissaries; (5) Coast Guard Buoy Maintenance and (6) leasing undeveloped lands.

  Last, there are many instances where public enterprises can be privatized without the need of further study. Included in this category are many of the Administration's previous proposals as well as the continuation of on-going contracting out efforts.

The following section provides a more detailed description of the Fiscal Year 1989 Privatization Plan. It includes many previously proposed initiatives and ongoing contracting out efforts as well as new initiatives.

1989 Privatization Plan

The 1989 Privatization Plan is designed to create an environment conducive to greater privatization successes by recognizing that each privatization opportunity is unique and that the process of implementing it must be tailored to special features. To link the opportunity with the process better, the Plan proposes three different implementation processes that have been developed based on the complexity of the subject and the public perception of each opportunity.

Comprehensive Studies

During 1989, comprehensive studies will be conducted on at least three major government enterprises to determine the benefits from privatization and recommend alternative implementation strategies. They include:

U.S. Postal Service (USPS): The USPS is the Nation's largest retail operation, generating $32 billion in 1987. Although the Postal Service has been granted a legal monopoly on first class mail by Congress, there are a number of important niches where private sector providers are allowed to operate, and where they are now serious competitors with USPS. These niches include package and express delivery, international first class and unaddressed third class mail. Evidence points to the likelihood that a private postal service could guarantee faster delivery for less than $0.22 an ounce. As one alternative form of privatization, the existing work force could be given a portion of the shares of a newly privatized postal service. According to some estimates of USPS net worth, such a distribution, even if limited to just a portion of the company, could be worth a substantial sum to each worker.

Because of the size and complexity of the USPS, additional, definitive information is necessary before a decision to privatize can be made and to determine the best method in which to proceed. During 1989, a study will be conducted by a well-respected, independent organization to resolve any areas of dispute.

Uranium Enrichment Facilities: America's uranium enrichment program is in serious trouble. It has accumulated, according to the General Accounting Office (GAO), a deficit of $8.8 billion in the civilian portion of the program. At the same time, it is losing market share to foreign competitors. Its former global monopoly has been destroyed as European state-owned enterprises compete for foreign market share. With the Japanese expected to complete their own production facility by the early 1990s, competitive pressure will only worsen. As a result of mounting costs and technological obsolescence, privatization in some form is becoming an increasingly attractive solution to these and other problems.

The debate over privatization needs not only to address the enrichment business but also ancillary issues such as the debt owed to the Treasury, the clean-up of radioactive sites, the status of mine workers, the choice of technology and facilities, the value of the enterprise, the impact on the United States' security and the likely impact on our international competitive position.

However, P. L. 100–202, a continuing appropriation bill for the fiscal year ending September 20, 1988, prohibits the use of any funds made available under the 1988 appropriation process or any other appropriation for the "study, review or to otherwise evaluate the transfer of the Federal ownership, management or control, in whole or in part, of the facilities, assets and functions of the uranium supply and enrichment program, until such activities have been specifically authorized by Congress." The administration therefore proposes that Congress specifically authorize and encourage the administration to study the feasibility of privatizing the federal government's uranium enrichment facilities. This request was submitted to Congress during 1988.

Although many of these issues have been dealt with separately, they need a comprehensive framework that will foster rational consideration of privatization alternatives. The proposed study will address all of these concerns and provide a detailed plan for future action.

National Institute of Health (NIH): The NIH has reported difficulties in recruiting and retaining top scientists in its intramural research labs, which make up about 10% of its budget. To address this problem, HHS plans to convene a study group to develop strategies for long-term excellence of the in-house NIH laboratories. The Administration believes a 4–5 month independent study of the various options, conducted by a broad base of individuals familiar with federal, university, and medical research entities will provide the Administration with information which will be useful to improve the NIH's efficiency. The study will focus on strategies to ensure the continued competitiveness of the NIH in-house laboratories. The study will consider the efficacy of: (1) establishing the NIH intramural laboratories as a free-standing government (within or outside HHS) or non-governmental research institute; (2) incremental changes to the status quo; (3) continuation of the status quo; and (4) other organizational structural or human resource changes.

Pilot Projects

Pilot projects for 1989 include:

Federal Prisons: A growing prison population, escalating costs and budget limitations are among the key factors prompting an examination of prison privatization. Private sector participation has already increased in state, local, and federal prisons in: (1) financing and construction of prisons; and (2) management, operation, and maintenance of prisons. Although the data from state and local prisons vary, most private prisons are operating at a lower cost. Additionally, there is some data which indicate that private prisons operate with a lower recidivism rate than their public counterparts.

At least 12 states have contracted for prison facilities, adding over 4,000 beds through some type of lease arrangement with the private sector. The federal government, too, has experimented with prison privatization, especially for confinement services. The Immigration and Naturalization Service (INS) has nine facility contracts for aliens awaiting deportation; the U.S. Marshall Service has contracted for two small 30-bed facilities; and the Federal Bureau of Prisons has a 60-bed facility for juvenile offenders. All federal half-way houses have been contracted out in the last few years.

A minimum of four pilot projects will be conducted to further test the viability of prison privatization. At least three prisons will be leased during 1989 and the Department of Justice will test private sector management and operation as well as provision of work programs at either a new prison and/or an existing minimum security prison.

Federal Prison Industries, Inc. (UNICOR): Private sector provision of work programs may hold the greatest promise for changing current confinement practices. The notion of a prison as a total work-like environment that operates on a profitable basis and pays inmates a fair wage is extremely appealing. It would allow inmates to contribute to the cost of confinement, increase the tax base, and cut welfare costs by providing income to prisoner families as well as provide training and productive work opportunities.

The Federal Prison Industries, Inc., known as UNICOR, provides work programs for the federal prison system. It is a major commercial endeavor which employs and trains inmates by operating industries that manufacture products for federal agencies. It generated over $300 million in revenues in 1987. As of December 1987, it employed over 1,200 federal employees and was training 15,000 inmates (48% of the federal prison population). The last several years have been a period of very rapid growth. Physical plants and equipment have been increased and modernized, and more federal funds have been requested for additional growth. However, by the end of its expansion phase it still will be unable to offer factory jobs to all inmates who want and are capable of holding one.

Private firms exist that perform the same functions in many state prison systems. During 1989, a pilot project will privatize a portion of UNICOR to allow the evaluation of true cost/benefits of privatization and create a workable structure of cooperation between all affected parties before considering a divestiture of the enterprise, in whole or in parts.

Commercial Cargo Inspection: The U.S. Customs Service is responsible for assessing tariffs, honoring quotas, enforcing shipping act requirements and preventing commercial fraud. While millions of dollars have been collected annually from shipper violations, only about 2% of imports are inspected. Internal audit and commercial cargo inspection resources are available from the private sector which regularly conduct documentary and physical verification for private parties. Privatization would cause cost savings for audit and inspection services or permit more inspections, increased tariff and penalty collection for the Treasury and allow Customs Service to devote its scarce resources to other pressing needs such as drug enforcement and border security. Customs conducted a privatization study in CY 1988 to identify feasible pilot projects to be implemented in at least three ports. In 1989, Customs will establish and implement these pilot programs using private sector cargo inspection and regulatory audit services.

Military Commissaries: Commissary stores, located on military installations in the U.S. and abroad, sell groceries to active duty, reserve, and retired military personnel. The system employs over 22,000 people with annual sales of more than $5 billion. Experience with contracting shows that savings as high as 40% can be achieved. Economies of scale are possible if large retailers are allowed to rely on their extensive networks to operate the facilities. During 1988/1989 the Department of Defense will complete a pilot program to determine if the private sector can operate and manage commissary facilities more efficiently than the Department of Defense.

Coast Guard buoy maintenance: The federal government owns and operates approximately half of the marine buoys currently in operation. In 1987 and 1988, the U.S. Coast Guard (USCG) agreed to contract out the operation of buoys at five service areas and will add another three stations in 1989. The USCG will also hire a private consulting firm to study the cost and benefits associated with private sector performance of additional buoy maintenance. The study will evaluate the USCG's cost allocation method, the quality of the service provided by the private sector contractors, as well as the public's acceptance of the private contractor's services. If the data indicate that the private sector is capable of providing the service on a cost-effective basis, the USCG will move to contract out more of its buoy maintenance operations.

Undeveloped lands: Federal ownership of land is extensive—comprising about 730 million acres or one-third of the nation. Federal management of these lands has been the subject of a great amount of contention over the years, precluding efficient management in some situations. This, together with growing experience in land management and ownership by environmental and conservation groups, may offer an opportunity to achieve better land management and provide more diverse benefits to society. Changing property rights and inventories may lead to improved management which ensures environmental protection, while permitting recreation and commercial activities under controlled circumstances. Revenues earned from the commercial activities could be used to manage better the entire parcel of land as well as fund other conservation activities.

The Department of Interior will establish at least ten pilot projects during 1989 which will allow private environmental/conservation organizations to obtain long-term leases to manage large tracts of undeveloped land throughout the United States at nominal fees. These pilots will be evaluated to determine the benefits to society of long-term leases and to assure the reduction in costs. Only if the pilots are successful would the program be expanded.

During 1988, the Department of Agriculture will conduct a study to determine if the program can be duplicated in the lands under its control. This study will evaluate any legislative or regulatory prohibitions which may limit privatization of the lands under the Department's control as well as the public policy implications associated with this proposal.

Full Privatization

In addition to the on-going privatization initiatives such as loan asset sales, credit and housing vouchers, the 1989 Budget will propose several new initiatives.

Tax dispute resolution procedures: The Internal Revenue Service (IRS) will develop regulations that permit taxpayers with disputes filed in the U.S. Tax Court to use private alternative dispute resolutions (ADR) firms to resolve their disputes. If a private ADR firm satisfies the provision of the IRS regulations, the taxpayer will be permitted to transfer his case from the Tax Court to the private ADR firm. The decision rendered by the ADR firm will be binding on both parties. Currently there are approximately 80,000 cases pending in the Tax Court involving over $20 billion in disputed Federal income taxes. The process takes an average of 24 months before a final decision is rendered. The private sector currently has in place an adjudication [time of] six months because of its ability to quickly adjust the number of judges as the docket changes. This approach is superior to the competing legislative proposals that would permit taxpayers, whether guilty or not, to settle automatically for a portion of the disputed claim rather than wait for a hearing in Tax Court.

Booking functions for concessional food programs: The Departments of Transportation (DOT) and Agriculture (USDA) and the Agency for International Development (AID) share responsibility for concessional food programs (Food for Peace, etc.) By the end of 1989, the USDA in cooperation with the DOT and AID will pursue private sector assessment and development of automated information needs leading to the ultimate privatization of automated information needs for transportation and commodity procurement-related programs. A recent GAO study estimated that between $12–$24 million could be saved annually and improved procurement practices and increased competition would result from such private sector participation.

Wastewater treatment plants. Privatization of wastewater treatment plants has been implemented successfully in a number of local communities. Currently over 50 cities contract out sewage plant operations. Private construction and operating costs generally run 20%–30% below publicly owned facilities; and construction time for a private plant is about two years compared with seven years when public funds are used. Many communities, especially in the Northeast, will have to rebuild their aging, 20- to 30-year-old plants in the near future. During 1989, the Environmental Protection Agency will establish an Office of Private Sector Initiatives, which will encourage and assist communities in developing innovative private investment strategies.

Employee housing: The Department of Defense will continue its efforts to increase private sector involvement through increased use of private housing stock. During 1989 private sector lease/construction, management and operation of Government housing will be used when private sector stock is unavailable and opportunities will be explored to develop similar programs at the Departments of Agriculture and Interior.

Mass Transit Projects: The Urban Mass Transportation Administration (UMTA) provides capital and operating assistance to public and private transit providers. UMTA has required all of its grant recipients to evaluate each new project to determine if it is amenable to privatization. Furthermore, all existing public mass transit services must be evaluated periodically to determine if they can be privatized. UMTA's grant recipients have reduced the cost of delivering mass transit service by 20% to 50% depending on the type of service contracted out. Unfortunately, legislative and external administrative barriers (such as the provision of the Urban Mass Transportation Act of 1964, as amended, which requires that the U.S. Secretary of Labor certify that UMTA-assisted projects do not adversely affect mass transit employees) have limited the ability of UMTA's grant recipients to implement privatization opportunities. These barriers have resulted in service not being offered or offered at a much higher cost. UMTA and OMB will work together to lessen these barriers to privatization.

National Finance Center: The Department of Agriculture, Office of Personnel Management, and Office of Management and Budget are currently working on a plan to privatize the National Finance Center (NFC) during 1989 using the Federal Employee Direct Corporate Ownership Opportunity Plan, or FED CO-OP. Located in New Orleans, the Center operates automated financial management systems for USDA and non-USDA Federal agencies. NFC activities include payments, accounts receivable, central accounting, payroll/personnel, and property management information. These are all commercial services available from the private sector.

Rural Telephone Bank: The Rural Telephone Bank (RTB) provides subsidized loans to rural telephone cooperatives for the construction and upgrade of rural telephone systems. Almost all RTB borrowers have the financial strength to borrow privately without any assistance from the government. Some RTB borrowers are subsidiaries of multibillion-dollar telecommunications holding companies who have a well-demonstrated ability to borrow from the private capital markets. Furthermore, over 96% of rural areas now have telephone service. The Administration therefore proposes that the RTB take the steps necessary to privatize the RTB, as called for in its authorizing statute, including setting aside $30 million per year to repurchase Treasury owned Class A stock of over $500 million (that pays a 2% annual dividend). The Administration's goal is to privatize the RTB by 1995.

Other Opportunities

In addition to the privatization opportunities being proposed for the first time as part of the 1989 Budget, the Administration will continue privatization efforts proposed in previous budgets. The more significant initiatives include:

Amtrak: With the successful sale of Conrail in 1987, the Administration will continue its efforts to get out of the rail business by severing its financial ties to Amtrak. For 1989, the Administration proposes a zero budget for Amtrak.

Naval Petroleum Reserves (NPR's): The federal government owns and operates two producing oil fields—Elk Hills, California, and Teapot Dome, Wyoming. The Administration proposes to sell these properties to private industry during 1989. Doing so would reduce the budget deficit an estimated $3.2 million in 1989. It would increase Federal, state, and local tax receipts several hundred-million dollars per year. It would also allow the government to improve civilian and military energy security since the NPR sales proceeds would be used to fill the 750-million-barrel strategic petroleum reserve at twice the current rate of 50,000 barrels per day and establish a 10-million-barrel defense petroleum inventory.

Alaska Power Administration: The 1989 Budget assumes divestiture of the Alaska Power Administration, which helps supply electricity in the Anchorage and Juneau areas. State and local groups in Alaska have submitted proposals to buy its two hydropower projects. Negotiations with these two groups have been completed and authorizing legislation was to be submitted to Congress in calendar year 1988, with the sale expected to be completed by the end of 1989.

Southeastern Power Administration: The Budget assumes a feasibility study of the divestiture of the Southeastern Power Administration. Proposed legislation to authorize this study was submitted to Congress last year. Assuming successful completion of the study and subsequent negotiations, divestiture is planned before the end of 1990.

Southwestern, Western and Bonneville Power Marketing Administrations: The Administration intends to pursue divestiture of the remaining three Power Marketing Administrations although no formal proposals have been made as yet. The Administration wants to be responsive to local and regional interest as it implements this initiative. Implementation plans for this proposal are still in the development process.

Federal Crop Insurance: The Administration has proposed a five-year phase down of the federal subsidy given to farmers on their crop insurance by: (1) decreasing the subsidy of farmer's premiums from 25% in 1988 to zero by 1993; (2) phasing-out subsidies for operating expense of reinsured companies and direct federal insurance over five years; (3) increasing premium rates charged to farmers to achieve an actuarially sound rate structure; and (4) streamlining the agency staff which will only oversee reinsurance. During 1989 the Administration will develop the legislation and regulations required to institute this program for 1990.

Helium processing, storage, and facilities: The Administration will continue its efforts to sell its helium processing operations. The Department of Interior will recommend how best to proceed by mid-1988. It is estimated that $53 million can be realized from such a sale.

Great Plains Coal Gasification Plant: The Department of Energy began marketing the Great Plains Coal Gasification Plant in North Dakota in 1987. The plant is the nation's only commercial-scale, coal-to-synthetic natural gas facility. The Energy Department received legal title to the facility in 1986, when the private sponsors withdrew from the project and defaulted on Federal loans. The sale is expected to be completed in 1988.

Railroad Retirement System: Railroad retirement is the only private industry pension administered by a federal agency. The Administration has recommended the rail pension system be privatized, and Congress has created a Commission on Railroad Retirement Reform to look into, among other things, establishing a privately funded and administered plan. During 1989, privatization of the system will put the rail pension on equal footing with other industry pensions. Social Security coverage could be extended to the rail sector, and a private entity created to administer the rail industry pension system.

Transportation Systems Center (TSC): Legislation has been transmitted to allow the Department of Transportation (DOT) to privatize TSC in Cambridge, Massachusetts. The proposal would allow the Secretary of Transportation to accept bids during 1989 for the sale of TSC, and select the most appropriate bid.

Federal National Mortgage Association (Fannie Mae)/Federal Home Loan Mortgage Corporation (Freddie/Mac): The Administration believes that because of Fannie Mae's and Freddie Mac's government-sponsored status, their securities enjoy an interest rate advantage in the credit markets. This gives Fannie Mae and Freddie Mac significant competitive advantages relative to private mortgage conduits. In 1982, the President's Housing Commission concluded that Fannie Mae and Freddie Mac impeded the growth of fully private mortgage conduits and recommended that the Administration seek to fully privatize them. The same conclusion was reached by the President's Private Sector Survey on Cost Control (Grace Commission) in 1983 and the President's Commission on Privatization in 1987.

The Administration supports the full privatization of Fannie Mae and Freddie Mac (beyond their private ownership), and is studying transitional steps needed to convert Fannie Mae and Freddie Mac to completely private status. Full privatization of Fannie Mae and Freddie Mac would eliminate the major hurdle private mortgage conduits face in playing a significant role in the nation's housing credit markets. However, while Fannie Mae and Freddie Mac continue to enjoy their government-sponsored enterprise status, private mortgage conduits will continue to have difficulty competing with them. In order to mitigate the effects of this unfair competition, the Administration is proposing legislation to:

- impose statutory market-based capital requirements on Fannie Mae and Freddie Mac mortgage-backed securities;
- increase capital requirements for their portfolio operations by mandating that capital equal 6% of total assets (using generally accepted accounting principles);
- subject their securities to SEC registration requirements; and
- prohibit them from purchasing mortgages in the top quartile of the home price distribution, not to exceed $168,700.

Executive Order 12615 – Contracting Out

In addition to the specific proposals outlined above, the Administration is encouraging the efficient use of scarce resources through contracting out activities which can be performed by private enterprise at less cost.

Some functions requiring federal funding or oversight can be performed by the private sector on a contract basis. Examples of such functions run the gamut from cleaning of federal buildings, operation of warehouses, motor pools, and ADP centers, to the management of entire military bases installations. Complete divestiture of such functions is impractical; however, by contracting with the private sector, the government can maintain the necessary oversight and still take advantage of the efficiencies, capabilities, and greater resources of the private sector.

Since the mid-1960s the federal government's policy of reliance on the private sector for the performance of these types of services has been set forth in OMB Circular A-76. The Circular requires a cost comparison of commercial functions currently operated by the government which could be performed by the private sector to determine if they should be contracted out. During this Administration, over 70,000 jobs have been studied, resulting in an annual savings of almost $700 million without loss of services. This is an annual savings of $10,000 per job studied.

The National Oceanic and Atmospheric Administration's (NOAA) A-76 program provides a representative example of the benefits which can be gained from contracting out. NOAA has completed 19 A-76 studies covering 599 employees. The government operation proved most cost effective in 10 of these studies with average savings of 26%, while the private sector was more efficient in 9 activities with average savings of 27%. Annual savings are over $9,300 per position studied and the return on the cost of conducting the studies was almost 5 to 1 in first year savings, and 25 to 1 in savings over the study period (three to five years). While these savings are impressive, the potential of competition to reduce government costs is much greater. To date, less than 10% of the positions that could be examined for contracting have been studied.

In recognition of the considerable opportunities which remain, the President issued Executive Order 12615, reinvigorating the policies of Circular A-76 and accelerating its implementation. The order provides:

- A senior official in each agency will be designated to coordinate studies and other privatization efforts and report progress to OMB.
- New requirements for commercial activities are to be provided by the private sector, except where excluded by statute, national security or costs.
- Agencies were to identify all government-operated commercial activities by April 30, 1988, and develop a review schedule for these activities by June 30, 1988.
- Agencies are to review at least 3% of their civilian work force per year until all commercial activities have been reviewed.
- Estimated savings will be included in agencies' annual budget proposals to OMB. Agencies may retain a portion of expected first-year savings to reward employees covered by studies for their productivity efforts or to use in other productivity enhancement efforts.
- Agencies will develop and maintain effective job placement programs and cooperate fully in interagency placements; and
- The Office of Personnel Management will review and revise, as necessary, personnel policies and procedures to give government managers the flexibility to organize in the most efficient manner and to reduce adverse effects of contracting out on employees.

Federal Employee Direct Corporate Ownership Plan—FED CO-OP

In addition to the revision of personnel policies and procedures and the development of effective intra- and inter-agency placement programs, incentives have been developed to allow employees working in federal commercial-type activities to take part in an alternative method of contracting—FED CO-OP. FED CO-OP is designed to share the financial benefits resulting from privatization with employees. Under FED CO-OP affected employees are offered participation in an Employee Stock Ownership Plan, which permits the employees to participate in the profits of firms winning bids to perform commercial activities. It also provides guaranteed employment for a limited period and high quality out-placement services for those employers who depart the firm within the first year. These benefits supplement other corporate benefits that may be provided by the employer.

Several activities have been identified as potential FED CO-OP opportunities and include medical centers, a data processing facility, the National Technical Information Service, the National Finance Center, and other administrative support activities. It is anticipated that at least two test cases will be completed in 1989.

Revised OMB Circular A-76

A change to OMB Circular A-76 will be made to incorporate the provisions of the Executive Order, employee equity participation, and other changes necessary to ensure that studies are accomplished in a fair and open manner. In addition, the revised Circular will provide more authority for agencies to contract activities without competitive cost comparisons when it makes economic sense to do so.

Emphasis on contracting out, under both OMB Circular A-76 and OMP's FED CO-OP, are essential ingredients in the Administration's commitment to provide better government at less cost and are a high priority in the budget.

Traces of Universal Wisdom in Management

William A. Jones, Jr.

In each profession there are certain fundamental "truths" that form the cornerstones of that particular field. These are the basic things that every practitioner of the discipline must know, the ABCs, the essential elements. To be a true professional, one must have a thorough knowledge of these kernels of wisdom to command the respect of peers.

The Peter Principle

As a service to all in the profession, this article will review a group of researchers whose works have not been adequately covered in current literature. We begin with a contemporary writer who broke conceptual ground—Laurence J. Peter. An astute observer, Peter was able to formulate the principle which proudly bears his name: "in a hierarchy every employee tends to rise to his level of incompetence." (See Laurence J. Peter and Raymond Hull, *The Peter Principles*, Bantam Books, 1969). How simple it is for us to relate to this knowledge—now that it has been discovered!

Of course people are promoted because of their competence! Of course the promotions stop when competence is lost! As Peter notes, it is fortunate that we usually have some number of employees who have not yet reached their "level." These are the people who accomplish the necessary work. This new science of hierarchiology may yield further flashes of brilliance.

Parkinson's Law

One of the earlier pioneers in this area of management research was the eminent British scholar C. Northcote Parkinson. As a result of his dedicated work, he was able to formulate the now famous law which bears his name. Many before him had, no doubt, observed that "work expands so as to fill the time available for its completion." (See *Parkinson's Law and Other Studies in Administration*, Ballantine Books, 1957.) Because of Parkinson's dedication, and his fervor to ferret out and understand basic truth, however, it was he who captured this important law in the written word. In capturing this important wisdom, Parkinson, almost single-handedly, became the founding parent of one important stream of contemporary management thought.

Reprinted with permission from *The Bureaucrat* (Winter 1987–88).

Related Findings

Parkinson provided insight that was instant and, at the same time, he provided broad shoulders upon which other scholars could stand and build. What practitioner among us would deny the existence of Parkinson's Law? Who would cast the first stone? Indeed, our debt to Parkinson runs far deeper.

In explaining the management of money, for example, his research led to the discovery of two kinds of people in the world: "those who have vast fortunes of their own and those who have nothing at all." An actual million dollars is real and understandable to persons of the first type, while to people such as professors a "million dollars is at least as real as a thousand, they having never possessed either sum."

In reality, of course, most people fall between these two extremes, and these are generally the people who sit on finance committees and other bodies that render decisions regarding important matters of high finance. In researching this third group, those who do most of the world's collective decisionmaking about money matters, Parkinson was able to isolate the important Law of Triviality.

Law of Triviality

This law, now well-known, states that ". . . the time spent on any item of the agenda will be in inverse proportion to the sum involved." Other researchers, generally being persons of more average intelligence and research skill, had previously believed that the time spent on an item and amount of money involved were positively correlated. In reality, of course, small sums and simpler items are far easier to understand and, as a result, can be debated by almost anyone! As sums grow larger and items become complicated, few wish to speak up and risk being exposed as ignorant about such matters! (It is sad to note that many of our younger colleagues are attempting to function in the real world without a full and detailed knowledge of Parkinson's discoveries. What will become of the younger generation?)

Other Research

Like giants in all fields, Parkinson was an inspiration to other serious researchers and scholars. Many others, those truly committed to the spirit of inquiry, have seized the momentum at hand and continued to press the frontiers of knowledge. While they are far too numerous to be fully chronicled in this short paper, a small sample will be presented from the work of such luminaries as Allan B. Jacobs, Carl Bellone, Arthur A. Sloane, Jeffrey Prottas, James Boren, Art Buchwald, and (of course) Anonymous.

Some are household words, while others are a bit obscure in the annals of our minds. In surveying these important writings, it must be emphasized that a brief review can never substitute for careful study of the originals.

Eyes Only, Jesus

The true origin of this category of research may have been accurately located by Jeffrey M. Prottas, His findings were reported in *The Washington Monthly* (February 1981) in a perceptive article entitled "Eyes Only, Jesus." Prottas writes of his amazing opportunity to review fragments of the Scripture chronicling the travels and teaching of Jesus. Archeologists had recently discovered these long-lost fragments inside a Gideon Bible in a Best Western Hotel near Jerusalem.

The fragments, a memorandum to Jesus of Nazareth from his administrative assistant, analyze the complications that resulted from Jesus's miracles. While noting the favorable publicity resulting from the miracles, the able staff assistant provides a thorough analysis and evaluation. Raising the dead Lazarus, for example, was found to have caused tremendous complications with regard to already-paid life insurance, social security payments, driver's license, and union card.

Another miracle, providing free fish (and bread) for the multitude, almost caused serious discontent among fishermen (a group that had been very loyal believers). The supply-demand balance and the fishermen's earnings were already in a precarious state. The teamsters were also quite upset because they had not been selected to transport the fish and bread to the multitude.

In addition to these complications, several government agencies were quite alarmed because no dispensing permits were obtained for either the food or the wine. The sanitation department also presented a bill for over $124,000 because this miracle left behind quite a mess. In closing his careful analysis of the Food for the Multitude Program, the administrative assistant emphasizes the potential dangers of allergies and bones when using fish. He urges a policy change to chicken sandwiches on white bread.

The Civil Service Giants

Much more recently, complications were reported in sports administration when the San Francisco Giants baseball team became civil service employees. Allan Jacobs provided an analysis for managers in "The Civil Service Giants" in *Harper's* (October 1979). It seems that a young, obscure attorney discovered that the team's 20-year stadium contract was with the city's Parks and Recreation Department. This was most significant as the city charter required all Parks-Rec employees be under civil service coverage.

The new status of Giants' team members, as city employees, naturally resulted in the application of all civil service rules and regulations. Failing pitchers sometimes filed grievances rather than turn the ball over to a relief player from the bullpen. Merit examinations and the precision of player position descriptions caused considerable consternation.

One amazing fact is that Carl Bellone reported very similar events in another area of sports management in his article in *Public Administration*

Review (November–December 1977), "A Merit System for Pro Football?" The universality of management is well-supported!

Creative Personnel Administration

Creative personnel administration in industry was Arthur Sloane's focus in a *Personnel Journal* article in September 1974. Writing about Louis LaRocco's distinguished career at Brooklyn Fast Freight, Sloane notes that LaRocco's motto was, "if you are ever absent without a compelling excuse, we are going to pay you a little visit." This was so effective that the absentee rate quickly neared zero.

Only one of LaRocco's ideas proved to be marginal. His widespread utilization of "Christ is the Answer" signs at strategic work-place locations produced mixed results. While this was probably the first known attempt to apply a higher-level approach to employee motivation, there was a discontent over the fact that the right answer is dependent on the exact nature of the question. It was pointed out that there is another answer for a question such as "What is the Capital of Montana?"

Boren Facts

One among us who combines the best of scholarship and practice is James Boren. His high post as president of the International Association of Professional Bureaucrats has facilitated his many accomplishments, including important testimony before the Congress of the United States. Speaking in a definitively orbital manner, he resonated prodigiously in nonresponsively elucidating the values of fuzzifying, pondering, orchestrating, and maturating all bureaucratical procedural clearances and decision avoidances. Boren has also noted the national impact of the bureaucratic movement (B.M. for short) in all areas of commerce, academia, and government. Among his many practical bits of wisdom is the heady suggestion that formed the title for his 1972 book *When in Doubt, Mumble.*

Data Famine

No review of contributors to management thought can conclude without mentioning at least one of the conceptual models provided by the sage of sages, Art Buchwald. While the reader can, no doubt, already cite several from memory, one does stand apart from the rest—"The Great Data Famine." (See Art Buchwald, *Getting High in Government Circles*, 1968). While the rest of the world has been busy building computers, fortunately Buchwald has recognized the possibility that there may be insufficient data to feed all of them.

As each new generation of computers becomes more sophisticated the likelihood of an information famine grows. It may prove necessary to limit daily plug-in time for computers, to expand government programs, and to initiate a computer birth-control program. To date these drastic measures have not been necessary. Having such important standby measures as deterents may have, as Buchwald would say, "saved our bacon."

Carefully Orchestrated Changes

Because the author is preparing this summary the old-fashioned way—with a pen—fingers are tiring. The end is near. Let us close with a citation from one of our most famous colleagues—Anonymous herself. It takes the form of a report prepared by a management consultant who had just returned from a visit to a symphony concert:

For considerable periods of time the four oboe players had nothing to do. The number should be reduced and the work spread out more evenly over the whole of the concert, thus eliminating peaks of activity.

All 12 violins were playing identical notes; this seems unnecessary duplication. The staff of this section should be drastically cut. If a larger volume of sound is required, it could be obtained by means of electronic apparatus.

It is remarkable that methods of engineering principles have been adhered to as well as they have. For example, it was noted that the pianist was not only carrying out most of his work by two-handed operation, but was also using his feet for pedal operations. Nevertheless there were excessive reaches for some notes on the piano, and it is probable that redesign of the keyboard to bring all notes within the normal working area would be of advantage to this operator.

Obsolescence of equipment is another matter into which further investigation could be made. It was reputed in the program that the leading violinist's instrument was already several hundred years old; if normal depreciation schedules had been applied, the value of this instrument should have been reduced to zero.

It was noted that excessive effort was being used occasionally by the players of wind instruments, whereas one air compressor could supply adequate air for all instruments under more accurately controlled conditions.

There seems to be too much repetition of some musical passages. Scores should be drastically pruned. No useful purpose is served by repeating on the horns a passage which has already been handled adequately by the strings. It is estimated that if all redundant passages were eliminated, the whole concert time of two hours could be reduced to 20 minutes, and there would be no need for an intermission.

The conductor agrees generally with these recommendations, but expresses the opinion that there might be some falling off in box-office receipts. In that unlikely event, it should be possible to close sections of the auditorium entirely, with consequent savings of overhead expenses, lighting, heat, etc. If worst comes to worst, the whole thing could be abandoned and the public could go to the movies instead.

Universal Wisdom

Yes, indeed friends, there are traces of universal wisdom in management! We must work harder to synthesize the fundamental knowledge of our discipline. This is a required first step if we are effectively to combat ignorance.

Serious readers are encouraged to consult W. Jack Duncan, "Humor in Management: Prospects for Administrative Practice and Research," *Academy of Management Review*, vol. 7, no. 1, 1982, 136–42; and, Paul B. Malone, III, "Humor: A Double-Edged Tool For Today's Managers?" *Academy of Management Review*, vol. 5, no. 3, 1980, 357–60.

Bibliography
Selected Public Management

Resource Material

This bibliography has two specific purposes. First, it will serve as a guide for readers desiring to explore the literature in more depth. This is something the authors certainly encourage. To facilitate such pursuit, the bibliography purposely does not present the reader with "information overload." Each item listed is well-worth an investment of time and energy. In most instances, each work included will also provide an additional bibliography.

The second purpose of the bibliography is to provide complete citations for books and articles that are mentioned within this text. Interested readers may wish to further pursue some references utilized by the authors.

1. Anthony, R. N., and R. E. Herzlinger. *Management Control in Nonprofit Organizations*. Homewood, Illinois: Irwin, 1980.

2. Appleby, Paul. *Big Democracy*. New York: 1945.

3. Ash, Roy. "Good Management—A Prized Commodity." *Civil Service Journal* (October-December 1973), 1.

4. Barnard, Chester. *The Functions of the Executive*. Cambridge, Masssachusetts: Harvard University Press, 1938.

5. Blau, Peter, and Marshall Meyer. *Bureaucracy in Modern Society*. 3rd edition. New York: Random House, 1987.

6. Block, Peter. *The Empowered Manager: Positive Political Skills at Work*. San Francisco: Jossey-Bass, 1987.

7. Boyer, William W. *Bureaucracy on Trial: Policy Making by Government Agencies*. New York: Bobbs-Merrill, 1964.

8. Bower, Joseph. "Effective Public Management." *Harvard Business Review* (March-April 1977), p. 140.

9. Brown, Brock, and Richard J. Stillman. *A Search for Public Administration: The Ideas and Career of Dwight Waldo*. College Station, Texas: Texas A & M University Press, 1986.

10. Carey, William D. "New Perspectives in Governance," in the Conference Board, *Challenge to Leadership: Managing in a Changing World*. New York: Free Press, 1973, p. 85.

11. Committee for Economic Development. *Improving Prodvctivity in State and Local Government*. New York, Committee for Economic Development, 1976.

12. Committee for Economic Development. *Public-Private Partnership*. New York, Committee for Economic Development, 1982.

13. Cranford, John. *Budgeting for America,* 2nd ed. Washington, D.C.: Congressional Quarterly Press, 1989.
14. Cummings, L. L., G. P. Huber, and E. Arendt. "Effects of Size and Special Arrangement of Group Decision-Making." *Academy of Management Journal* (December 1974).
15. Davis, Ralph C. *The Fundamentals of Top Management.* New York: Harper & Row, 1951.
16. Dror, Yehezkel. *Public Policymaking Reexamined.* Scranton, Pennsylvania: Chandler, 1968, pp. 72–73.
17. Dye, Thomas R., and Harmon Zeigler. *The Irony of Democracy.* 8th ed. Pacific Grove, California: Brooks/Cole, 1990.
18. Easton, David. *A Framework for Political Analysis.* Englewood Cliffs, New Jersey: Prentice-Hall, 1965.
19. Edwards, G. C., II. *Implementary Public Policy.* Washington, D. C.: Congressional Quarterly Press, 1984.
20. Elkouri, Frank, and Edna Asper Elkouri. *How Arbitration Works.* 4th edition. Washington, D. C.: Bureau of National Affairs, 1985, p. 98.
21. Etzioni, Amitai. "Mixed Scanning: A 'Third' Approach to Decision-Making." *Public Administration Review,* Vol. 27 (December 1967), pp. 385–392.
22. Gerth, H. H., and C. W. Mills, eds. and trans. *From Max Weber: Essays in Sociology.* Fair Lawn, New Jersey: Oxford University Press, 1946.
23. Goodnow, Frank. *Politics and Administration.* New York: Macmillan, 1900.
24. Goodsell, Charles T. *The Case for Bureaucracy.* 2nd ed. Chatham, New Jersey: Chatham House, 1986.
25. Gulick, Luther, and L. Urwick. *Papers on the Science of Administration.* New York: Institute of Public Administration, 1937.
26. Hess, S. *The Government-Press Connection.* Washington, D.C. Congressional Quarterly Press, 1984.
27. Hinrich, Harley H., and Greme M. Taylor. *Systematic Analysis.* Pacific Palisades, California: Goodyear, 1972, p. 111.
28. Howitt, H. M. *Managing Federalism: Studies in Intergovernmental Relations.* Washington, D.C.: Congressional Quarterly Press, 1984.
29. Janis, Irving L. *Victims of Groupthink.* Boston: Houghton-Mifflin, 1972.
30. Jones, Charles O. *An Introduction to the Study of Public Policy.* 3rd ed. Belmont, California: Wadsworth, 1984.
31. Jung, John J. "Management by Objectives in the Public Sector." *Public Administration Review.* (January-February, 1976).
32. Lasswell, Harold. *Politics: Who Gets What, When, Where, How.* New York: McGraw-Hill, 1936.
33. Lindblom, Charles, E. *The Policy-Making Process.* 2nd ed. Englewood Cliffs, New Jersey: Prentice-Hall, 1980.
34. Madison, James, Alexander Hamilton, and John Jay. *The Federalist.* New York: Modern Library, 1937.

35. McCaskey, Michael B. *The Executive Challenge: Managing Change and Ambiguity.* Boston: Pitman, 1982.
36. McCaskey, Michael B. "An Introduction to Organizational Design." *California Management Review* (Winter 1974), p. 13.
37. Miner, John B. *The Human Constraint.* Washington, D.C.: The Bureau of National Affairs, Inc., 1974, p. 65.
38. Mintzberg, Henry, *The Nature of Managerial Work.* New York: Harper & Row, 1973.
39. Morrisey, George L. *Management by Objectives and Results in the Public Sector.* Reading, Massachusetts: Addison-Wesley, 1976.
40. Mosher, Frederick C. "Features and Problems of the Federal Civil Service." In Wallace S. Sayre, ed., *The Federal Government Service.* 2nd ed. Englewood Cliffs, New Jersey: Prentice-Hall, 1965.
41. Musolf, Lloyd D. *Promoting the General Welfare: Government and the Economy.* Chicago: Scott, Foresman, 1965.
42. Nigro, Felix A., and Lloyd G. Nigro. *Modern Public Administration.* 7th ed. New York: Harper & Row, 1989.
43. Newman, William. *Constructive Control: Design and Use of Control Systems.* Englewood Cliffs, New Jersey: Prentice-Hall, 1975, pp. 202–203.
44. Odiorne, George S. "MBO in State Government." *Public Adminstration Review* (January-February 1976.)
45. Ouchi, W. *Theory Z.* Reading, Massachusetts: Addison-Wesley, 1980.
46. Perry J. L., and K. L. Kraemer, eds. *Public Management: Public and Private Perspectives.* Palo Alto, California: Mayfield, 1983.
47. Peters, T., and R. H. Waterman. *In Search of Excellence.* New York: Harper & Row, 1982.
48. Quinn, J. B. *Strategies for Change: Logical Incrementalism.* Homewood, Illinois: Irwin, 1980.
49. Roethlisberger, F. J., and W. J. Dickson. *Management and the Worker: An Account of a Research Program Conducted by the Western Electric Company, Hawthorne Works,* Chicago; with the assistance and collaboration of Harold A. Wright. Cambridge, Massachusetts: Howard University Press, 1939).
50. Robbins, Stephen. *Organization Theory: Structure, Design and Applications.* 3rd ed. Englewood Cliffs, New Jersey: Prentice-Hall, 1990.
51. Shafritz, J. M., and A. C. Hyde. *Classics of Public Administration* 2nd ed. Chicago: Dorsey, 1987.
52. Simon, Herbert A. "The Changing Theory and Changing Practice of Public Adminstration." In Ithiel de Sola Pool, ed. *Contemporary Political Science: Toward Empirical Theory.* New York: McGraw-Hill, 1967, pp. 87–88.
53. Starling, Grover. *Managing the Public Sector.* 3rd ed. Homewood, Illinois: Dorsey, 1986.
54. Straussman, J. D. *Public Administration.* New York: Holt, Rinehart and Winston, 1985.
55. Waldo, Dwight. *The Enterprise of Public Administration.* Novato, California: Chandler and Sharp, 1980.

56. Wildavsky, Aaron. *The Politics of the Budgetary Process.* 4th ed. Boston: Little, Brown, 1984.
57. Wildavsky, Aaron. *Speaking Truth to Power: The Art and Craft of Policy Analysis.* Boston: Little, Brown, 1979.
58. Wilson, Woodrow. "The Study of Administration." *Political Science Quarterly.* June 1887, p. 209.
59. Wright, Deil S. "Intergovernmental Relations: An Analytical Overview." *The Annals of the American Academy of Political and Social Science.* (November 1974).
60. Yates, Douglas. *The Politics of Management.* San Francisco: Jossey-Bass, 1985.

Index